Interfaces between second language acquisition and language testing research

Edited by

Lyle F. Bachman

University of California, Los Angeles

and

Andrew D. Cohen

University of Minnesota

CAMBRIDGE
UNIVERSITY PRESS

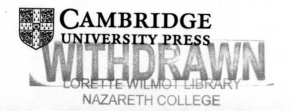

CAMBRIDGE UNIVERSITY PRESS
Cambridge, New York, Melbourne, Madrid, Cape Town, Singapore, São Paulo

Cambridge University Press
The Edinburgh Building, Cambridge CB2 2RU, UK

Published in the United States of America by Cambridge University Press, New York

www.cambridge.org
Information on this title: www.cambridge.org/9780521640237

© Cambridge University Press 1998

First published 1998

A catalogue record for this publication is available from the British Library

Library of Congress Cataloguing in Publication data

Interfaces between second language acquisition and language testing
research / Lyle F. Bachman and Andrew D. Cohen, editors.
p.   cm.
Includes bibliographical references.
ISBN 0-521-64023-7 (hc. : alk. paper). – ISBN 0-521-64963-3 (pbk. :
alk. paper)
1. Second language acquisition – Research.   2. Language and
languages – Ability testing – Research.   I. Bachman, Lyle F.
II. Cohen, Andrew D.
P118.2.I577   1998
401'.93 – dc21   98-24269
                                                          CIP

ISBN-13 978-0-521-64023-7 hardback
ISBN-10 0-521-64023-7 hardback

ISBN-13 978-0-521-64963-6 paperback
ISBN-10 0-521-64963-3 paperback

Transferred to digital printing 2005

Contents

Contributors

Lyle F. Bachman, University of California, Los Angeles
Geoff Brindley, Macquarie University
Carol A. Chapelle, Iowa State University
Andrew D. Cohen, University of Minnesota
Dan Douglas, Iowa State University
Elana Shohamy, Tel Aviv University
Elaine Tarone, University of Minnesota

Series editors' preface

Two of the fastest growing, and most technical, areas of applied linguistics are second language acquisition (SLA) and language testing. Perhaps because of the degree of specialization required of those doing research in either one, together with the advent of separate conferences and journals for each, dialogue between practitioners in the two fields has been sporadic at best, and nonexistent in many cases.

This state of affairs is clearly unproductive. Advances in SLA in recent years, for example, have thrown new light on such crucial notions for test developers as "acquisition" and "proficiency," on learnability and teachability, and on the relevant criteria for student placement for the purpose of instruction, leading in some quarters to requests for tests that are "interlanguage-sensitive," or "developmental," and that take the individual learner as the unit of analysis. Yet many test designers remain unaware of such developments and continue to produce ever more sophisticated proficiency measures, of high reliability, but obtained via norm-referenced, group-level statistics, and of questionable validity when used to cluster learners for teaching purposes. Advances in language testing, conversely, are sometimes a closed book for many SLA researchers, whose training too often lacks a sufficiently rigorous grounding in research methods in general, and in measurement in particular. The result can be studies that are theoretically innovative and insightful, but of questionable validity due to inadequate measurement of the variables of interest, including second language abilities and development.

Interfaces between Second Language Acquisition and Language Testing Research is an attempt to begin to remedy the situation. Professors Bachman and Cohen have brought together a group of respected researchers, most of whom are active in both SLA and testing, and have asked them to address specific topics that they feel will benefit from greater contact across subdisciplinary borders. The result is a volume whose contributors draw on a rich base of empirical studies in discussing such problematic issues as construct validity, the operationalization and measurement of variables in SLA studies, interlanguage variation, individual differences, test-taking strategies, rating scales, potentially idiosyncratic psycholinguistic dimensions of context and discourse domain, and relationships among traditional notions of data elicitation tasks and language tests. The editors not only provide insightful discussion of those chapters but contribute new work of their own.

This book should be of considerable interest to language teachers, teacher educators, and program administrators, and to faculty and graduate students in applied linguistics. Its treatment of cutting edge issues in contributions that are accountable to empirical findings makes it an appropriate addition to the Cambridge Applied Linguistics Series.

Michael H. Long
Jack C. Richards

Preface

For many years, a relatively small number of applied linguists whose research interests straddle second language acquisition (SLA) and language testing (LT) have incorporated insights from both areas into their own research – if not explicitly, at least in the kinds of research questions they ask, and in the interpretations they offer of their results. These individuals have also employed similar tools in their research, such as interviews, observation, structured elicitations, rating scales, questionnaires, and language tests. More recently, a relatively small number of these individuals have become increasingly concerned with the general lack of recognition among their colleagues of the interfaces between these two areas of applied linguistics research. It was clear to them that the majority of individuals who were in the mainstream of either SLA or LT research were largely ignorant of the other field, both in knowing the major issues and research questions, and in knowing the research approaches and methods commonly used.

It was this concern with the need for a more extensive dialogue between SLA and LT researchers and a deeper understanding and sharing of common research and methodological issues that led to the organizing of a colloquium at the annual meeting of the American Association for Applied Linguistics in Seattle in 1992. The purpose of this colloquium was to stimulate discussion among SLA and LT researchers by exploring areas of common interest, both substantive and methodological, from a variety of perspectives. Individuals who are at the "cutting edge" of research in various aspects of SLA and LT research were invited to write original papers addressing areas of interface between SLA and LT research from the perspective of their particular area of interest. To provide a common point of departure, these individuals were all asked to read Bachman's article "Language Testing – SLA Interfaces," in Volume 9 of the *Annual Review of Applied Linguistics,* which is included as the Appendix to this volume. The colloquium was very well received and generated considerable interest, and thus it was felt that there was a need to make the papers available to a wider audience. In discussing the idea of publishing the papers as a collection, a number of the colloquium participants, including the editors, agreed that it would be useful to include additional perspectives in the collection, and three additional papers were subsequently invited.

A variety of issues, both those that prompted the colloquium and those that were of concern to the individual authors, are dealt with in the chapters of this book. In Chapter 1, Bachman and Cohen provide an update of Bachman's 1989 article, outlining a number of issues and questions that continue to be of concern to both SLA and LT researchers, discussing some recent studies that illustrate ways and areas in which these two aspects of applied linguistics can be integrated, and suggesting ways in which SLA and LT researchers can learn from one another.

Chapelle (Chapter 2) deals with the need that SLA researchers have to justify their interpretation of a given test as an indicator of a particular construct. She points out that in order to do so, they must define the construct that the test is intended to measure. Her chapter offers three theoretical perspectives toward construct definition: trait, behaviorist, and interactionalist. Each perspective is illustrated by demonstrating how interlanguage vocabulary might be defined within the perspective and how that perspective is reflected in vocabulary testing. Since current applied linguistic theory favors an interactionalist perspective to construct definition, Chapelle explains the implications of this definition for valid inquiry, including investigation of construct validity and the consequences of testing. Her chapter thus provides an excellent overview of issues related to validity that arise in many of the other chapters.

Tarone raises the issue of interlanguage variation in Chapter 3, calling attention to research indicating that the language production of second language learners varies in grammatical accuracy and fluency (as well as in other language components) in response to contextual changes. She concludes from this that SLA research findings, such as those regarding SLA universals, must be viewed with some skepticism since few studies control carefully for interlanguage variation. Also, given the variable of learner performance, the impact of a given test task will not be identical across learners, suggesting the importance of multiple tasks in order to build profiles of individual learners.

Cohen (Chapter 4) examines the role of test-taking strategy data in validating language tests. The use of verbal report measures to identify test-taking strategies represents an approach to research that has been more commonly used in SLA research than in LT research. The concern is to consider the processes in test taking so as to determine the effects of test input upon the test taker – that is, the processes that the test taker makes use of in order to produce acceptable answers to questions and tasks, and perceptions about tests before, during, and after taking them. Cohen concludes that SLA and LT researchers would be advised to consider validating the testing measures that they use through triangulation, which would include the collection of test-taking strategy data on sub-samples of respondents, as in the Anderson et al. study (1991).

In Chapter 5, Brindley examines the validity of behavioral rating scales from an SLA perspective. Rather than focusing on the measurement properties of rating scales, he looks more specifically at the nature and status of the verbal descriptors that define different levels of ability. After considering the extent to which behavioral rating scales can be said to characterize SLA, he then utilizes findings from both LT and SLA research to assess the validity of the text, task, and skill hierarchies typically described in such behavioral scales. He concludes with suggestions based on both SLA and LT research for assisting in the construction and validation of such rating scales.

Douglas (Chapter 6) focuses on the discourse domain, which he views as a cognitive construct created by the language learner as a context for interlanguage development. He sees the discourse domain as mediating between the specific context of language use (situation, setting, domain, environment, task, content, topic, schema, frame, script, and background knowledge) and the respondents' language competence. He discusses the need for LT and SLA researchers to design tests that have instructions, contents, genre, and language directed toward specific populations.

Shohamy discusses the interfaces between SLA and LT research in discourse analysis in Chapter 7. She contends that while language testers have contributed to SLA research by defining the construct of language ability and the component of discourse within that construct, they need to expand their repertoire of assessment procedures by experimenting with a variety of elicitation tasks that SLA researchers use.

It is often only by considering our own research interests and approaches in relief that we fully understand and appreciate their potential. Such is the case, we believe, with LT and SLA research. In the process of editing this volume, we have seen the papers evolve in ways that neither we nor the individual authors could have anticipated at the beginning. We have altered our perceptions of our own research and gained greater appreciation of the complementarity of these two fields of applied linguistics. We believe that this book offers a fresh look at ways in which LT and SLA research has been conducted and suggests exciting directions for how it can be integrated. We thus hope that this collection will provide a stimulus for a continuing and expanding dialogue between SLA and LT researchers. If the conversation that has already been generated in the chapters included here is any indication, this hope is already becoming a reality.

Lyle F. Bachman
Andrew D. Cohen

References

Anderson, N., L. F. Bachman, K. Perkins, & A. Cohen. 1991. An exploratory study into the construct validity of a reading comprehension test: Triangulation of data sources. *Language Testing, 8*(1), 41–66.

1 Language testing – SLA interfaces: An update

Lyle F. Bachman
Andrew D. Cohen

For some years, language testing (LT) research and second language acquisition (SLA) research have largely been viewed as distinct areas of inquiry in applied linguistics. Since the late 1980s, however, we have seen an increasing number of studies in which these two subfields of applied linguistics come together, both in terms of the substantive issues being investigated and the methodological approaches used. An overview of the areas of overlap, or interfaces, was provided in Bachman (1989; reprinted as an appendix in this volume). There have been many developments in both areas since then, and in this chapter we identify what we see as some of the continuing contrasts – contrasts that we view as natural and healthy outgrowths of the differing interests and foci of LT and SLA research. We then discuss several areas and issues that have been discussed more or less independently by LT and SLA researchers, and that we believe constitute *interfaces* between these two fields of applied linguistics, briefly illustrating these interfaces with some recent research studies. Finally, we list some of the challenges and questions that we feel suggest areas for future research for both LT and SLA. It is not our purpose to present a comprehensive review of the research literature in LT and SLA. Rather, we would like to suggest a conceptual framework and approach for building more extensive and substantial interfaces between LT and SLA research in the future, and point to some directions for addressing many of the complex and thorny issues that have, in the past, generally been dealt with in a rather compartmentalized manner by LT and SLA researchers.

Different foci of SLA and LT research

Although the making of broad contrasts between traditional SLA research and traditional LT research necessitates some oversimplification, the following are several of the more noticeable tendencies that were mentioned by Bachman in 1989, and that we feel are still relevant today. SLA research has tended to concern itself with the description and explanation of how second language ability develops, focusing on interlanguage as a language with rules and conventions in its own right and on the processes and factors that are involved in the development of interlanguage. LT research, on the other hand, has attempted to arrive at a model of language ability that can provide a basis for describing and assessing this ability for a given individual or group of individuals at a given stage of development, using a given norm or standard of target language use as a point of reference. While SLA research has concerned itself more with the factors and processes that affect or are part of language acquisition, LT research has tended to focus on components and strategies that are part of language ability. Thus, while SLA has looked for antecedents of language ability, LT research has studied the results of acquisition. The two fields also differ in their theoretical goals: SLA research has concerned itself with theories of language acquisition, while LT research has focused on theories of language test performance and the correspondence between test performance and nontest language use. In addition to having different substantive foci, the two fields have tended to use different research methodologies. SLA research has historically utilized the linguistic analysis of learners' interlanguage utterances, descriptive case studies, ethnographic research, and experimental and quasi-experimental designs, while LT research has more typically employed *ex post facto* correlational methods. These contrasts are summarized below:

SLA research	*LT research*
Research perspective	
Longitudinal view of interlanguage development.	"Slice of life" view of language ability at a given stage of development, with reference to a given norm or standard of language use.
Focus of research	
Antecedents of interlanguage ability: factors and processes that affect or are part of language acquisition, e.g., contextual features, learner characteristics, processes.	Results of language acquisition: components and strategies that are part of language ability, e.g., grammatical competence, pragmatic competence, strategic competence.
Goals of research	
To develop and empirically validate a theory of SLA that will (1) describe how SLA takes place and (2) explain why SLA takes place.	(1) To develop and empirically validate a theory of language test performance that will describe and explain variations in language test performance; and (2) to demonstrate the ways in which language test performance corresponds to nontest language use.

Research methodology

Variety of research approaches: discourse analysis, case studies, ethnography, experimental, quasi-experimental, *ex post facto* correlational.

Dominant research approach: *ex post facto* correlational; increasing use of qualitative analysis of test content and test takers' responses, verbal reports of test taking.

Interfaces: Some areas of common interest and cross-fertilization

Despite the differences in foci, several researchers (e.g., Bachman 1989; Shohamy 1994) have recognized that there is considerable commonality of interests and potential for cross-fertilization between LT and SLA researchers, both in terms of the research questions they address and the empirical approaches they take in dealing with these questions. These common areas of interest, or interfaces, can be seen as deriving from an issue that is of central concern to both LT and SLA research: describing and explaining variability in language acquisition (SLA) and test performance (LT). Ellis (1985) and Bachman (1990) have proposed frameworks for considering sources of variability in SLA and LT, respectively. Ellis considers all variations in language-learner language to be part of variability, and classifies these into two main categories: systematic variability, which includes individual variability and contextual variability, and nonsystematic variability, which includes what he calls *free variability* and *performance variability* (Ellis 1985: 75ff).

For Bachman, on the other hand, the distinction of prime interest and importance is not that between systematic variation and nonsystematic, or random, variation, but rather that between two types of systematic variation: (1) variation due to differences across individuals in their language ability, processing strategies, and personal characteristics (e.g., cultural and background knowledge, affective schemata), and (2) variation due to differences in the characteristics of the test method, or test tasks. Tarone (Chapter 3, this volume) makes a similar distinction, arguing that the term *individual difference* should be used for differences in performance across individuals, and the term *variation* should be reserved for "synchronic situation-related variation in the use of a second language." Variation, she goes on to point out, "ought to be reserved to refer to shifts *within* the performance of any given individual" (p. 73). We agree that this distinction in terminology is useful, and will follow it in this chapter.

Considering the major sources of variability that have been identified and investigated in the two fields, clearly a large number of factors need to be considered in both LT and SLA research. However, we focus here on three sources of variability that we believe are central to both fields:

1. Individual differences in the *language abilities* that are acquired or measured
2. Individual differences in the *strategies and other processes* that individuals employ in language use, as well as on language test tasks and SLA elicitation tasks
3. Variation in the *tasks and context* and their effects on language use, as well as on performance on language test tasks and SLA elicitation tasks.

The nature of the language abilities acquired or measured

HISTORICAL OVERVIEW OF THE EVOLUTION OF A MULTICOMPONENTIAL, INTERACTIONALIST VIEW OF LANGUAGE ABILITY

Let us begin this discussion by making a distinction between language and language ability. We would argue that it is not language per se that is measured or acquired, but language ability. That is, even though we speak of language acquisition and language testing, what we are primarily interested in, in both cases, is not the system of language itself, but rather the learner's capacity for acquiring and using a language system either for, or as part of, various processes, such as socialization, psychological orientation, and communication. We would further argue that both LT and SLA researchers make inferences or assumptions about the nature of language ability in their research, and that a clear definition of this construct is thus essential to both LT and SLA research. (See Chapelle, Chapter 2 of this volume, for a detailed discussion of the issues involved in defining language ability as a construct.)

Because of its historical focus on assessing language ability, with its attendant accountability, in terms of actual practice, LT research has understandably been generally more concerned with defining this construct than has the field of SLA. The view of language ability, or proficiency, that dominated the field of language testing during the 1960s and 1970s was one that derived largely from a structuralist linguistics view that saw language as being composed of discrete components (e.g., grammar, vocabulary) and skills (listening, speaking, reading, writing), and a trait psychology view of ability as a unidimensional attribute of which different individuals have greater or lesser amounts.[1]

1 Chapelle (Chapter 2, this volume) provides an excellent discussion of the trait perspective toward defining constructs. Lado (1961) and Carroll (1961) provide discussions of the so-called skills and components approach to defining second

Early SLA research, as did contrastive analysis and error analysis, drew on essentially the same linguistic paradigm for its theoretical grounding.[2] As the field developed, however, many SLA researchers fairly quickly embraced a *homogeneous competence model,* based largely on transformational, generative linguistics, in which linguistic competence is clearly distinguished from nonlinguistic, or pragmatic, knowledge, which "does not need to be taken into account when explaining linguistic competence" (Ellis 1985: 77). At the same time, other SLA researchers broadened their theoretical base to include what Ellis calls a *heterogeneous competence model,* in which "the user's knowledge of the language rules is interlocked with his knowledge of when, where, and with whom to use them" (Ellis 1985: 77). This broader view of language ability as communicative, rather than linguistic, competence incorporates insights from both functional linguistics and sociolinguistics. In addition to enlarging their theoretical view of language ability, SLA researchers began looking more toward cognitive information-processing models of learning for theoretical inspiration.

Thus, as the fields of LT and SLA developed during the seventies and into the eighties, they paid allegiance to different theoretical paradigms, both in linguistics and in psychology. Language testing clung tenaciously to a skills and components model of language proficiency and a trait psychology view of ability, with a brief flirtation, in the early eighties, with the view of language proficiency as a single unitary trait. At the same time, SLA became much broader and more eclectic, embracing a wide range of theoretical perspectives in linguistics, sociolinguistics, sociology, anthropology, psychology, and cognitive science. Nevertheless, even though its theoretical base had expanded a great deal, much of the empirical research in SLA continued to focus rather narrowly on acquisition of the linguistic aspects of language ability, such as morphology, syntax, and lexicon, just as language testing continued to focus on these same elements. That is, even though LT and SLA research had become quite diverse in terms of the theoretical frameworks that generated their research questions and guided their interpretations, the data on language ability that the two sets of researchers collected were still very similar, focusing largely on language skills and language components.

The view of language ability as *communicative competence* currently

language ability. See Oller (1979) for a discussion of the "unitary trait hypothesis" of language ability, a hypothesis that he and the majority of language testers have long since abandoned.
2 See Lado (1957) and Wardhaugh (1970) for early discussions of contrastive analysis; see Corder (1967, 1971) and Richards (1974) for early discussions of error analysis. We would be remiss if we did not point out that neither of these concepts, in its original formulation, is current in SLA. The description of interlanguage differences and learner errors does, nevertheless, continue to be a part of SLA research, albeit within more recent linguistic paradigms.

accepted by many LT researchers represents a major paradigm shift from the structuralist, "skills and components," trait view outlined earlier.[3] The notion of communicative competence, or communicative language ability, has evolved in the following four ways in the past decade:

1. Recognition of a much broader range of components
2. Recognition that these components are not discrete, and that they interact with each other
3. Consideration of how components of competence interact with other cognitive abilities and processes
4. Recognition that language ability includes the capacity for interacting with the context.[4]

Current views of communicative competence in applied linguistics can be traced, to a large extent, to Hymes's (1972) work in this area and to Canale and Swain's (1980) description, which itself drew heavily on work of Hymes (1972), Savignon (1972), and Halliday (1976). Although Canale and Swain (1980) and Canale (1983) provided an expanded view of the components involved in communicative competence, theirs was essentially a static framework, with little discussion of how these expanded components interacted with each other, if at all, or of how communicative competence enables language users to interact with the characteristics of the context of situation, including other language users, in a speech event. Bachman's (1990) description of *communicative language ability* built upon the Canale and Swain description, retaining essentially the same components as theirs, but expanding the role of strategic competence, which Canale and Swain had considered to be limited largely to compensatory communication strategies for dealing with breakdowns in communication or for enhancing communication. Bachman's description of the functions of strategic competence in planning, assessment, and execution provided a means for explaining how the various components of language competence (grammatical, textual, pragmatic, sociolinguistic) interact with each other, and with features of the language use situation.

A recent expansion of this framework is that of Bachman and Palmer (1996), which elaborates further the role of strategic competence as metacognitive strategies (goal setting, assessment, and planning) and includes a discussion of the roles of topical knowledge, or knowledge schemata, and affective schemata in language use. According to Bachman and Palmer's formulation, *goal setting* involves the language user or test taker

---

3 See McNamara (1996) for a thorough historical treatment and critique of the models of language ability proposed by Hymes (1972), Canale, and Swain (1980), and Bachman (1990). Bachman (1990) also provides an overview of these models, as well as those of Lado (1961) and Carroll (1961).

4 This view of language ability is essentially what Chapelle (Chapter 2, this volume) calls an "interactionalist" approach to defining the construct.

in identifying and selecting one or more tasks that he or she might attempt to complete, and deciding whether or not to attempt to complete the task(s). The *assessment component* operates in three ways: (1) assessing the language use or test task to determine whether it is either desirable or feasible to attempt the task, and what linguistic and knowledge resources are likely to be required for this; (2) assessing the individual's own linguistic and knowledge resources to determine whether the knowledge needed is available for use; and (3) assessing the correctness or appropriateness of the response to the task. The *planning component* involves (1) the retrieval of the relevant items from linguistic and topical knowledge, (2) the formulation of one or more plans for responding to the task, and (3) the selection of one plan for initial implementation in a response (Bachman & Palmer 1996: 71–73).

This multicomponential view of language ability has provided a particularly productive theoretical basis for both research and practice in language testing. As part of the background research in preparation for the TOEFL 2000 project, Chapelle, Grabe, and Berns (1997) have provided a description of *communicative language proficiency* and discuss the implications of this model for test development. Several test development projects based explicitly on multicomponential definitions of language ability are included in Brindley (1995). McDowell (1995) uses Bachman's 1990 model of communicative language ability as a basis for developing an English proficiency test as part of a procedure for qualifying nonnative English speakers as language teachers in Australia. Clarkson and Jensen (1995) draw on Bachman's 1990 model to develop rating scales for specific task components, for the purpose of assessing learner achievement in English for occupational purposes courses. Grierson (1995) also utilizes Bachman's 1990 model, along with a systemic functional model of language use (Halliday 1985), to develop an observational checklist for use by teachers in assessing communicative ability in spoken discourse in secondary Intensive English Center classrooms in Australia. McKay (1995) uses Bachman and Palmer's (1996) more elaborated model of language ability, along with considerations of content and contextual features, as a basis for constructing rating scales for use in assessing the ESL proficiency of primary and secondary school students.

STUDIES THAT PROVIDE INSIGHT INTO SPECIFIC COMPONENTS OR ASPECTS OF LANGUAGE ABILITY AND THEIR MEASUREMENT

Now let us consider some studies in which the interplay of SLA and LT research has helped to enhance our understanding of some specific components or aspects of language ability and its acquisition and measurement. The following are some of the many areas that have been explored: the development and role of discourse domains in language acquisition and test performance; the nature of second language (L2) ability, pedagogical factors that affect its development in classroom settings; and social and individual factors that affect its development in majority and minority language settings; interrelationships among L2 ability, foreign language aptitude, and intelligence; the communicative interaction among speakers and learners of a language; communicative grammar; breadth of lexical knowledge; type of cognitive activity in L2 essay writing; multilingual versus monolingual language learning; sociolinguistic ability; and cross-cultural pragmatic ability.

Development and role of discourse domains in language acquisition and test performance. The multicomponential view of language ability has provided a theoretical basis for research not only in LT but in SLA as well. Douglas and Selinker (1985; Selinker & Douglas 1985, 1989; Douglas 1986, and Chapter 6 in this volume), for example, draw on the assessment function of strategic competence to develop the notion of discourse domain as a dynamic, evolving sociopsychological construct that test takers may construct temporarily as a means for dealing with variation across different types of language test tasks. They suggest that these discourse domains may also provide a basis for mediating between the context of language use and language ability, becoming part of the learner's interlanguage competence.

The nature of L2 ability and factors that affect its development in classroom settings, and in majority and minority language settings. In the Development of Bilingual Proficiency (DBP) project (Allen, Cummins, Mougeon, & Swain 1983; Harley, Allen, Cummins, & Swain 1987, 1990), a massive longitudinal study that investigated issues relevant to both the assessment and the acquisition of bilingual proficiency, the Canale and Swain model of communicative competence provided the theoretical definition of language proficiency. The DBP project included both quantitative and qualitative studies, which investigated the nature of language proficiency, the pedagogical factors that affect its development in classroom settings, and the social and individual factors that affect its development in majority and minority language settings. With respect to the nature of language proficiency, the results were mixed: Although confirmatory factor analysis did not support the construct hypothesized by the Canale-Swain model, other analyses "did provide some support for the hypothesis that these constructs are distinguishable and also educationally relevant" (Harley, Cummins, Swain, & Allen 1990: 24). Other findings were that academic tests tended to be related, that academic skills were strongly related across languages, that cognitive factors were more strongly related to discourse competence and writing than to grammatical competence, and that "language proficiency must be conceptualized within a developmental context as a function of interactions that students or learners experience in their languages" (p. 25).

Interrelationships among L2 ability, foreign language aptitude, and intelligence. In a study that included both quantitative and qualitative research approaches, Sasaki (1993a, b) investigated the relationships among components of second language proficiency and two individual factors that have long been investigated in the SLA literature: foreign language aptitude and intelligence. The results of her quantitative analyses provide support for a multicomponential model of second language proficiency, for a cognitive ability that includes both intelligence and language aptitude, and for Bachman's (1990) hypothesis that second language ability "is related to but not identical with, general cognitive abilities" (Sasaki 1993a: 337). The results of her qualitative analyses of verbal report protocols suggest that a general factor of second language proficiency is related to the amount of information processing involved in correctly solving certain types of tasks. In addition, the verbal report protocols reveal that high proficiency subjects were better able to use available information to answer cloze test items correctly, spent more time planning, and used a greater variety of strategies than did the low proficiency subjects. This study thus provides some tantalizing insights into the nature of language proficiency and its relationship to general cognitive abilities. In addition, it demonstrates that by combining quantitative and qualitative approaches to research one can investigate both the process of problem solving and its product. Since SLA tends to focus on the process of language acquisition, and LT on its product, the combining of qualitative and quantitative approaches would appear to provide a particularly powerful paradigm for future research in this interface.

Assessing word order through communicative interaction. Perhaps one of the first areas in which SLA research informed the design of more communicative speaking tests was that of interactional analysis. SLA researchers wanted to capture interaction, but felt that traditional approaches to testing speaking were not assessing these interactions well, if at all. There is now a series of SLA studies that inform language testing because they suggest the kinds of interactive tasks that are likely to produce interactional data. An example of these studies is that reported by Ellis (1989), which looked at the extent to which classroom and naturalistic acquisition are the same.

The article reports a study of the classroom acquisition of German word order rules by adult foreign language learners of varied language backgrounds in two institutions in London. Data elicited by an information gap task performed by 39 foreign learners of German at two points in time were used to describe the sequence of acquisition of three obligatory word order rules. The learners worked in pairs. A picture composition was cut up and two pictures were given to each learner. Each learner was asked to describe his or her pictures in German without showing them to the partner so that they could jointly work out the story, creating a two-way communication task. The pairs completed the task three times, the first serving as a warm-up, followed by each learner's producing a monologue of one of the complete stories. The tasks were conducted in a language laboratory and the stories were recorded, both as a pre- and a posttest.

Ellis compared the word order sequence observed with that reported in the literature on naturalistic learners of German and found no difference, despite the fact that the order in which the rules were introduced in the curriculum and the degree of emphasis given to the rules in the instruction differed from the naturalistic order. The classroom learners, however, did appear to be more successful than the naturalistic learners in that they reached higher levels of acquisition in a shorter period of time. The results of this study supported the claim that the classroom and naturalistic L2 acquisition of complex grammatical features such as word order follow similar routes. The results also suggest that classroom learners may learn more rapidly. In addition to the substantive findings about SLA, this study's use of paired tasks constituted an effort to use LT tasks that were genuinely communicative. The learners were recorded on a pre- and posttest basis by performing a task in a language laboratory whereby they had to communicate back and forth until they reconstituted picture compositions for which each learner had been given two pictures. Then in each case one of the learners had to tell the complete story in German. The elicitation task was designed to tap unmonitored, informal language use.

Assessing grammar in communicative contexts.   Some studies have by their very nature been suggestive of how to design measurement tasks in areas that have been a challenge to assess. One such area is that of assessing grammatical competence in immersion education programs. In an effort to produce L2 speakers who have truly functional ability, immersion programs have at the same time produced speakers who lack control of grammar. Day and Shapson (1991) conducted a study to evaluate the degree to which focusing on form affects French immersion students' proficiency. Their contribution to the language testing literature was to demonstrate an approach to measuring form within a communicative situation.

Although far from unique, their efforts do constitute an example of applying SLA insights to test construction. The researchers designed a teaching/learning unit focusing on the conditional in natural, communicative situations, and administered it for three 45- to 60-minute periods over a period of five to six weeks. The learning was reinforced with systematic linguistic games, and metalinguistic awareness was encouraged through self-evaluation activities. Group work and cooperative learning were encouraged. Pre-, post-, and follow-up tests were administered to 315 seventh grade early immersion and control classes (also to French immersion classes, without focus on form). The instruments included a written version of a French dialogue with 30 verbs omitted (to be filled in mostly with the conditional form); a 15-minute composition titled "If I were . . . ," to be completed with reference to a comic character or a famous person; and an oral interview designed to elicit the use of the conditional in hypothetical situations. The results indicated that the classes that experienced an approach integrating formal analytic and functional communicative activities in teaching the conditional made significantly higher gains in their ability to use this form in writing than did classes that had not experienced this approach. While the group differences in speaking were not significant, there still appeared to be greater and more consistent growth in speaking for the experimental than for the control classes. This study demonstrated the interface of SLA with LT by addressing an SLA issue – focus on form – and then developing measures to try to assess the forms in question.

Breadth of lexical knowledge.   Although researchers have explored lexical knowledge to some extent, they have until recently made few innovations in assessment (see, e.g., Read 1993; Chapelle 1994; Wesche & Paribakht 1996). We are beginning to see studies in which SLA researchers are defining new ways to assess vocabulary knowledge. Verhallen and Schoonen (1993), for instance, conducted a study with the aim of gaining insight into the lexico-semantic knowledge of bilingual children growing up in a second language submersion environment. The research focused on aspects of lexical knowledge relevant for school success. They were seeking a more detailed picture of the underlying semantic knowledge of individual words than that typically obtained from vocabulary tests, and so they constructed a series of extended word definition tasks.

Data were obtained by asking 40 monolingual Dutch and 40 bilingual Turkish children (9- and 11-year-olds) to explain the meanings of common Dutch nouns in an extended word definition task. In a structured interview, the children were requested to provide all the meaning aspects they could think of for a series of words. Hence, the interview tasks went beyond elicitation of formal definitions, such as "How would you explain what an X is?", "What do you see if you look at an X?", "What kinds of X's are there?", "What can/must you do with an X?", and "Can you make three sentences with the word X?" Data analysis looked at both the number of meaning aspects expressed and the nature of meaning relations involved. Compared to the monolingual Dutch children, the

Turkish children tended to allot less extensive and less varied meanings to Dutch words. This article demonstrates how SLA researchers can broaden the aspect of language ability that testers are looking for – in this case, broader lexical knowledge.

Type of cognitive activity in L2 essay writing.   Another study suggested ways of broadening essay writing tasks by making explicit the type of cognitive activity desired. In a process-oriented SLA study, Kobayashi and Rinnert (1992) investigated English composition writing by 48 Japanese university students. The students were requested to compose their essays in two different ways – writing in Japanese and then translating, as well as writing directly in English. The finding was that the translations were rated higher (in content and style) than were the direct essays. This demonstrated the interface of SLA with testing in that testers would traditionally not consider the possible role of mental translation and overt translation in the writing process. The study revealed certain advantages of translation: Ideas were easier to develop, thoughts and opinions could be expressed more clearly, and words could be more easily found through the use of a dictionary. Respondents reported being able to think more deeply and better express their thoughts and opinions using this approach. The main point is that a process approach characteristically reserved for SLA studies might suggest the benefits of requesting respondents to perform different types of writing tasks at the cognitive level – that is, tasks calling for composition in the L1 and then translation, and tasks that are to be composed directly in the L2.

Multilingual versus monolingual language learning.   Another SLA study demonstrated ways in which language learners who were already multilingual (i.e., competent in three or more languages) may perform differently on language tests from learners who are monolingual (minimal or no proficiency in languages other than their native language). Nayak, Hansen, Krueger, and McLaughlin (1990) investigated the hypothesis that people with multiple language skills have different language acquisition strategies than do people with language skills in a single language. Twenty-four multilingual subjects (i.e., rated at least 6 on a scale of 1 to 7, in at least three or more languages) and 24 monolingual subjects learned a miniature linguistic system under instructions to "memorize" or to "discover" rules. In the "memory" condition, subjects were told to memorize each sentence presented. In the "rule discovery" condition, subjects were told that the order of the words in the sentences presented was determined by a complex set of rules and that their task was to try to discover these. A computerized vocabulary task was constructed with 15 exemplars of five different types of items. The subjects were asked to indicate whether the word and its referent were items learned in the learning phase. The instructions stressed both accuracy and speed. The subjects also took a test of syntax that required them to determine whether 48 sentences were grammatically acceptable in the language. The subjects also provided verbal reports as to which strategies they were using in the course of the learning phase, and these protocols were analyzed for the frequency of four types of strategies: (1) focusing on the syntactic structure of the sentences, (2) listing sets of words as appearing in specific positions, (3) referring to a real-world object by its shape, and (4) trying to construct normal lexical items from consonant-vowel-consonant artificial words.

Although not superior overall, multilingual subjects were better able to adjust their learning strategies according to the requirements of the task, as indicated through verbal report data. For example, the multilingual subjects used a wider variety of different strategies in the rule discovery than in the memory condition, and no such difference existed in the monolingual subjects. Although these differences in strategy use did not yield significant advantages in overall performance, we feel that the finding that multilingual subjects showed greater flexibility in switching strategies has important implications with respect to interpreting the results of performance on language tests. In a study like this one, SLA researchers contribute to language testing the message that respondents' language background must be taken into account when interpreting test results.

Assessing sociolinguistic ability.   SLA researchers have already contributed to the assessment of sociocultural and sociolinguistic ability (e.g., Cohen & Olshtain 1981; Raffaldini 1988; Cohen 1994). What has been lacking is sufficient volume of such studies to give language testers a clear picture of forms of sociocultural and sociolinguistic assessment that are both needed and feasible. One example of a recent effort in this direction is a study by Lyster (1994), which investigated the effect of teaching foreign language immersion students functional aspects of sociolinguistic competence, specifically, sociostylistic variation in the use of the French pronominal forms *tu* and *vous*. The sample consisted of 106 eighth grade French immersion students in five classrooms from three schools in Toronto. All students were native English speakers and had been enrolled in immersion school since kindergarten. At the eighth grade level, 50 percent of the school day was still conducted in French. The treatment was administered by three out of the five French immersion classroom teachers during French language arts over five weeks. The treatment materials consisted of a curriculum unit written by the researcher and highlighting sociolinguistic variation, context, participant roles, and speech acts. The focus was on how language varies according to social context (formal vs. informal) and geographic context (Canadian vs. European lexical variants). Grammar exercises, role plays, letter and invitation writing, and intensive reading activities all highlighted verb patterns using both *tu* and *vous*.

Three measures of sociolinguistic competence were given as a pretest, immediate posttest, and delayed posttest to the experimental classes and to the comparison classes. The measures included an oral production task (requesting or giving directions, requesting help in math, offering to help carry books in formal and informal contexts), a written production task (writing an informal note and a formal letter), and a multiple choice task of stylistic choice (choosing the appropriate style for the given context or the appropriate context for a given style). Findings showed improvement in the experimental group in three ways: (1) ability in oral production to appropriately and accurately use *vous* in formal situations, (2) ability in written production to appropriately use *vous* in formal letters, and in the short run, to use polite closings in formal letters, and (3) ability to recognize contextually appropriate French. The study represents an SLA study that affects language testing because it demonstrates not only how sociolinguistic features can be taught and learned, but how they can be assessed on a large-scale basis.

Assessing cross-cultural pragmatic ability. Hudson, Detmer, and Brown (1992) present a framework for developing methods that assess cross-cultural pragmatic ability. The framework was designed for Japanese and American cross-cultural contrasts and focuses on the variables of social distance, relative power, and the degree of imposition within the speech acts of requests, refusals, and apologies. Evaluation of performance is based on recognition of the speech act, amount of speech, forms or formulae used, directness, formality, and politeness. In a subsequent report, Hudson, Detmer, and Brown (1995) provide an updated description of their efforts to generate instruments for assessing cross-cultural pragmatics that might make research comparable across studies and languages. They describe the process through which six forms of cross-cultural assessment were developed for ESL learners: two forms each of indirect discourse completion tests, oral language production, and self-assessment. The procedures involve the assessment of requests, apologies, and refusals. The models are intended for use with L2 learners of other languages.

Strategies and processes in LT and SLA

Language use strategies are mental operations or processes that learners consciously select and apply when attempting to accomplish language use tasks. These strategies constitute test-taking strategies when they are applied to language assessment tasks. For the purposes of this volume (and as further discussed by Cohen in Chapter 4), test-taking strategies are viewed as those test-taking processes that the respondents have selected and that they are conscious of, at least to some degree. In other words, the notion of strategy implies an element of selection. Otherwise, the processes would not be considered strategies. The ability of learners to use language strategies was referred to by Canale and Swain (1980) as their strategic competence – a component of communicative language use. As indicated earlier, Bachman (1990) and Bachman and Palmer (1996) have expanded this view of strategic competence to include metacognitive strategies.

A number of studies have now emerged that have attempted to describe the processes involved in the implementation of language assessment instruments. We briefly review here some illustrative studies that deal with the learning and recall of vocabulary, the strategies involved in taking listening and reading comprehension tests, the validation of self-assessment, and the relationship between metacognitive and cognitive strategies and performance on language tests. Cohen (Chapter 4, this volume) provides a more extensive review and discussion of test-taking strategies and processes.

THE RELATIONSHIP BETWEEN METACOGNITIVE AND COGNITIVE STRATEGIES AND PERFORMANCE ON LANGUAGE TESTS

A study by Purpura (1996) utilized a questionnaire to investigate the relationships among self-reported metacognitive and cognitive strategy use and different areas of EFL proficiency. The questionnaire he used included two of the components from the questionnaire item bank on test-taker characteristics that was developed by Bachman, Purpura, and Cushing (1993), and the EFL proficiency test he used was the English Language Test developed by the University of Cambridge Local Examinations Syndicate for use as an anchor test in equating different Cambridge EFL proficiency tests. Purpura obtained responses to the strategy questionnaire and anchor test from 1,382 nonnative speakers of English and analyzed these responses with structural equation modeling to investigate the relationships among the strategy variables and scores on the different parts of the EFL test.

His results suggest that two factors of language ability – reading and grammar – are tapped by the test, and that cognitive processes are grouped into three factors: comprehending, memory, and retrieval. Furthermore, he found that the metacognitive process variables loaded on a single factor, and that this was positively related to the three cognitive process factors, suggesting that "metacognitive processes consist of a set of overarching control processes, where metacognitive processing basically involves assessment with goal-setting and planning characterized as special cases of assessment" (Purpura 1996: 218). Purpura found that the cognitive factors – comprehending and memory – had slight negative effects and large negative effects, respectively, on the grammar ability factor, whereas the retrieval factor had a strong positive effect. Purpura speculates that these relationships may indicate that memory processes are more closely associated with learning than with language use or test taking, and that "'good' test taking strategies might be empirically defined as the ability to retrieve information from long-term memory without spending time trying to 'learn' or 'remember' during the test" (p. 226). Purpura also proposes a construct, test-taking style, which "can be characterized along a continuum from learning-oriented to product or testing-oriented" (p. 227), and that can be defined "according to the type of cognitive processes a test taker invokes during testing and the degree to which test takers use cognitive processes" (p. 228). This study provides valuable insights into the nature of learning and test-taking strategies, and suggests that these may be fruitfully considered not as separate types of strategies, but rather as a common set of strategies applied to different types of language learning and language use tasks.

PROCESSES INVOLVED IN TAKING LISTENING AND READING COMPREHENSION TESTS

With specific regard to the testing of listening, Buck (1994) utilized introspective verbal reports to examine the processes involved in responding to second language listening comprehension tasks, and then related the verbal reports to performance on a listening comprehension test. Using a structured interview procedure, six Japanese-speaking ESL students studying at a British university were asked to introspect while taking a short-answer listening comprehension test – with ongoing questions after each section. The resulting protocols were then analyzed to ascertain the knowledge, skills, and abilities that influenced item performance. Results indicated that items typically required a variety of subskills of listening for successful performance, and that these usually differed from one respondent to another. This was primarily a language testing study, and it can be used to demonstrate how process approaches to test taking can help to validate listening comprehension tests by attempting to determine what the items are actually assessing.

With regard to reading, a study by Anderson, Bachman, Perkins, and Cohen (1991) used data from think-aloud protocols, content analysis of test tasks, and statistical indices of item difficulty and discrimination to investigate the relationships among the strategies used by nonnative readers on reading tests, the characteristics of the test tasks, and performance on those tasks. The subjects for this study were 28 native speakers of Spanish studying in an intensive English program at a U.S. university. All subjects took three measures of reading comprehension: (1) a reading comprehension subtest from a test of language skills, (2) a measure of ability to read college-level textbook prose (Textbook Reading Profile), and (3) an alternate form of the reading comprehension test. After the first two tasks, the participants provided retrospective think-aloud protocols describing the strategies they used while reading the textbook material and while answering the comprehension questions. On the third task, respondents were asked to provide think-aloud protocols after reading each passage and answering the comprehension questions for that passage.

Data from verbal report protocols were classified into 47 processing strategies, which were then grouped into the following five categories:

1. *Strategies for supervising strategy use* (e.g., stating failure to understand a portion of text, confirming an inference)
2. *Support strategies* (e.g., skipping unknown words, skimming reading material for a general understanding)
3. *Paraphrase strategies* (e.g., translating a word or phrase into the L1, breaking lexical items into parts)
4. *Strategies for establishing coherence in text* (e.g., reading ahead, using background knowledge)
5. *Test-taking strategies* (e.g., looking for the answers in chronological order in the passage, selecting an alternative through deductive reasoning).

In addition to the data from the participants' retrospective think-aloud protocols of their reading and test-taking strategies, two other kinds of data were collected. These included (1) content analyses of the reading comprehension passages and questions, one based on the test designer's specifications and the second on a taxonomy that had been used in previous studies (Sarig 1987), and (2) classical indices of item difficulty and discrimination. The data indicated that respondents used certain strategies differently, depending on the type of question that was being asked. For example, the strategies of "trying to match the stem with the text" and "guessing" were reported more frequently for inference type questions than for the other question types, such as direct statement or main idea. The strategy of "paraphrasing" was reported to occur more in responding to questions involving a direct statement than those involving the main idea or inference. This study exemplifies the use of different types of data – verbal reports of processing strategies, content analyses of test tasks, and indices of item difficulty and discrimination – in construct validation. It also illustrates how construct validation research can provide one paradigm for investigating research questions that are of interest to both LT and SLA researchers.

PROCESSES IN THE LEARNING AND RECALL OF VOCABULARY

SLA research aimed at describing the processes learners go through in order to perform language tasks has provided valuable insights into the interpretation of the results obtained from language tests. Mangubhai (1991), for example, provided a case-study analysis of the processes used by five native English-speaking adult learners of Hindi as a second language in their efforts to learn and recall words. The input was from 20 Total Physical Response sessions over one month. Concurrent think-aloud protocols, as well as immediate and delayed retrospective reports, were collected over the 20 sessions. At the end of the sessions, all subjects carried out three tasks that were audiotaped: performing an action in response to 30 utterances, sentence repetition with 20 items, and summarizing in English two short conversations in Hindi.

While the first and third tasks were the kinds of tasks conventionally used in language tests, the second was more the type of measure used in SLA studies (see Bley-Vroman & Chaudron 1994; Munnich, Flynn, & Martohardjono 1994). The study is an example of the impact of SLA work on language testing in both its integration of SLA and testing types of measures and its collection of verbal report data to assist in interpreting the product results. Mangubhai was able to describe the processing of lexical items by his respondents – that is, whether the focus was on form, on meaning, or on storage and retrieval.

These studies reflect a clear shift in perspective from a view of language ability and other abilities as traits that learners possess to varying degrees, to an interactionalist view of language ability as the capacity for language use. This capacity, then, involves a dynamic, information-processing interaction among components of language competence, metacognitive strategies and processes, knowledge schemata, affective schemata, and the characteristics of the context in which language use takes place.[5]

VARIATIONS IN TASKS AND CONTEXT AND THEIR EFFECTS ON LANGUAGE USE

As is discussed at length by Tarone (Chapter 3, this volume), research on interlanguage variation has shown that it is common for the language production of L2 learners to vary systematically in grammatical accuracy and fluency (among other characteristics) in response to contextual changes. Such systematic variation may lead to seeming inconsistencies among respondents on language tests or SLA research tasks from one task to the next. It is in part the work of the test developers or researchers to specify the situational features, or characteristics, of the tasks they design so as to facilitate the investigation of the degree to which variations in performance, or interlanguage output on the task, are in fact an artifact of task characteristics. As Tarone notes, researchers in language testing may wish to join forces with SLA researchers in joint research

---

5 Skehan (1994) discusses the role of metacognition and cognitive processes, or what he calls "general cognitive abilities," in foreign language aptitude and language ability.

projects to establish exactly what task characteristics tend to be related to what sorts of systematic variation in particular interlanguage forms. An understanding of this relationship could enable language testers to systematically manipulate task characteristics with a clear understanding of the sorts of choices those manipulations lay before learners.

It is now well established that the way individuals use language, and perhaps their ability to use language, for communication varies as a function of features in the language use context or situation (e.g., Cathcart 1986; Tarone 1988; Bayley 1991, 1994; Young 1991, 1993; Tarone & Liu 1995). Research on interlanguage variation has shown that it is common for the language production of L2 learners to vary systematically in grammatical accuracy and fluency (among other characteristics) in response to contextual changes (see Tarone, Chapter 3).

PERFORMANCE ON SLA ELICITATION TASKS

As illustrated through 75 SLA studies discussed in Tarone (1988), variation in language production by the same L2 learner is common, and shifts in accuracy may be triggered by such contextual factors as shifts in the identity of the interlocutor and the learner's relationship with that interlocutor, topic, degree to which the learner was encouraged to focus on accuracy, or communicative pressure (defined as the speaker's perception of the interlocutor's need for the information being transmitted), among others. A recent longitudinal case study, for example, demonstrated the effects of context on the elicitation of SLA data. The study was of a 6-year-old Chinese boy acquiring English as a second language in three contexts, each distinguished by the interlocutors with whom the boy was interacting and his role relationships with those interlocutors (Liu 1991; Tarone & Liu 1995). As Tarone points out in Chapter 3 (this volume), the boy's movement through five developmental stages of question formation in English was affected differentially by each situational context. Each new stage of question formation generally appeared first in interaction with a friendly and interested adult friend during "play sessions" in the boy's home, later in interactions in the classroom with the boy's peers in desk work, and last (often weeks later) in interactions with the boy's teacher in class. Thus, at any given time, this boy's use of English questions appeared most advanced in the first context and least advanced in the third.

PERFORMANCE ON LANGUAGE TESTS

Systematic variation within language learners not only shows up in SLA tasks but may lead to seeming inconsistencies among respondents on language tests from one task situation to the next. This has long been the subject of research and discussion in the LT literature and continues to be an area of active interest. Hoekje and Linnell (1994), for instance, evaluated three instruments of spoken language assessment: the Spoken Proficiency in English Assessment Kit (SPEAK), the ACTFL Oral Proficiency Interview (OPI), and their own Interactive Performance (IP) test. The IP test required candidates to give a 10-minute videotaped presentation on a topic from their prospective teaching fields and to answer questions from a panel of evaluators. The panel consisted of three ESL specialists and, in some cases, an undergraduate student. Throughout the IP presentation, the panelists were to interrupt and ask questions in order to (1) elicit paraphrase, defense of an opinion, and negotiation of meaning, and (2) have the candidate speak extemporaneously on a related but, perhaps, unprepared topic. Hoekje and Linnell's analyses of the test data indicated that these three instruments differed from one another primarily with regard to the effect of the interlocutor on the performance of the same respondent. Specifically, the tests varied with regard to whether or not an interlocutor was present, the number of interlocutors present, and the power of the speaker (to control turn taking and topic) in relation to the interlocutor(s). The three instruments were found to have a differential impact on the learner's length of turn and use of discourse markers.

It has also been empirically demonstrated that even when tasks are identical, topic can affect interlanguage performance. Smith (1992) found that the pronunciation, grammar, fluency, and overall comprehensibility of many teaching assistants (TAs) were all subject to variation in relation to changes in topic, and in relation to particular test tasks. Smith's results showed that individual TAs' scores on a SPEAK test differed strikingly, depending on whether they were given a field-specific topic or a general topic for otherwise identical test tasks (see Tarone, Chapter 3 in this volume, for more details).

There is also empirical evidence from a number of studies that variations in the specific characteristics of individual test tasks or items is related to test performance. In a study that examined the relationship between characteristics of EFL vocabulary test items and item difficulty, Perkins and Linnville (1987) used both objective measures (e.g., frequency, distribution, number of syllables) and subjective ratings (e.g., abstractness, evaluation, potency, activity) of characteristics of EFL vocabulary test items and related these to the performance on these items by students in two different levels of ESL courses and by native English speakers. Their results indicated that while very few of the variables examined were related to item difficulty, word length, frequency, and abstractness consistently predicted item difficulty across three different levels of English proficiency.

Freedle and Kostin (1993) investigated the extent to which the content characteristics of TOEFL reading comprehension items predict item difficulty. They used both objective measures (e.g., number of words in the item stem, number of sentences in the passages) and subjective measures – involving either rating (e.g., degree of coherence or abstractness) or counting (e.g., number of negations, referentials) – as indicators of item content. Although they found that a large number of the predictor variables, taken individually, were correlated significantly with item difficulty, the sizes of these correlations were generally small enough so as to raise the question of whether they are meaningful. Using multiple regression analysis, they found that only 8 of the 91 predictors included in the study were significantly related to item difficulty.[6] Their reported R^2s, however, were sizable (.303 and .524 for samples of 213 and 98 items, respectively), and on this basis they concluded that "a substantial amount of the variance [in item difficulty] can be accounted for by a relatively small number of . . . predictors" (p. 166).

Bachman, Davidson, and Milanovic (1996) investigated the relationships between expert ratings of the test method characteristics of individual test items and difficulty indices of these items. Following Bachman (1990), a content analysis of test method characteristics and components of communicative language ability was performed by five raters on six forms of the First Certificate of English, which is administered by the University of Cambridge Local Examinations Syndicate. The relationships between the content analysis ratings and two-parameter item response theory (IRT) item difficulty estimates were investigated using multiple linear regression analysis. Although neither test method nor ability ratings by themselves yielded consistent predictions of item difficulty across the six forms examined, fairly high predictions were consistently obtained when method and ability ratings were both used as predictors.

Careful analysis of contextual differences in assessment instruments led Douglas (Chapter 6, this volume) to conclude that any factor in the test domain that researchers change can lead to changes in an interlanguage user's perceptions and assessment of the communicative situation, and thus to changes in interlanguage performance on the test. He suggests that rather than attempting to minimize the effects of test method on the interpretation of results, LT and SLA researchers should employ them to design tests that are appropriate for particular populations.

Taken together, the results of these studies not only support the hypothesis that test performance varies across different tasks, but they also provide evidence that performance varies as a function of specific task characteristics that may be common to a number of different tasks.

6 We would note that in multiple linear regression, it is the number of independent variables that actually enter a given regression as predictors, and not the total number of independent variables in the study design, that is relevant to determining the adequacy of the sample and the need to adjust for shrinkage by using the adjusted R^2.

Directions for future research

Characterizing authenticity and the nature of language use tasks

As noted earlier, many SLA researchers consider authentic, unmonitored language use (vernacular) to be the primary source of data for the investigation of language acquisition, and hence place great value on "authentic" tasks for SLA research (Tarone, Chapter 3, this volume). Language testers have also argued that in order to make inferences about language ability that will generalize beyond the language test, we need to design test tasks that correspond to nontest language use tasks (Bachman & Palmer 1996). It may appear to be relatively straightforward to base research on observations of specific instances of authentic language use and to make inferences about language acquisition and language ability in general on the basis of such observations. However, there are two dilemmas that make these activities particularly problematic for LT and SLA researchers. First, there is the so-called observer's paradox (Labov 1972), which refers to the problem that the very act of observation may change, in fundamental ways, the nature of the language use that is being observed. This implies that it is virtually impossible to observe authentic language use naturalistically, let alone to collect instances of it through LT test tasks or SLA elicitation tasks. Candidates in an oral interview, for example, are generally quite aware that this is a test, and the extent to which their responses to the interviewer's questions are affected by this awareness will diminish their authenticity. Similarly, those SLA elicitation tasks that require subjects to respond in prescribed ways, so as to elicit specific structures or lexical items, impose artificial constraints that may yield responses that are less authentic than the language the subjects may use in real-life situations.

The second dilemma is the so-called bandwidth fidelity dilemma (Cronbach 1984: 174–175), which refers to the problem that broad, authentic samples of language use yield more generalizable but less accurate inferences about components of language ability, while narrow, less authentic samples yield more accurate but less generalizable inferences. This can be illustrated by two different approaches that might be used to collect data on the acquisition of, say, tense and aspect in English. One approach might be to collect a broad range of authentic samples of language use, and then go through these to identify and analyze the specific utterances that include data relevant to the research question. With this approach, inferences made about the acquisition of tense and aspect may generalize to a relatively wide range of situations, but the precision or accuracy of these inferences may be limited by the specific local contexts in which the subjects happen to use the structures in question. Another approach would be to design some highly structured elicitation tasks that focus on the use of tense and aspect in both obligatory and nonobligatory contexts. With this approach, inferences made about the acquisition of tense and aspect may be quite accurate with respect to specific contexts, but these inferences may not generalize beyond the types of elicitation tasks that are used.

We would argue that as long as LT and SLA researchers view authenticity as an *absolute* quality that resides solely in the language used in naturally occurring real-life discourse, and conceive of the contexts and tasks in which such discourse occurs as holistic entities, these two dilemmas will continue to cloud the inferences they make on the basis of their research. Rather than accepting this source of indeterminacy in our research, we believe we need to reconceptualize authenticity as a *relative* quality: the degree to which the language use we observe and sample in our research corresponds to real-life language use. In order to assure that relativeness does not become a license for imprecision in our research, we need a means for describing the characteristics of tasks in precise terms.

Bachman and Palmer (1996) have developed an approach for characterizing and designing test tasks that correspond to nontest language use tasks.[7] Although they present the approach for designing and developing or for selecting test tasks, we believe it also provides a basis for developing or selecting SLA elicitation tasks and for investigating the degree to which and how such tasks correspond to real-life tasks. At the heart of their approach is the principle that if we use performance on test tasks to make inferences about individuals' language ability, then performance on these tasks must correspond, in demonstrable ways, to test takers' language use in nontest situations. Their notion of authenticity pertains to this correspondence between test tasks and real-life tasks. We would argue that this same principle can be applied to the use of SLA elicitation tasks to make inferences about L2 acquisition.

The idea of using actual instances of real-life language use as criteria of authenticity for either selecting test tasks or defining the domain to which inferences about language ability generalize has long been a topic of controversy in LT. The controversy has centered on the problem of distinguishing real-life language use from performance on language tests. Bachman (1990) discusses this problem at length, arguing that because real-life language use does not constitute a well-defined domain, there is no basis for determining where real-life language use ends and test language use begins. Furthermore, as Bachman and Palmer (1996) argue,

---

7 We do not discuss Bachman and Palmer's approach in its entirety here, but simply mention the concepts that are central to their view of authenticity. Readers interested in a discussion of how these concepts can be operationalized in the design and development of language tests should consult their book.

"because language use, by its very nature, is embedded in particular situations, each of which may vary in numerous ways, each instance of language use is virtually unique, making it impossible to list all the possible instances" (p. 44). Consider, for example, the problem of listing all the instances of language use in even a fairly narrowly constrained domain such as that of an airline flight attendant. Even if all instances of language use could be listed, which of the following would you consider to be representative of this domain?

Describing safety regulations and procedures to be followed in the event of an emergency
Asking passengers' preferences for refreshments
Explaining why a particular request cannot be granted
Giving passengers information about connecting flights
Assuring passengers that they will not miss their connecting flight, even though this flight is going to arrive late
Requesting a passenger to refrain from smoking in the aisle

This example illustrates the difficulty of determining whether a given instance of real-life language use is representative of a particular domain. Bachman argues that in order to address this problem, we need to characterize instances of language use in terms of their essential characteristics, rather than as holistic language use situations, and proposes a set of such features for the purposes of language testing research and development.

In their approach to language test design and development, Bachman and Palmer (1996) begin by defining the notion of *language use task,* drawing on both the SLA literature (e.g., Crookes & Gass 1993; Duff 1993; Pica, Kanagy, & Falodun 1993) and the psychometric literature (e.g., Carroll 1993), as follows:

an activity that involves individuals in using language for the purpose of achieving a particular goal or objective in a particular situation. We would note that this definition of language use task thus includes both the specific activity and the situation in which it takes place. (p. 44)

It is worth noting that there is nothing in this definition that precludes, a priori, either LT tasks or SLA elicitation tasks. Bachman and Palmer then define two additional key notions of their approach: target language use domain and target language task, which provide the basis for their definition of authenticity. Drawing on Bachman's notion of essential features, they argue that it is possible to identify certain distinguishing characteristics of language use tasks and to use these characteristics to describe target language use domains, or those specific domains in which the test takers are likely to use language. They define a *target language use domain* as follows:

a set of specific language use tasks that the test taker is likely to encounter outside of the test itself, and to which we want our inferences about language ability to generalize.[8]

A language use task that is within a specific target language use domain is called a *target language use task.*

In order to illustrate how these notions can be defined in operational terms, Bachman and Palmer (pp. 49–50) describe a framework of task characteristics, which they believe provides a basis for test developers and test users to investigate the degree of correspondence between target language use tasks and test tasks, which, they argue, is at the heart of authenticity.[9] We believe this approach to defining authenticity in relative terms and to characterizing the nature of tasks as collections of characteristics is valuable for two reasons. First, it enables us to *demonstrate* the relative authenticity of the language samples we observe or elicit, rather than simply argue for their authenticity. Second, it provides a clear delineation of the domain(s) of language use to which our inferences about language ability or language acquisition may generalize.

Some questions for future research

The multicomponential, information-processing view of language ability discussed here, along with the recognition of the complexity of language use tasks, poses a number of challenging questions for both LT and SLA research. Rather than attempting to discuss these in detail, we will simply list those that appear to us to be particularly challenging and interesting.

DEVELOPMENT OF L2 ABILITY

1. To what extent does the acquisition of the different components of language ability follow distinct developmental sequences, or is the development of these components interrelated? For example, research into the acquisition of various syntactic, lexical, and morphological features of languages suggests fairly well-defined developmental sequences. To

---

8 Bachman and Palmer (1996) further distinguish two general types of target language use domains that are of particular interest to the development of language tests. One type of domain consists of situations in which language is used essentially for purposes of communication. They refer to these as *real-life domains.* The other type of domain consists of situations in which language is used for the purpose of teaching and learning language, which they refer to as *language instructional domains.* These two domains are not necessarily mutually exclusive, since much of the research and thinking in language teaching methodology since the late 1970s have been aimed at creating teaching and learning tasks in which the purpose for using language is to communicate, and not simply to learn.

9 The task characteristics described by Bachman and Palmer are essentially the same as the "test method facets" described in Bachman (1990).

what extent does the acquisition of pragmatic features, such as language functions, and sociolinguistic features, such as register and politeness, also follow regular patterns of development? What are regular patterns of development for language functions, register, and politeness, and how can we measure these? To what extent are the acquisition of formal characteristics and the acquisition of functional characteristics of languages related? How does this vary across different languages? Answers to these questions would have important implications not only for the way we design language tests and interpret their scores, but also for the specification of pedagogical grammars and the design of language teaching syllabi, tasks, and materials.

2. Under what specific conditions do the different components of language ability in a given language operate in more or less the same way across a variety of language use contexts? Under what conditions do they operate differently? This question focuses on the situated nature of language use and its acquisition. For example, does a businessperson need to learn a huge number of combinations of situations, functions, and lexico-grammatical features in order to conduct business in the foreign language, or are there some generalizations about how these co-occur that might minimize the learning task? Similarly, are there generalizations across home, market, and educational settings that might aid language planners? To what extent can we investigate these variations with SLA elicitation tasks or LT tasks?

ROLES OF COGNITIVE STRATEGIES AND PROCESSES

3. To what extent are the same cognitive strategies and processes involved in the acquisition and use of different components of L2 ability?

4. To what extent are the same cognitive strategies and processes involved in both second language acquisition and L2 use?

5. To what extent are these strategies and processes qualitatively different from each other, as opposed to being a common set of metacognitive components and cognitive strategies that are applied differentially in response to different tasks? It has been fairly common, for example, to discuss test-taking strategies as different from language learning and language use strategies. Cohen (Chapter 4, this volume), however, argues that a common set of strategies may be activated by language users, learners, and test takers as a function of the particular type of task encountered. If this hypothesis were supported by research results, it would have important implications, not only for the way we design language tests but also for how and whether we attempt to teach such strategies to language learners and language users.

ROLES OF TASK CHARACTERISTICS[10]

6. To what extent do task characteristics differentially affect an individual's perceptions of the relative authenticity of tasks? To what extent do these differing perceptions of authenticity affect an individual's performance, and hence the kinds of inferences made on the basis of observation, elicitation, and test scores? Suppose, for example, that a male respondent were asked in a speaking task to apologize for bumping into someone and knocking a bag of groceries out of that person's hands. If the respondent viewed this as an absurd situation, because he would never be so careless, would the task be relatively inauthentic? If the respondent were not able to extrapolate from this particular situation to one that required a sincere and explicit apology, would this limit the evaluator's ability to make inferences about the respondent's ability to apologize appropriately or about his acquisition of appropriate strategies for apology?

7. To what extent do the characteristics of assessment or elicitation tasks affect or determine the domains to which our inferences from test scores or SLA elicitation results generalize? For example, to what extent would inferences about reading that were based on a test that included several academic science passages generalize to other topics or genres? If a candidate in an oral interview is not asked to discuss topics about which she has professional expertise, to what extent can we infer that she is capable of addressing such topics effectively in speaking? If a subject is asked to participate in a role play involving peers, as a means for investigating the acquisition of appropriate request forms, to what extent do the inferences we make, based on his responses, generalize to interactions with adults?

References

Allen, P., J. Cummins, R. Mougeon, & M. Swain. 1983. The development of bilingual proficiency: Second year report and appendices. Toronto: Modern Language Centre.

Anderson, N., L. F. Bachman, K. Perkins, & A. Cohen. 1991. An exploratory study into the construct validity of a reading comprehension test: Triangulation of data sources. *Language Testing, 8*(1), 41–66.

Bachman, L. F. 1989. Language testing–SLA research interfaces. *Annual Review of Applied Linguistics, 9*, 193–209.

Bachman, L. F. 1990. *Fundamental considerations in language testing.* Oxford: Oxford University Press.

---

10 See Douglas (Chapter 6, this volume) for a related discussion of the role of contextual cues in language use.

Bachman, L. F., F. Davidson, & M. Milanovic. 1996. The use of test method characteristics in the content analysis and design of EFL proficiency tests. *Language Testing, 13*(2), 125–150.

Bachman, L. F., & A. S. Palmer. 1996. *Language testing in practice: Designing and developing useful language tests.* Oxford: Oxford University Press.

Bachman, L. F., J. E. Purpura, & S. T. Cushing. 1993. Development of a questionnaire item bank to explore test-taker characteristics. Interim report on the Cambridge-UCLA Language Testing Project, submitted to the University of Cambridge Local Examinations Syndicate.

Bayley, R. 1991. Variation theory and second language learning: Linguistic and social constraints on interlanguage tense marking. Doctoral dissertation, Stanford University, Stanford, CA.

Bayley, R. 1994. Interlanguage variation and the quantitative paradigm: Past tense marking in Chinese-English. In E. E. Tarone, S. M. Gass, & A. D. Cohen (eds.), *Research methodology in second-language acquisition* (pp. 157–181). Hillsdale, NJ: Lawrence Erlbaum.

Bley-Vroman, R., & C. Chaudron. 1994. Elicited imitation as a measure of second-language competence. In E. E. Tarone, S. M. Gass, & A. D. Cohen (eds.), *Research methodology in second-language acquisition* (pp. 245–261). Hillsdale, NJ: Lawrence Erlbaum.

Brindley, G. (ed.). 1995. *Language assessment in action.* NCELTR Research Series No. 8. Sydney: National Centre for English Language Teaching and Research.

Buck, G. 1994. The appropriacy of psychometric measurement models for testing second language listening comprehension. *Language Testing, 11*(2), 145–170.

Canale, M. 1983. On some dimensions of language proficiency. In J. W. Oller, Jr., (ed.), *Issues in language testing research* (pp. 333–342). Rowley, MA: Newbury House.

Canale, M., & M. Swain. 1980. Theoretical bases of communicative approaches to second language teaching and testing. *Applied Linguistics, 1,* 1–47.

Carroll, J. B. 1961. Fundamental considerations in testing for English language proficiency of foreign students. In *Testing the English proficiency of foreign students* (pp. 30–40). Washington, DC: Center for Applied Linguistics.

Carroll, J. B. 1993. *Human cognitive abilities: A survey of factor analytic studies.* Cambridge: Cambridge University Press.

Cathcart, R. 1986. Situational differences and the sampling of young children's school language. In R. Day (ed.), *Talking to learn: Conversation in second language acquisition* (pp. 118–140). Rowley, MA: Newbury House.

Chapelle, C. A. 1994. Are C-tests valid measures for L2 vocabulary research? *Second Language Research, 10*(2), 157–187.

Chapelle, C., W. Grabe, & M. Berns. 1997. *Communicative language proficiency: Definitions and implications for TOEFL 2000.* TOEFL Monograph Series No. 10. Princeton, NJ: Educational Testing Service.

Clarkson, R., & M-T. Jensen. 1995. Assessing achievement in English for professional employment programs. In G. Brindley (ed.), *Language assessment in action* (pp. 165–194). NCELTR Research Series No. 8. Sydney: National Centre for English Language Teaching and Research.

Cohen, A. D. 1994. *Assessing language ability in the classroom* (2nd ed.). Boston: Newbury House/Heinle & Heinle.

Cohen, A. D., & E. Olshtain. 1981. Developing a measure of sociocultural competence: The case of apology. *Language Learning, 31*(1), 113–134.

Corder, S. P. 1967. The significance of learners' error. *International Review of Applied Linguistics, 5,* 161–170.

Corder, S. P. 1971. Idiosyncratic dialects and error analysis. *International Review of Applied Linguistics, 9,* 147–159.

Cronbach, L. 1984. *Essentials of psychological testing* (4th ed.). New York: Harper & Row.

Crookes, G., & S. M. Gass (eds.). 1993. *Tasks and language learning: Integrating theory and practice.* Clevedon: Multilingual Matters.

Day, E. M., & S. M. Shapson. 1991. Integrating formal and functional approaches to language teaching in French immersion: An experimental study. *Language Learning, 41*(1), 25–58.

Douglas, D. 1986. Communicative competence and tests of oral skills. In C. W. Stansfield (ed.), *Toward communicative competence testing: Proceedings of the second TOEFL invitational conference* (pp. 156–174). Princeton, NJ: Educational Testing Service.

Douglas, D., & L. Selinker. 1985. Principles for language tests within the "discourse domains" theory of interlanguage: Research, test construction and interpretation. *Language Testing, 2*(2), 205–226.

Duff, P. 1993. Tasks and interlanguage performance: An SLA research perspective. In G. Crookes & S. M. Gass (eds.), *Tasks and language learning: Integrating theory and practice* (pp. 57–95). Clevedon: Multilingual Matters.

Ellis, R. 1985. *Understanding second language acquisition.* Oxford: Oxford University Press.

Ellis, R. 1989. Are classroom and naturalistic acquisition the same? *Studies in Second Language Acquisition, 11*(3), 305–328.

Freedle, R., & I. Kostin. 1993. The prediction of TOEFL reading item difficulty: Implications for construct validity. *Language Testing, 10*(2), 131–170.

Grierson, J. 1995. Classroom-based assessment in intensive English centres. In G. Brindley (ed.), *Language assessment in action* (pp. 195–238). NCELTR Research Series No. 8. Sydney: National Centre for English Language Teaching and Research.

Halliday, M. A. K. 1976. The form of a functional grammar. In G. Kress (ed.), *Halliday: System and function in language* (pp. 7–25). Oxford: Oxford University Press.

Halliday, M. A. K. 1985. *An introduction to functional grammar.* London: Edward Arnold.

Harley, B., P. Allen, J. Cummins, & M. Swain. 1987. *The development of bilingual proficiency: Final year report. The nature of proficiency* (Vol. 5). Toronto: Modern Language Centre.

Harley, B., P. Allen, J. Cummins, & M. Swain (eds.). 1990. *The development of second language proficiency.* Cambridge: Cambridge University Press.

Harley, B., J. Cummins, M. Swain, & P. Allen. 1990. The nature of language proficiency. In B. Harley, P. Allen, J. Cummins, & M. Swain (eds.), *The development of second language proficiency* (pp. 7–25). Cambridge: Cambridge University Press.

Hoekje, B., & K. Linnell. 1994. "Authenticity" in language testing: Evaluating spoken language tests for international teaching assistants. *TESOL Quarterly, 28*(1), 101–126.

Hudson, T., E. Detmer, & J. D. Brown. 1992. A framework for testing cross-cultural pragmatics. Technical Report No. 2. Honolulu: Second Language Teaching and Curriculum Center, University of Hawaii at Manoa.

Hudson, T., E. Detmer, & J. D. Brown. 1995. Developing prototypic measures of cross-cultural pragmatics. Technical Report No. 7. Honolulu: Second Language Teaching and Curriculum Center, University of Hawaii at Manoa.

Hymes, D. 1972. On communicative competence. In J. B. Pride & J. Holmes (eds.), *Sociolinguistics* (pp. 269–293). Harmondsworth: Penguin.

Kobayashi, H., & C. Rinnert. 1992. Effects of first language on second language writing: Translation versus direct composition. *Language Learning, 42*(2), 183–215.

Labov, W. 1972. *Sociolinguistic patterns.* Philadelphia: University of Pennsylvania Press.

Lado, R. 1957. *Linguistics across the cultures.* Ann Arbor: University of Michigan Press.

Lado, R. 1961. *Language testing.* New York: McGraw-Hill.

Liu, G. 1991. Interaction and second language acquisition: A case study of a Chinese child's acquisition of English as a second language. Doctoral dissertation, La Trobe University, Melbourne, Australia.

Lyster, R. 1994. The effect of functional-analytic teaching on aspects of French immersion students' sociolinguistic competence. *Applied Linguistics, 15*(3), 263–287.

Mangubhai, F. 1991. The processing behaviors of adult second language learners and their relationship to second language proficiency. *Applied Linguistics, 12*(3), 268–298.

McDowell, C. 1995. Assessing the language proficiency of overseas-qualified teachers: The English language skills assessment (ELSA). In G. Brindley (ed.), *Language assessment in action* (pp. 11–29). NCELTR Research Series No. 8. Sydney: National Centre for English Language Teaching and Research.

McKay, P. 1995. Developing ESL proficiency descriptions for the school context: The NLIA bandscales. In G. Brindley (ed.), *Language assessment in action* (pp. 31–64). NCELTR Research Series No. 8. Sydney: National Centre for English Language Teaching and Research.

McNamara, T. 1996. *Measuring second language performance.* London: Longman.

Munnich, E., S. Flynn, & G. Martohardjono. 1994. Elicited imitation and grammaticality judgment tasks: What they measure and how they relate to each other. In E. E. Tarone, S. M. Gass, & A. D. Cohen (eds.), *Research methodology in second-language acquisition* (pp. 227–243). Hillsdale, NJ: Lawrence Erlbaum.

Nayak, N., N. Hansen, N. Krueger, & B. McLaughlin. 1990. Language-learning strategies in monolingual and multilingual adults. *Language Learning, 40*(2), 221–244.

Oller, J. W., Jr. 1969. *Language tests at school.* London: Longman.

Perkins, K., & S. E. Linnville. 1987. A construct definition study of a standardized ESL vocabulary test. *Language Testing, 4*(2), 125–141.

Pica, T., R. Kanagy, & J. Falodun. 1993. Choosing and using communicative tasks for second language instruction. In G. Crookes & S. M. Gass (eds.), *Tasks and language learning: Integrating theory and practice* (pp. 9–34). Clevedon: Multilingual Matters.

Purpura, J. 1996. Modeling the relationships between test takers' reported cognitive and metacognitive strategy use and performance on language tests. Doctoral dissertation, University of California, Los Angeles.

Raffaldini, T. 1988. The use of situation tests as measures of communicative ability. *Studies in Second Language Acquisition, 10*(2), 197–216.

Read, J. 1993. The development of a new measure of L2 vocabulary knowledge. Paper presented at the 15th Language Testing Research Colloquium, Arnhem, Holland, August.

Richards, J. 1974. *Error analysis: Perspectives on second language acquisition.* London: Longman.

Sarig, G. 1987. High-level reading in the first and in the foreign language: Some comparative process data. In J. Devine, P. L. Carrell, & D. E. Eskey (eds.), *Research in reading in English as a second language* (pp. 105–123). Washington, DC: TESOL.

Sasaki, M. 1993a. Relationships among second language proficiency, foreign language aptitude, and intelligence: A structural equation modeling approach. *Language Learning, 43*(3), 313–344.

Sasaki, M. 1993b. Relationships among second language proficiency, foreign language aptitude, and intelligence: A protocol analysis. *Language Learning, 43*(4), 469–505.

Savignon, S. J. 1972. *Communicative competence: An experiment in foreign language teaching.* Philadelphia: Center for Curriculum Development.

Selinker, L., & D. Douglas. 1985. Wrestling with "context" in interlanguage theory. *Applied Linguistics, 6,* 190–204.

Selinker, L., & D. Douglas. 1989. Research methodology in contextually-based second language research. *Second Language Research, 5,* 93–126.

Shohamy, E. 1994. The role of language tests in the construction and validation of second-language acquisition theories. In E. E. Tarone, S. M. Gass, & A. D. Cohen (eds.), *Research methodology in second-language acquisition* (pp. 133–142). Hillsdale, NJ: Lawrence Erlbaum.

Skehan, P. 1994. Foreign language ability: Cognitive or linguistic? *Thames Valley University Working Papers in English Language Teaching,* No. 2.

Smith, J. 1992. Topic and variation in the oral proficiency of international teaching assistants. Doctoral dissertation, Department of Linguistics, University of Minnesota.

Tarone, E. 1988. *Variation in interlanguage.* London: Edward Arnold.

Tarone, E., & G. Liu. 1995. Situational context, variation and second-language acquisition theory. In G. Cook & B. Seidlhofer (eds.), *Principles and practice in the study of language and learning: A Festschrift for H. G. Widdowson* (pp. 107–124). Oxford: Oxford University Press.

Verhallen, M., & R. Schoonen. 1993. Lexical knowledge of monolingual and bilingual children. *Applied Linguistics, 14*(4), 344–363.

Wardhaugh, R. 1970. The contrastive analysis hypothesis. *TESOL Quarterly, 4,* 123–130.

Wesche, M., & T. S. Paribakht. 1996. Assessing vocabulary knowledge: Depth vs. breadth. *Canadian Modern Language Review, 53*(1), 13–40.

Young, R. 1991. *Variation in interlanguage morphology.* New York: Peter Lang.

Young, R. 1993. Functional constraints on variation in interlanguage morphology. *Applied Linguistics, 14*(1), 76–97.

2 Construct definition and validity inquiry in SLA research

Carol A. Chapelle

In second language acquisition (SLA) research, some form of measurement is frequently used to produce empirical evidence for hypotheses about the nature and development of communicative competence. For example, SLA researchers test learners to investigate such aspects of interlanguage vocabulary[1] as the acquisition of semantic (Kellerman 1978) and syntactic (Ard & Gass 1987) features of words, the structure of the L2 lexicon (Meara 1984; Singleton & Little 1991), lexicon size (Nation 1993), strategies associated with vocabulary use (Blum-Kulka & Levinson 1983), and automaticity of lexical access (Chitiri, Sun, Willows, and Taylor 1992). Tests are used for investigating vocabulary, as well as for SLA research in general, to elicit learners' performance in a defined context. In other words, taking the complement to Douglas's (Chapter 6, this volume) view of language tests as SLA elicitation devices, I consider SLA elicitation devices from the perspective of two principles that underlie language testing: construct definition and validation.

These principles are important in SLA research because learners' performance on elicitation devices – like performance on language tests – is used to make inferences extending beyond the observed performance. For example, inferences are often made concerning the learner's underlying competence, which is a construct. Justification of the inferences made on the basis of performance is validation. On SLA elicitation devices, researchers would seldom rely on a single observation of performance to make inferences. Instead, performances are typically summarized across observations to produce scores or other descriptions of performance consistency. In SLA research – like language testing (LT) research – demonstration of performance consistency is significant because when learners' consistent performances across observations are summarized, the resulting score or profile is more dependable than any one idiosyncratic observation can be. When researchers summarize performance consisten-

---

1 Interlanguage vocabulary is used here to indicate learners' vocabulary that is less developed than that of a native speaker. As explained in this chapter, this term can be viewed from all three perspectives of construct definition. Interlanguage vocabulary refers to one component within a broad definition of communicative language ability.

cies and use those summaries to make inferences beyond the actual performance, they are working within the domain of psychological measurement – a domain that supports theory and practices relevant to the use of measurement in SLA research. In particular, measurement theory offers perspectives on (1) defining the construct(s) believed to be reflected by consistent performance and (2) justifying test performance as a valid indicator of the construct(s).

The purpose of this chapter is to explore how principles of construct definition and validity inquiry apply to SLA research. Using research on interlanguage vocabulary as an example, the first part examines the nature of construct definition. It explains three theoretical perspectives toward construct definition – trait, behaviorist, and interactionalist – by demonstrating how interlanguage vocabulary can be defined within each and how each is reflected in vocabulary testing. In my view, current theory in applied linguistics favors an interactionalist approach to construct definition.[2] Therefore, the second part of the paper explains the implications of such a definition for validity inquiry. It defines validation as the ongoing process of justifying particular interpretations and uses of test results, and it explores implications of an interactionalist approach to construct definition for investigating construct validity and the consequences of testing.

Construct definition

Because SLA researchers study interlanguage constructs, it is crucial to define the term. A *construct* is a meaningful interpretation of observed behavior. When a researcher interprets a learner's score on a vocabulary test, for example, as an indicator of vocabulary knowledge, then "vocabulary knowledge" is the construct that gives meaning to the score. The fundamental requirement for interpreting observed behavior as a construct is that the behavior reflect performance consistency. The consistency requirement has caused some researchers to question the usefulness of tests in SLA research and practice (e.g., Lantolf & Frawley 1988; Swain 1990) because of the variable and changing nature of interlanguage. However, as Bachman (Appendix, this volume) points out, the intention of SLA research is to document and explain the learner's changing interlanguage, and to do so, researchers need reliable descriptions of language at its various stages of development. Reliable pictures of interlanguage

2 I interpret the work on communicative competence and communicative language ability as pointing to the need to hypothesize an interactionalist construction for language measurement. Note, in contrast, however, that Eckman (1994) assumes that the trait-oriented construct definition (i.e., the linguist's notion of "competence") is the obvious way of approaching construct definition in SLA research.

are obtained when consistent performance is observed because consistencies allow researchers to

move from the level of discrete behaviors or isolated observations to the level of measurement. This is not to say that scores for individual items of discrete behaviors are not often of interest but, rather, that their meaning and dependability are fragile compared with response consistencies across items or replications. (Messick 1989: 14)

Observation of performance consistency is therefore fundamental to the use of empirical performance data to infer constructs such as "interlanguage vocabulary." The problem of construct definition is to hypothesize the source of performance consistency.

Theorists' various perspectives of construct definition, therefore, can be understood by identifying how they explain response consistency (Messick 1981). *Trait theorists* attribute consistencies to characteristics of test takers, and therefore define constructs in terms of the knowledge and fundamental processes of the test taker. A trait perspective on interlanguage vocabulary must include the dimensions of vocabulary knowledge (e.g., size) and fundamental processes (e.g., lexical access) that have been investigated in SLA research. *Behaviorists* attribute consistencies to contextual factors (e.g., the relationship of participants in a conversation), and therefore define constructs with reference to the environmental conditions under which performance is observed. A behaviorist definition of interlanguage vocabulary must specify features of the context that SLA researchers have identified as affecting vocabulary use. *Interactionalists* see performance as the result of traits, contextual features, and their interaction. An interactionalist definition of vocabulary will include dimensions of both trait and context, although each will be constrained by the other. In addition, this definition must include the strategies required to mediate between the person and the context (e.g., goal setting based on an assessment of the context).

In the following sections, the three approaches to construct definition are introduced by citing the SLA research supporting each and outlining the components of each type of definition. Since SLA researchers' definitions of interlanguage have implications for the types of tests they choose (e.g., Skehan 1987), some of the principles and methods of measurement implied by each type of definition will be explained. Discussion of the three types of definitions and their uses will show that much of the research on interlanguage vocabulary appears to assume a trait-oriented definition, but it is the interactionalist perspective that is consistent with current theory in applied linguistics (Bachman & Cohen, Chapter 1, this volume). Taking the interactionalist perspective as most relevant to future SLA research, I then discuss how validity inquiry for tests used in SLA research can be informed by an interactionalist construct definition.

A *trait perspective of interlanguage vocabulary*

A trait definition of interlanguage would attribute test performance to the characteristics of the learner, because "for trait theorists (and cognitive theorists as well), scores are largely signs of underlying processes or structures" (Messick 1989: 15). Strictly speaking, a trait is defined as "a relatively stable characteristic of a person – an attribute, enduring process, or disposition – which is consistently manifested to some degree when relevant, despite considerable variation in the range of settings and circumstances" (Messick 1989: 15). The notion of stability is not essential to the trait definition, however, because a trait can be expected to change as the result of deliberate study (Carroll 1993: 7) or other special conditions, as in the case of second language (L2) development. The primary identifying feature of a trait is that it can be defined as a person characteristic that is displayed across a variety of settings and therefore can be defined without careful specification of the settings in which it might be observed.[3]

Interlanguage researchers have hypothesized trait-type theories of interlanguage by attributing performance across relevant measures to underlying characteristics. Trait-type construct definitions of language have been articulated and used by SLA researchers such as Bialystok and Sharwood Smith (1985), who describe interlanguage as a system that "depends upon the dual influence of the learner's level of analysis of knowledge and control of cognitive procedures." Learners' performance or "product is a description of essentially the values which occur on these dimensions" (p. 116). In their view, the focus of construct definition for SLA researchers is describing the learner's underlying "system," which is responsible for "products." Figure 2.1 illustrates the assumed relationship between a construct conceived as an underlying system and observed products which appear as performance consistency. In other words, performance consistency is attributed to underlying characteristics of the learner.

TOWARD A TRAIT DEFINITION OF VOCABULARY

A trait theorist's view of interlanguage vocabulary attempts to define "implicit knowledge" (Ard & Gass 1987) and fundamental processes that would be relevant to vocabulary performance across a variety of contexts. A trait-oriented definition would therefore consist of the four knowledge and process dimensions that SLA researchers have investigated,

---

3 Of course, all performance is the result of contact between person and context; therefore, even a trait theorist would agree that context does influence performance. The point is that the focus of construct definition (to interpret performance consistency) is on person characteristics, and particularly on those characteristics believed to behave similarly in different contexts.

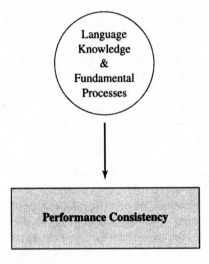

Figure 2.1

each of which is defined without reference to a context of language use. The first dimension, *vocabulary size,* denotes the absolute number of content words a person knows. Estimates of absolute native speaker vocabulary size differ (Aitchison 1987), but as learners' second language develops, the size of their vocabulary grows (Blum-Kulka & Levinson 1983).

The second dimension is *knowledge of word characteristics,* including phonemic, graphemic, morphemic, syntactic, semantic, and collocational features. During the process of acquisition, knowledge of specific words can be incorrect, incomplete, or unanalyzed (Bialystok & Sharwood Smith 1985). Incorrect knowledge refers to lexical representations that do not correspond to the target language, such as erroneous orthographic or semantic representations. Incomplete knowledge refers to the gaps in the learner's knowledge of a word, which may result in confusion between two words with similar forms (Laufer 1990). Unanalyzed knowledge is what the learner knows as a unit but cannot break up or use creatively. For example, in early stages the learner often knows words as they occur in phrases but does not know how to change them morphologically or use them in other phrases.

The third dimension of the trait definition, *lexicon organization,* refers to the way morphemes and words are represented in the mental lexicon, as well as the way they are connected to one another by, for example, semantic and phonological features. The change in vocabulary organization that accompanies acquisition is termed *restructuring* (McLaughlin 1990) or *reanalysis* (Gass 1988). Although debate continues on the representation of morphemes in the mental lexicon (e.g., Henderson 1985; Sternberger & MacWhinney 1988), most agree that the connections among words in a native speaker's mental lexicon are primarily semantic. In contrast, the lexicon of the low ability L2 learner has been described as more loosely organized (Ard & Gass 1987), with connections made on the basis of phonological features (Meara 1984).

The fourth dimension of a trait definition is a set of fundamental vocabulary processes (Sternberg 1977) associated with lexical access. Vocabulary processes would include the following: attending to relevant vocabulary features in written or spoken input, encoding phonological and orthographic information into short-term memory, accessing structural and semantic properties from the lexicon (e.g., Yang & Givon 1993), integrating the semantic content of the word with the emergent semantic representation of the input text (Marslen-Wilson 1989), parsing words into their morphological components, and composing words morphologically (Olshtain 1987).[4] These fundamental processes are tied closely to the three aspects of language knowledge defined earlier. For example, speed of lexical access is believed to depend, in part, on the organization of the lexicon (Frenck-Mestre & Vaid 1992). Furthermore, Olshtain (1987) describes morphological parsing and composing as both "word formation processes" and "knowledge of word formation rules" (p. 221). In short, the processes appear to be viewed by SLA researchers as specific to the vocabulary trait. What these four dimensions of the trait definition – size, knowledge of word characteristics, organization, and fundamental processes – have in common is that each is defined and studied independently of the context of language use.

MEASUREMENT IMPLICATIONS OF A TRAIT DEFINITION

In interlanguage vocabulary research, trait approaches to construct definition are apparent not only by the way researchers define vocabulary constructs but also by the principles they use for test construction and validity justification. In constructing tests, trait theorists rely on random sampling of content from the relevant domain so that test performance can be considered an accurate sign of vocabulary ability across a wide variety of contexts. For example, taking a trait perspective of vocabulary, Nation (1993) explained ideal procedures for sampling from a dictionary to develop tests of vocabulary size. He notes that if the researcher follows these sampling procedures, "it is possible to make an estimation of vocabulary size that can be generalized beyond the particular dictionary

---

4 The processes associated with production are hypothesized to be more difficult than those required in comprehension because when a word is produced, its formal properties must be accessed and composed morphologically to fit properly into the linguistic output (Teichroew 1982).

studied" (p. 32). A second principle of test construction for the trait theorist is to minimize the effects of context on performance by placing vocabulary items within a minimal discourse context. For example, the trait
"vocabulary organization" has been investigated by researchers who
have chosen such tests as the word association test, which presents words
in isolation (Meara 1978, 1984), and grammaticality judgments, which
present words in isolated sentences (Ard & Gass 1987). Word recognition processes (i.e., accessing semantic features) have been assessed by
presenting subjects with isolated pairs of words (one in the native language
and the other in the target language) and timing test takers' judgment of
whether or not the pair is the same semantically (Yang & Givon, 1993).
All three of these tests, in keeping with principles of trait theory, present
language in settings other than the type of discourse context that would
require learners to perform tasks encountered during normal communicative discourse.

In justifying the use of tests chosen to measure vocabulary traits, researchers use both judgmental and empirical arguments. For example,
Ard and Gass (1987) justify their choice of grammaticality judgment tests
as follows: "We are attempting to understand the implicit knowledge that
learners have about the relationships among words in their mental lexicon. This is only ascertainable through specific probings of intuitions,
which provide a much more direct window on implicit knowledge than
do other types of data (cf. Bialystok 1981)" (p. 238). Justifying the choice
of two tests for investigating learners' "lexical confusions," Laufer (1990)
supplies the following rationale: "The fact that test version A tested syn-
forms [i.e., lexical confusions] in sentences, while test version B tested
them in isolation, does not mean we wanted to check context effect on
synform confusion. The versions were simply two elicitation methods"
(p. 285). This use of different test methods solely for the purpose of
double-checking that the trait was measured accurately epitomizes the
trait theorist's ideal that observed performance be attributable to the underlying capacity of the test taker and not to features of the operational
setting (i.e., the test). The researcher states no interest in "context effect"
(which here refers to the context of the sentence in the test items) on performance. Instead, performance is to be attributed to a trait dimension –
the quality of word representation in the mental lexicon (i.e., knowledge
of word characteristics).

A behaviorist perspective of interlanguage vocabulary

A behaviorist's view of interlanguage vocabulary would include the features of context relevant to vocabulary use. In contrast to trait theorists,
who interpret performance as a sign of underlying characteristics,

in psychological measurement, behaviorists and social behaviorists usually interpret scores as samples of response classes. A response class is a set of behaviors all of which change in the same or related ways as a function of stimulus contingencies, that is a class of behaviors that reflect essentially the same changes when the person's relation to the environment is altered (Messick 1989: 15)

For behaviorists, then, the relevant dimensions are not person characteristics, but characteristics of the context in which performance occurs. Accordingly, the scores obtained from tests are interpreted by behaviorists as "derived from responses made to [carefully defined] stimuli for the purpose of predicting responses made to similar naturally occurring stimuli found in vocational, academic, and other settings" (Tryon 1979: 402).[5]

A behaviorist construct definition is implicit in the work of some SLA and LT researchers. SLA researchers focusing on the contextual features influencing performance have discussed the issue in terms of "variability" in interlanguage (e.g., Tarone, Chapter 3, this volume). Although appearing to be the opposite of the performance consistency of interest to LT researchers, some variability – that recognized as "systematic" variability (e.g., Ellis 1989) – refers to performance consistency under particular conditions. Conditions might include the linguistic environments or the sociolinguistic contexts in which particular interlanguage forms are most likely to appear (Ellis 1989). When SLA researchers attempt to explain systematic variability by specifying the contextual factors influencing performance, they are defining performance consistency within particular contexts. Use of contextual factors to explain performance consistency reflects a behaviorist approach to construct definition.

From the same theoretical stance, LT researchers working within the tradition of performance testing attempt to create test methods that replicate the conditions of the settings for which they wish to predict the test taker's future performance. Wesche (1987) describes the rationale as follows:

Since it appears to be impossible to establish the communicative load of . . . different kinds of knowledge precisely because they interact with each other in a compensatory way in performance, it will probably not be possible to establish context-free, universally fair language tests. Rather one might hope to improve the predictive validity of tests by recreating those contextual features that theory and experience suggest may have an important influence on language performance. (Wesche 1987: 31)

Representing the modern behaviorist position implicit in performance testing, Wesche's statement indicates that the learner's underlying knowledge

5 In SLA research the "other settings" of interest to the researcher are "target language use" settings: the contexts in which learners will use the target language (Bachman & Palmer 1996).

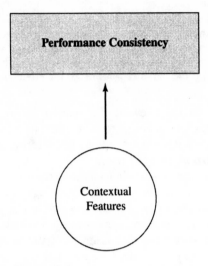

Figure 2.2

is too elusive to define, and therefore, as Figure 2.2 illustrates, the objective of construct definition becomes context definition. In other words, performance consistency is attributed to the context in which it occurs.

TOWARD A BEHAVIORIST DEFINITION OF VOCABULARY

A behaviorist definition of vocabulary would therefore comprise the descriptions of contexts believed to affect vocabulary performance. Relevant contexts are often described imprecisely, by using phrases such as "vocabulary knowledge in reading comprehension" (Luppescu & Day 1993: 263–264) or by referring to local discourse contexts of vocabulary as defined by "phrasal constraints" or "situational utterances" (Nattinger & DeCarrico 1989). Recognizing the importance of context, SLA researchers are beginning to take a more comprehensive view of context definition. For example, in an attempt to better understand the construct of task, Duff (1993) examined the role of task characteristics like "direction of interaction" and "nature of gap between subject and interviewer on task" in predicting interlanguage performance (p. 65). In his work on nonnative speakers' use of inflectional morphology, Young (1989) has suggested that the essential elements to include in such a definition would be those Hymes (1967) identified: *setting, participants, ends* (i.e., purpose), *art characteristics, communicative key, instrumentality* (e.g., spoken vs. written), *norms* (i.e., sociolinguistic rules of conversation), and *genre*. Although his research investigated only the role of participants, Young hypothesized that each of these features of context would affect learners' use of inflectional morphemes (i.e., one aspect of vocabulary), and therefore that observed performance must be explained with reference to these features of context. Because little work has attempted to add to our understanding of a behaviorist definition of vocabulary, these features of context are adopted here to illustrate the behaviorist approach to construct definition. In other words, from a behaviorist perspective, consistency in vocabulary performance might be hypothesized to be defined by Hymes's eight features of context.

MEASUREMENT IMPLICATIONS OF A BEHAVIORIST DEFINITION

One measurement implication of a behaviorist perspective as explained by Wesche (1987) is that tests must be designed by carefully constructing test environments that mirror the contexts in which the test writer wishes to predict performance (see the "target language use situation"described by Bachman & Palmer 1996). In other words, tests cannot be constructed through random selection of items from a large domain of possible items. The behaviorist does not assume that performance will be generalized over a wide variety of contexts, but only to those contexts which are similar to the test setting. In constructing a test of "reading vocabulary," then, the behaviorist would attempt to mirror the context in which the learner will be reading in the future. If researchers used Young's behaviorist construct definition to design such a test, Hymes's features of context would guide comparison of the elements of the test setting to those of the reading context. For example, a test of reading comprehension vocabulary might be constructed to fit the following contextual specifications. Test takers read at home *(setting)* alone *(participants)* to answer questions at the end of the chapter *(ends)*; this would be treated as an important class assignment in a real class, so the text must be read for its meaning *(art characteristics)*. The reading consists of a written text *(instrumentality)* composed by an unknown, respected scientist who uses formal language *(communicative key)* conforming to the norms of academic written language *(norms)* and containing the specific linguistic signals that identify the content and structure of an academic text of its type *(genre)*. Performance on such a test would be interpreted as a sample of performance in target language use settings that reflect similar contextual values.

A second measurement implication follows from the first: Because target language use situations consist in part of language in discourse contexts, the behaviorist's vocabulary test must present and elicit vocabulary within a discourse context. Unlike Laufer (1990), who did not want to "check context effect on synform confusion" (p. 285), the behaviorist attempts to create a test that will check the relevant context effects. The behaviorist considers the well-chosen discourse context in a vocabulary test to be essential to the test, unlike the trait theorist, who views it as a source of error in observed performance.

TABLE 2.1. MEASUREMENT PRINCIPLES ASSOCIATED WITH TRAIT
AND BEHAVIORIST DEFINITIONS OF INTERLANGUAGE VOCABULARY

	Trait principles	*Behaviorist principles*
Meaning of performance	A sign of underlying characteristics.	A sample of performance across similar contexts.
Construct definition	Implicit characteristics must be specified independent of context.	Implicit characteristics cannot be specified. Context must be specified.
Test construction	Random sampling of content allows generalizability across all contexts. Contextual influences are considered irrelevant. Minimize these by presenting and eliciting language out of context.	Careful selection of content allows generalizability across similar contexts. Contextual influences are considered relevant. Maximize these by presenting and eliciting language in relevant contexts.
Validity justification	Compare performance on different test methods to distinguish method error from the trait variance.	Compare the test context to the context of interest to identify similarities and differences.

Because the behaviorist views performance as a sample, justification of test use (i.e., test validity) requires the researcher to demonstrate that test performance is a good sample of the behavior that would occur in a real setting. Therefore, some researchers attempt to document the authenticity of the test setting relative to the context in which the test user wishes to make predictions. This approach to testing research has resulted in attempts to define and investigate "authenticity" (see, for example, volume 2, number 1 of *Language Testing*, 1985), which compare characteristics of the test setting with those of the target language use situation. Researchers also attempt to demonstrate that significant variance cannot be accounted for by irrelevant aspects of the operational test setting, but that variance can be attributed to facets of the test methods that reflect the same contextual values present in the target language use setting.

Table 2.1 clarifies the contrasts between the measurement assumptions underlying the trait and behaviorist perspectives. Despite the polarity of the two approaches, SLA and LT researchers increasingly recognize that progress in understanding language development and use rests on understanding how traits and contexts interact during the process of communication. This interactionalist perspective requires that the contrasts between the trait and behaviorist perspectives be seen as complements in an interactionalist construct definition that specifies how language traits are put into use in contexts.

An interactionalist perspective of interlanguage vocabulary

The third approach to construct definition, the interactionalist approach, requires the researcher to specify the relevant aspects of both trait and context. Interactionalist perspectives of construct definition (e.g., Zuroff 1986) represent "intermediate views, attributing some behavioral consistencies to traits, some to situational factors, and some to interactions between them, in various and arguable proportions" (Messick 1989: 15). Despite the fact that the interactionalist construct definition includes both trait and context, it cannot be derived by simply adding trait and behaviorist definitions together. Instead, when trait and context dimensions are included in one definition, the quality of each changes. Trait components can no longer be defined in context-independent, absolute terms, and contextual features cannot be defined without reference to their impact on underlying characteristics. From the interactionalist perspective, *performance is viewed as a sign of underlying traits, and is influenced by the context in which it occurs, and is therefore a sample of performance in similar contexts.* Moreover, to incorporate a dimension of interaction between trait and context, an interactionalist definition must include metacognitive strategies responsible for mediating between the two. For example, the language user's metacognitive strategies (e.g., "assessing the context") would intervene between the context of language use and the user's knowledge during performance to assess the relevant features of context (e.g., level of formality) and decide which aspects of knowledge (e.g., which words) were needed.

SLA AND LT RESEARCHERS AS INTERACTIONALISTS

There is strong support for an interactionalist perspective in both SLA and LT theory. In SLA, the interactionalist perspective has been fueled primarily by the theory of communicative language use, which suggests that communicative competence refers to both knowledge of language and the ability to put language to use in context (Hymes 1972; Canale & Swain 1980; Widdowson 1983). In addition, many "variability" researchers who examine performance data conclude that performance is the result of "both learner internal and environmental (i.e., input) sources" (Ellis 1989: 25), and therefore a need exists for "studies showing the ways in which these various influences *interact* in normal communication" (Tarone 1988: 136; emphasis in original). Some researchers have attempted to outline the strategies required for communication in context (Faerch & Kasper, 1983) and to identify methods for studying such strategies (Cohen & Robbins 1976; Cohen 1984; Faerch & Kasper 1987).

In LT the interactionalist perspective has gained empirical support through research which has found that traits and methods (the latter interpreted as realizing contextual variables) each contribute unique variance to test performance (Bachman & Palmer 1982; Bachman, Davidson, & Foulkes 1993). On the basis of this empirical work and communicative competence theory, Bachman (1990) composed a general interactionalist construct definition of communicative language ability, which includes "both knowledge, or competence, and the capacity for implementing, or executing that competence in language use" in context (Bachman 1990: 84). An interactionalist definition includes the language knowledge and fundamental processes of the trait theorist as well as the context of the behaviorist. When these two parts appear in a single construct definition, the need for a component controlling the interaction between the two is apparent. Bachman defined this as "strategic competence," the metacognitive strategies required for assessing contexts, setting goals, constructing plans, and controlling execution of those plans (Faerch & Kasper 1983). In other words, an interactionalist construct definition comprises more than trait plus context; it includes the metacognitive strategies (i.e., strategic competence) responsible for putting person characteristics to use in context.

TOWARD AN INTERACTIONALIST DEFINITION OF VOCABULARY

To hypothesize a framework for an interactionalist definition of interlanguage vocabulary, it will be necessary to revisit the trait and context dimensions outlined earlier. When traits and contexts are considered together, however, both lose their general relevance. Trait dimensions must be specified more precisely with reference to the context of language use, as Table 2.2 indicates. "Vocabulary size," for example, cannot be defined in an absolute sense but instead is a meaningful construct only with reference to a particular context (Dollerup, Glahn, & Hansen 1989). Similarly, the "linguistic characteristics" a learner knows about individual words would be prompted by and would depend on the contextual factors occurring when those words are used. Moreover, from the interactionalist perspective, word knowledge must include the word's pragmatic features – knowledge of the appropriate contexts of word use and the perlocutions the word can produce in those contexts. "Vocabulary organization" would not be fixed at any stage of development, but the connections the language user made between words would depend on contextual factors prompting those connections (Votaw 1992). Fundamental lexical processes would also be defined relative to the context of language use so that a researcher, rather than investigating "lexical recognition," might investigate lexical recognition during reading processes (Chitiri et

TABLE 2.2. HYPOTHESIZED INFLUENCES ON PERFORMANCE ACCORDING
TO TRAIT, BEHAVIORIST, AND INTERACTIONALIST DEFINITIONS
OF INTERLANGUAGE VOCABULARY

Performance influence	*Trait definition*[a]	*Behaviorist definition*[b]	*Interactionalist definition*[c]
Knowledge	Size Linguistic characteristics Organization		Size in context Linguistic and pragmatic characteristics in context Organization in context
Process	Fundamental lexical processes		Fundamental lexical proc- esses in context
Context		Setting Participants Ends Art characteristics Key Instrumentation Norms Genre	Field Tenor Mode
Metacognitive strategies			Assessment Goal setting Planning Execution

[a]Comprising trait dimensions investigated by interlanguage researchers. One
might find additional dimensions that could be added to a trait definition.
[b]Based on Young's (1989) suggestion for the study of interlanguage variation.
One might choose other features of context.
[c]My hypothesis of how trait and context might be combined at the theoretical
level.

al. 1992) in particular contexts. In short, according to the interactionalist definition, the dimensions of the trait definition of interlanguage vocabulary will differ qualitatively depending on the context in which vocabulary is used, and therefore must be specified with reference to that
context.

The context dimension of an interactionalist definition must provide
a theory of how the context of a particular situation within a broader
context of culture constrains the linguistic choices a language user can
make during linguistic performance. Systemic theory provides a general
theory to do just that. Encompassing Hymes's (1972) features of context
while allowing flexibility to add additional features, Halliday and Hasan

(1989) present a theory of context comprising three theoretical components: field, tenor, and mode. Reflecting applied linguists' understanding of context, these three components are intended to be complex and overlapping. They work together in any language use situation to define a range of potential language that may occur. Field refers to the location(s), topic(s), and action(s) present in a particular language use context. Tenor includes the participants, their relationships, and objectives. Mode includes the channel, texture, and genre of situated language. These three context constructs of systemic theory work together to define a particular "contextual configuration," which consists of specific values for field, tenor, and mode. To use this theory of context in consort with the trait dimension "vocabulary size," for example, it would be necessary to define vocabulary size within a particular field, tenor, and mode. Learners' vocabulary size would be expected to differ depending on whether they were reading a psychology text at home, for example, or listening to a biology lecture in a classroom.[6] These differences, according to the interactionist definition, are important for defining and assessing vocabulary size.

In addition to trait and contextual features, an interactionist definition must include the metacognitive strategies required for vocabulary use in context. The strategies Bachman (1990) defined as strategic competence – assessing the situation, setting goals, planning language use, and controlling execution of plans (Faerch & Kasper 1983) – are not specific to vocabulary but are an important part of the definition of interlanguage vocabulary. Metacognitive strategies are different from the fundamental processes defined by the trait theorist because the former are tied directly to the context of language use, and therefore in order to be defined meaningfully must be specified with reference to a particular context of language use. For example, Blum-Kulka and Levinson (1983: 126) have identified some of the strategic plans associated with vocabulary use: circumlocution, paraphrase, language switch, appeal to authority, change of topic, and semantic avoidance. These strategies, unlike fundamental processes such as lexical access or morphological parsing, are "situation bound" (Blum-Kulka & Levinson, 1983: 126). Figure 2.3 illustrates the multiple influences the interactionist construct definition hypothesizes

6 According to Halliday and Hasan's (1989) theory of context, "reading a psychology text at home" and "listening to a biology lecture in a classroom" could be specified at various levels of delicacy through the field, tenor, and mode constructs. A key problem in an interactionist definition is finding an optimal level of delicacy for defining contexts that are meaningful to test users and in which consistent performance can be observed. In other words, even when the future language use context (e.g., academic reading [EFL] in international universities) is identified, the question remains of how specifically one needs to define such a context (e.g., "all academic reading," "science reading," "chemistry reading," "research articles in chemistry," "research articles on a particular topic within chemistry" . . .).

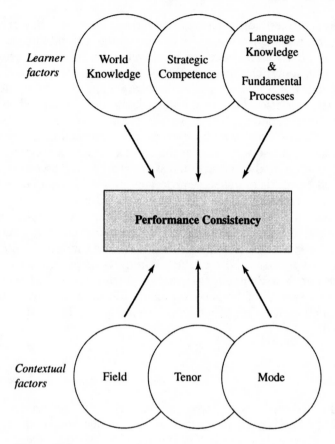

Figure 2.3

for performance consistency. Performance consistency is attributed to
learner characteristics (knowledge and processes, metacognitive strategies,
and world knowledge) and the values of the contextual variables of field,
tenor, and mode.

MEASUREMENT IMPLICATIONS
OF AN INTERACTIONALIST DEFINITION

An interactionalist approach to construct definition poses difficult problems for measurement because it combines two philosophies that embody
contrasting ideals, as indicated in Table 2.1. With respect to construct
definition, interactionalist theory, like trait theory, requires that implicit
knowledge be specified. What the researcher must specify are the knowledge and fundamental processes that are required within a particular context as well as the metacognitive strategies controlling performance in

that context. In test construction, interactionalist theory, like behaviorist theory, requires that test content be the result of careful sampling from the context of target language use. However, unlike the behaviorist, who might rely on superficial similarities between the test methods and the future language use context (e.g., "authenticity"; Spolsky 1985), the interactionalist must also consider the underlying abilities judged to be required in the test context. Test construction using language in a discourse context is also the ideal for the interactionalist. But unlike the behaviorist, who simply attempts to mirror the context of future language use to improve prediction, the interactionalist attempts to use discourse to elicit the defined linguistic knowledge, processes, and metacognitive strategies during test performance.

Justification of test use within an interactionalist framework also poses some unique dilemmas because the interactionalist construct definition ascribes observed performance consistency to the combined influence of person characteristics and contexts. This view of performance consistency presents a challenge for traditional testing research. Fortunately, modern theory and methods of test validation meet this challenge with an expanded conception of what validity means and how it can be investigated.

Validity inquiry

SLA and LT researchers alike are concerned that the interpretations they make on the basis of test performance are well justified. With respect to vocabulary research, for example, Sharwood Smith has pointed out that "experimental data cannot of themselves inform us about the nature of the learner's current mental lexicon" (1984: 239). His point is that researchers make interpretations on the basis of their observed data, and as a result, the justification of their interpretations is crucial. For example, the sustainability of Meara's conclusion, mentioned earlier, about the nature of L2 vocabulary organization rests on the validity of his interpretation of performance on word association tests as a sign of vocabulary organization. The value of Young's findings, about participant influence on inflectional morpheme use rests on the quality of the observed performance as a sample obtained from the relevant contextual configuration. In both cases, inferences are made on the basis of performance in a setting that acts as an operational definition of the construct the researcher wants to assess. When the setting where performance consistency is observed is a test, the operational definition can be specified in terms of test method facets (Bachman 1990) or task characteristics (Bachman & Palmer 1996). This is illustrated in Figure 2.4, which shows that performance consistency is observed within a setting that often can be

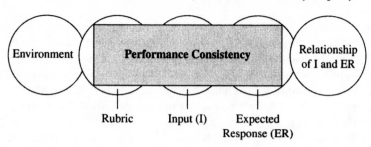

Figure 2.4

described by test method facets or task characteristics. (The test method or task characteristics are good descriptors for operational settings that are language tests or SLA elicitation devices, but it is not clear that they would be the best descriptors for other settings.) Sufficient justification of the interpretations made from test performance in an operational setting is needed so that tests can be used appropriately for decision making in educational contexts or for theory construction in research settings. The process of securing sufficient justification is validation.

Measurement researchers' conceptions of validation have evolved considerably throughout the 1980s and 1990s in ways that are relevant to the use of the interactionalist construct definition. Messick (1989) defines validity as "the degree to which empirical evidence and theoretical rationales support the adequacy and appropriateness of interpretations and actions based on test scores" (p. 13). "Empirical evidence and theoretical rationales" refer to justifications for test interpretation and use. Justifications for the interpretation and use of vocabulary tests include evidence about their construct validity and about their relevance and utility in a particular setting. In addition, justifications refer to the consequences resulting from test use. The types of construct validity evidence that can be used to justify test interpretation and use include such arguments as results of content analysis and correlational studies that support the hypothesis that test performance reflects the intended construct. Implications of an interactionalist definition for five types of construct validity evidence are discussed later in this chapter.

Another type of validity justification is the evidence pertaining to the relevance and utility of testing. Such evidence would demonstrate the usefulness of a test for achieving particular objectives in a given context. For example, in a setting where instructors need diagnostic information pointing to the needs of individual students, a vocabulary test that meets those needs from the instructors' and students' perspectives could be shown to have utility in that context. Such evidence, of course, would not stand alone in justifying test use but would need to be supported by construct evidence indicating that the test measured the desired aspects of vocabulary. For example, in a study of interlanguage vocabulary (Singleton & Little 1991), learners' responses to C-test items were used to make inferences about vocabulary processes and strategies, but because no construct evidence supported such inferences, Chapelle (1994) suggested that the test had no utility for its research purpose – to inform theories of vocabulary organization, a vocabulary strategy, and the strategy's context of use. Because relevance and utility evidence are use-specific, and because there has been little work in this area, I will not discuss this facet of validity inquiry here.

Justification of testing through examination of a test's consequences requires the researcher to clarify the value implications underlying interpretation and use of a particular test as well as its impact on the test use context and beyond. Value implications are attached to the nature of the construct definition a test reflects. As explained earlier, each perspective on construct definition encompasses beliefs about what can and should be defined, how tests should be designed, and what the priorities for validation should be. These beliefs are formulated in socioacademic communities that implicitly support particular perspectives on construct definition through the use of particular types of tests. The objective of clarifying the value implications associated with particular test interpretations and uses is to assess consciously the values implied by the choice of a test for a particular purpose. Other consequences refer to the actions resulting from test use in a particular context and its unintended side effects beyond the immediate test use context.

For example, some tests that begin as research instruments eventually make their way to classrooms, where they provide implicit guidance to teachers about what to teach and to students about what to study. As an illustration, I will examine the value implications and social consequences of the trait-oriented vocabulary tests used in vocabulary research. I will explain why examination of values and consequences associated with a test must be informed by an understanding of the construct definition underlying the test. However, because all validity questions rest on an understanding of construct validity, I begin by explaining methods for investigating construct validity within an interactionalist perspective of construct definition.

Construct validity evidence

Construct validity evidence refers to the judgmental and empirical justifications supporting the inferences made from test scores. Because test performance is used to make inferences about a construct believed to be reflected in test performance, the nature of the researcher's construct definition is fundamental to the manner in which construct validity evidence is produced and interpreted. The confusion resulting from disparate perspectives toward construct definition is apparent from Shohamy's (Chapter 7, this volume) interpretation of Tarone's (Chapter 3, this volume) finding that subjects performed differently on two versions of a speaking test. Tarone's point, consistent with behaviorist and interactionalist construct definitions, was that the two sets of data varied because they were samples from two different contexts, and therefore could not be interpreted as if they had been affected by the same set of factors. Shohamy, viewing the same results from a trait perspective (as signs of speaking ability), offered the following explanation: "One wonders if Tarone's conclusions can be interpreted as an indication of variation or of method effect" (p. 162). From the trait perspective, of course, "method effects" refer to error introduced into performance data resulting in inconsistent performance (i.e., variation) across test methods. From a behaviorist or interactionalist perspective, these method effects would not be error; they would be evidence of the expected influence of context on performance.

In short, rational interpretation of this and other evidence attempting to explain performance must be tied to an understanding of how the measured construct is defined. This understanding of the theoretical construct definition can then be used to evaluate the adequacy of the operational definition (i.e., the test) in eliciting the relevant performance as signs, samples, or both. The interactionalist perspective, which views the operational definition as eliciting both a sign of learner capacities and a context-constrained sample, is illustrated in Figure 2.5. The figure shows that performance consistency, which is attributed to both learner characteristics and aspects of context, is observed within an operational setting, which can be defined through the use of test method facets or task characteristics.

The process of construct validation requires evidence supporting the use of performance within the operational setting as an indicator of the defined construct. Five types of construct validity evidence are examined here: (1) content analysis, (2) empirical item investigation, (3) task analysis, (4) relationships between test scores and other measures, and (5) experimental research identifying performance differences over time, across groups and settings, and in response to experimental interventions.[7]

CONTENT ANALYSIS

Content analysis consists of experts' judgments of what they believe a test measures at the operational level (e.g., Carroll 1976; Bachman,

---

7 Another type of construct validity evidence, of course, demonstrates that observed test performance exhibits theoretically appropriate consistency.

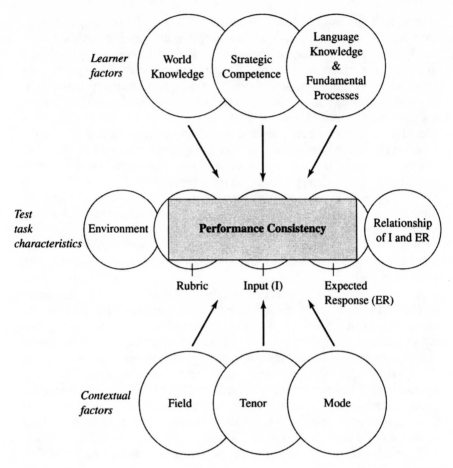

Figure 2.5

Kunnan, Vanniarajan, & Lynch 1988; Bachman, Davidson, Ryan, & Choi 1995). These judgments are then used to argue for or against the use of test performance as an indicator of the theoretically defined construct that the test is intended to measure as well as to inform empirical validity inquiry. With respect to tests of interlanguage vocabulary, for example, performance on word association tests has been judged as indicative of the trait "lexical organization" (Meara 1978, 1984). In Meara's judgment, word association tests "are a useful way of investigating the way a speaker's knowledge of his language is structured and stored" (Meara 1978: 208). It was on the basis of results from word association tests that Meara concluded that learners' mental lexicons were not semantically organized. Another test, the C-test, has also been judged a measure of vocabulary organization by other researchers (Singleton & Little 1991), but the results obtained from that test led the researchers to a different conclusion – that learners' lexicons were organized semantically. Particularly in view of the contradictory conclusions drawn from the use of the two different tests, a content analysis of each test based on the same interactionalist construct definition would be informative.

An interactionalist content analysis should hypothesize how the test operationalizes – during test taking – all of the theorized influences on performance. Such an analysis would use the test method facets to organize judgments about the operational constructions of the learner factors (language knowledge, fundamental processes, strategies, and world knowledge) and contextual factors (field, tenor, mode). For example, Douglas (Chapter 6, this volume) hypothesizes that the instructions (a test method facet) are associated with the test takers' conception of the discourse domain (the operational level the test taker creates for values of field, tenor, and mode). The discourse domain then influences the test taker's goal setting and planning (the operational level of strategic competence), which in turn – along with other test method facets – influence the language knowledge employed (the operational level of language knowledge).

Because the test taker encounters test method facets sequentially during test taking (i.e., first the environment is perceived, then the instructions are read or heard, then the input is encountered . . .), Chapelle and Douglas (1993) have suggested that content analysis should also be process-oriented, allowing for judgments about the nature of the operational setting as it is constructed during test taking. Indeed, such an analysis becomes very complex. As Palmberg (1987) put it in his discussion of learners' performance on a vocabulary test used in classroom research, "it is hazardous to speculate about the factors that made the pupils think of the very words that they actually produced [on the test]" (Palmberg, 1987: 209). Although it may be hazardous, theory-based speculation about the nature of the operational test performance is essential if a content analysis is to provide results that can be compared to a theoretical interactionalist construct definition. Such a comparison is a crucial source of construct validity evidence.

EMPIRICAL ITEM INVESTIGATION

Empirical item investigation, or identification of factors affecting item difficulty and discrimination (Carroll, 1989), provides statistical evidence relevant to researchers' understanding of the operational level of the construct definition. In vocabulary testing, for example, Perkins and Linnville (1987) investigated the operational construct definition of a multiple choice vocabulary test by assessing the extent to which item difficulty could be attributed to test method facets, including the characteristics of the stimulus words (e.g., frequency, abstractness) and the keyed responses (e.g., number of synonyms for each response). Their findings that the combinations of item characteristics predicting item difficulty depended on the level of subjects' proficiency led them to conclude that the operational construct meaning of the test varied as a function of proficiency level – evidence useful in the interpretation of scores for learners at different levels. If we were to interpret such item analysis results with reference to the theoretical construct the test is intended to measure, however, the operational variables to be investigated could be chosen on the basis of their hypothesized reflection of aspects of the theoretical definition.

From an interactionalist perspective, the test method facets to investigate would be those reflecting the influences of specific learner factors (language knowledge, fundamental processes, strategies, and world knowledge) and contextual factors (field, tenor, and mode). For example, one predictor of difficulty in a vocabulary test might be frequency of the lexical item (as Perkins and Linnville hypothesized); however, that variable defined from an interactionalist perspective would have to refer to frequency within a particular context, and the results would be interpreted relative to that context. Another test method facet that has been investigated in this manner in cloze tests is the distance from the blank of the clue needed for supplying the correct lexical item. The distance variable might be chosen to represent the metacognitive strategies required for figuring out what goes in each blank; the prediction is that the farther the clue is from the blank, the more difficult the item. Results are interpreted to indicate that the predicted metacognitive strategies do indeed come into play in the operational definition. The construct validity question is whether or not these similar strategies are also included in the theoretical construct definition of what the test is supposed to measure.

This type of validity inquiry places difficult demands on construct definition because it requires predictions linking theoretical sources and levels of difficulty with empirical item difficulty. Such a theory of item difficulty (Campbell 1961; Carroll 1989; Abraham & Chapelle 1992) can best be informed by a construct definition with components specified in terms of their levels of development. For example, the trait or interactionalist definition informed by SLA research would specify that idiomatic senses of words would be acquired later than literal senses (Kellerman 1978). This developmental assertion predicts that a test response requiring knowledge of an idiomatic sense will be more difficult than responses requiring knowledge of literal senses. Accordingly, item analysis research might choose the item characteristic "literal/idiomatic" as a predictor of difficulty. Similarly, native speakers' acquisition of word meaning has been found to be a gradual process (Marshalek 1981) so items requiring vague knowledge of meaning (e.g., recognition items) are hypothesized to be easier than those requiring precise knowledge of meaning (e.g., items requiring test takers to produce definitions). Work is needed to hypothesize the developmental dimensions of other aspects of the interactionalist construct definition to make it more applicable to our understanding of operational definitions through the study of item difficulty.

EMPIRICAL TASK ANALYSIS

As Cohen (Chapter 4, this volume) explains, empirical task analysis attempts to document the metacognitive strategies that learners use as they complete test tasks. The primary methodology is qualitative, probing the metacognitive strategies employed in the operational setting. The operational performance is then compared to an interactionalist construct definition at the theoretical level. For example, Feldman and Stemmer (1987) documented the test-taking strategies used in an operational setting to complete the lexical items deleted from a C-test (see also Stemmer 1991). They found that a wide variety of metacognitive plans were executed to complete blanks when lexical items were not retrieved automatically. The results of such research, suggesting that the plans (and therefore knowledge) used to arrive at responses vary across items and learners, present a challenge for construct validity inquiry. Messick describes the problem as follows:

The notion that a test score [or profile] reflects a single uniform construct interpretation or that validation should seek to defend (or challenge) a single test-construct match becomes illusory. Indeed, that a test's construct interpretation might need to vary from one type of person to another (or from one setting or occasion to another) is a major current conundrum in educational and psychological measurement. It suggests that the purview of construct validation should include delineation of the alternative construct meanings of test scores. (Messick 1989: 55)

These multiple construct meanings implied by the idiosyncratic metacognitive strategies used in an operational setting are the precise target of empirical task analysis.

The kind of information provided by empirical task analysis makes it uniquely suited to investigating the operational settings associated with interactionalist construct definitions. For example, Dollerup et al. (1989) present a definition of "vocabularies in the reading process" that includes "(a) a 'word knowledge store,' (b) strategies for decoding words, and (c) the special linguistic context. It implies that individual vocabularies in reading exist instantaneously, and that they are, in effect, fluid entities which change every time they are generated by the reading of specific texts. *Vocabularies differ not only in time but also from text to text with the same reader*" (pp. 30–31; emphasis in original). Investigation of a test associated with this interactionalist conception of vocabulary would have to probe the strategies individuals used in the operational setting of the test. Findings would address the conundrum of individual differences in score meaning.

CORRELATIONS WITH OTHER TESTS AND BEHAVIORS

Similarities among different operational settings can be identified by calculating correlations among sets of scores obtained in operational test (and other) settings. Insofar as the researcher understands the connections between operational tests and their underlying theoretical construct definitions, such correlations can provide a source of validity evidence. The need to use other methods of validity inquiry to hypothesize the bridge between operational and theoretical levels was voiced by early educational measurement researchers (e.g., Gulliksen 1950) and has been echoed more recently by LT researchers (e.g., Vollmer 1983; Grotjahn 1986; Bachman 1990; Alderson 1993). Grotjahn expresses the problem of using correlational evidence at the operational level as follows:

> Construct validation of a language test with the help of other language tests presupposes the construct validity of these tests, which is normally at best only partially established, and if at all, then only with the help of correlational analysis. The potential circularity of this approach should be obvious. (Grotjahn 1986: 161)

The operational circle can be broken when the theoretical constructs underlying performance on tests inform the design and interpretation of correlational research. The best-known paradigm for systematizing theoretical predictions of correlations obtained at the operational level is the multitrait-multimethod (MTMM) research design (Campbell & Fiske 1959). To conduct research within this paradigm, as some language testing researchers have done (e.g., Bachman & Palmer 1982; Arnaud 1989; Swain 1990), the researcher administers several tests – each intended to measure a language trait. Tests must be chosen intentionally so that each trait is measured using several different methods. Observed variance attributed to the context (which is realized by the test methods) is viewed as evidence against the test's validity. In other words, context (or method) variance is viewed as measurement error. Observed variance attributed to the trait that the test is intended to measure is considered evidence for the test's validity. Trait variance is good. The researcher has found evidence for the construct validity of the tests if the correlations among tests of the same trait are higher than are correlations among tests of different traits or among tests using the same method of measurement. In other words, this research design, consistent with the trait theorist's measurement principles, treats method effects as error, predicting that ideally strong covariance should occur only as the result of similar traits underlying test performance.

The MTMM research design offers valuable perspectives for the use of correlational methods in validation research; however, to work within the interactionist construct perspective, researchers need to reconceptualize the "trait as good variance" and "method as systematic error variance" as more general notions – "construct-relevant variance" and "construct-irrelevant variance," respectively. According to the interactionalist definition (as illustrated in Figure 2.3), variance should be contributed by both test-taker and context factors. To the extent that the test method facets play a role in operationalizing both of these aspects of the theoretical definition, they cannot be treated as error. Instead of assuming that only trait variance is construct relevant and that all method variance is irrelevant, the researcher working within an interactionalist construct definition is obligated to theorize exactly what should be considered relevant sources of variance and what should be considered irrelevant.

Moreover, because the interactionalist perspective hypothesizes multiple contributors to observed performance consistency, the researcher must consider the expected proportions of relevant variance that should be shared with various types of tests. For example, Chapelle and Green (1992) have suggested the need to hypothesize the expected shared variance between language and nonlanguage tests (e.g., Marshalek 1981; Chapelle & Abraham 1990) in order to interpret observed correlations. Such hypotheses must rest on an understanding of both theoretical and operational construct meaning of all the tests involved because interpreting such correlations requires a construct theory that allows a researcher to hypothesize a "network of relationships of a test to other measures" (Embretson 1983: 180). The general interactionalist construct definition moves in this direction by including all of the factors believed to affect performance; however, it fails to specify the predicted relative strengths of influence from any of the factors. This additional specification would be needed to make predictions about the strengths of observed correlations. Correlational research that systematically selects operational definitions of various aspects of the interactional construct definition can help to develop an understanding of the general construct definition.

EXPERIMENTAL STUDIES OF TEST PERFORMANCE

Experimental manipulations of subjects or test methods enable the researcher to examine hypotheses about test performance by systematically modifying test conditions to verify that observed performance behaves in consort with theory-based predictions. This type of research can investigate differences in test performance between native speakers and nonnative speakers, between learners before and after instruction, or between the same learner's performance on different forms of a test. The latter type of research can be most useful when it is informed by the interactionalist construct definition. The interactionalist definition provides a framework for hypothesizing aspects of the theoretical definition as they emerge within the operational setting. In a study comparing a general and a field-specific speaking test, for example, Douglas and Selinker (1992) demonstrated the use of the interactionalist perspective in this type of research:

It is our view that testing language for specific purposes involves more than just changing content; specific purpose testing requires a change in discourse domain (Douglas & Selinker 1985), which involves the language user's assessment of the communicative situation and her subsequent planning of a linguistic response to the situation [i.e., the operational level of strategic competence] ... This change in discourse domain is brought about in turn by contextualization cues, culturally conventional, highly redundant language signals such as voice tone, pitch, tempo, rhythm, code, topic, style, posture, gaze and facial expression, that interactants attend to in assessing the communicative situation (Gumperz 1976). (Douglas & Selinker, 1992: 318).

In an operational setting, these contextual features (which fall within the field, tenor, and mode constructs) are identified through test method facets and their interpretation by the test taker. In other words, in a given test the features of the input (a test method facet) would specify particular values for cues such as voice tone (an aspect of tenor), and a particular test taker would interpret those values to create a discourse domain during test taking.

An important question to be investigated in validity research is whether changes in test method facets can produce the theorized changes in all aspects of the operational setting, including the test takers' construction of context and use of strategic competence. As Douglas (Chapter 6, this volume) points out, an understanding of the role of the test method facets in creating an operational setting is essential to progress within the interactionalist perspective:

I have argued that we need to *capitalize* on [method effects] by designing tests for specific populations – tests that contain instructions, content, genre, and language [i.e., test method facets] directed toward that population. The goal is to produce tests, useful to both LT and SLA professionals, that would provide information interpretable as evidence of communicative competence in context. (p. 153)

Research investigating the role of subtle differences in test method facets as operational instruments of theoretical learner and context factors will provide an essential foundation for work seeking to realize this objective.

Each of these research methods used for investigating construct validity offers a unique type of evidence pertaining to the meaning of consistent test performance. In each case, however, a rational approach to designing and interpreting the research rests on a clearly articulated construct definition. The collective possibilities for construct validation may appear overwhelming to researchers wishing to use tests rather than endlessly investigating their construct validity. As Shepard (1993) expresses the problem, "If construct validity is seen as an exhaustive process that can be accomplished over a 50-year period, test developers may be inclined to think that any validity information is good enough in the short run" (p. 444). The alternative Shepard suggests is to focus on those questions essential to the consequences of testing. For example, Perkins and Linn-ville's (1987) object of investigation was a test used for placement at different levels; therefore, their most immediate concern was the consistency of the operational construct definition across different levels, causing them to choose to investigate validity through a study of empirical item difficulty. If testing consequences are to direct validity inquiry, however, it will be necessary to identify the consequences of tests used in SLA research.

Consequences of test use

According to Messick's (1989) definition of validity, the consequences of testing serve as additional justifications that can build upon our understanding of score meaning by identifying the value and sociological implications of testing. In particular, Messick identifies two interrelated questions that should underlie investigation of testing consequences: What are the value implications of the interpretations made from testing? What are the social consequences of test use? These difficult questions are just beginning to be explored by LT researchers. Addressing educational uses of tests, Alderson and Wall (1993) point out that specific consequences of language tests have not been clearly documented, and therefore an essential aspect of consequential validity inquiry is to hypothesize the nature and scope of test consequences. Addressing test consequences from the perspective of educational and psychological measurement in general, Shepard suggests that "the validity framework appropriate to [an educational] test use will have a different focus than one for the same measure used to operationalize a construct in a research setting" (1993: 445). In applied linguistics research, however, the distance between laboratory and classroom is often negligible; the constructs developed by researchers often end up affecting the classroom. I will therefore consider research on testing to affect both L2 research and classrooms.

I will illustrate the testing impacts relevant to validity by discussing the apparent consequences of two test methods associated with the trait-oriented perspective of interlanguage vocabulary: the word association test and the Y/N vocabulary recognition test. The former method has been used in a number of different forms, but the basic principle is that the test taker is required to produce one or more words that come to mind each time the experimenter presents a word. Meara (1978, 1984) believes that the word association test assesses the trait dimension "vocabulary organization." The Y/N test requires learners to indicate whether or not they think they recognize words that are presented to them in isolation. Test items are composed of both actual target language words and sequences of letters that are not real words in the language. Meara believes that this test measures the trait "absolute vocabulary size" (Meara & Buxton 1987;

Meara 1989). Both tests, consistent with their underlying construct definitions, present vocabulary items out of context and choose items without regard to the context in which they might occur in language use.

The validity of interpretations and uses of these tests should be examined by considering evidence for their construct validity with reference to the construct each is intended to measure, their relevance and utility in a particular setting, and their consequences. Here, however, I will consider only the consequences in terms of value implications and their societal consequences.

SOCIETAL IMPLICATIONS OF INTERLANGUAGE VOCABULARY TESTING

In SLA research, the tests used to elicit language samples are typically viewed as instruments acting as one piece of a larger research design. As Loevinger (1957) pointed out many years ago, however, the tests used in research help to define researchers' views of the constructs they investigate. The use of a given instrument is tied to a particular perspective toward construct definition, which is built upon assumptions and values about constructs and their measurement. Tests and their associated construct definitions, in turn, affect the nature of the theories that L2 researchers develop. One purpose of validity inquiry, therefore, is to clarify the values underlying the interpretations made from a given test in order to compare these implicit test-embedded values with the researcher's explicit values and with those of others in the field. I explain here how identifying the nature of the construct definition underlying a particular test is essential to an investigation of the values underlying test interpretation. In particular, I will speculate on two value-related implications of the trait-oriented word association and Y/N test: their impacts on the perceptions of researchers and on the nature of SLA theory.

The word association test and its underlying trait definition appear to have influenced the perceptions of some interlanguage vocabulary researchers. Since Meara's 1978 study, other researchers have continued to use varieties of word association tests in L2 lexicon research (e.g., Palmberg 1987; Soderman 1989) and to discuss "vocabulary organization" from a trait perspective (e.g., Ard & Gass 1987; Gass 1988; Singleton & Little 1991). In fact, after finding that a word association test was inadequate as a proficiency measure, Kruse, Pankhurst, and Sharwood Smith (1987) concluded that word association tests "may conceivably be a useful tool in future explorations of lexical interlanguage. A study of the associative responses given by learners might still contribute to the discovery of developmental processes that take place in language learners' mental lexicons" (p. 153). On the basis of this recommendation and the lack of additional insight into the validity of word association tests for making inferences about lexicon organization, future researchers may indeed continue to investigate the trait conceptions of vocabulary using word association tests.

Meara, on the other hand, later advocated the Y/N test, which is intended to measure the trait dimension "absolute vocabulary size," but he also suggests it for a proficiency measure.

The prototype version of the test [estimates vocabulary size] in 10 minutes, scores itself automatically and produces very high correlations with an extended test of overall ability in EFL which normally requires an hour and a half to administer. We think this is a significant development, particularly for research purposes, since it will allow researchers to assess the proficiency level of their subjects in a very simple way and help us to get away from the messy and unreliable labels which characterize much current research (Meara & Buxton 1987: 150–151)

It is not yet clear whether or not other researchers will adopt the Y/N test for measuring vocabulary size (or for proficiency). What is apparent is that the trait-oriented construct definitions underlying both of these tests must be recognized and their impacts evaluated.

A validity study investigating the values underlying the use of a word association test or the Y/N test would first identify the trait-oriented construct definition underlying the tests and then examine the impact of this trait definition on the test use context. Because the word association test and the Y/N test are believed to affect perceptions of interlanguage vocabulary researchers, consistency between the field's conception of interlanguage and the construct definition implied by a test should be examined. These tests apparently play a role in maintaining a trait perspective of interlanguage vocabulary despite the fact that the interest in applied linguistics has shifted to an interactionalist perspective. One might argue against the use of such tests in research on the basis of this discontinuity.

A second value-related consequence of tests used in vocabulary research is their impact on the nature of theory about the acquisition of L2 vocabulary. In the case of the Y/N test, the "neat and reliable" underlying trait definition extends into a trait-oriented *theory of L2 vocabulary development*. Meara's theory of vocabulary development hypothesizes that "the underlying structure [of vocabulary acquisition] can be seen as a transitional probability matrix" (Meara 1989: 73). The research associated with this theory would focus on prediction and observation of increases in vocabulary size without reference to other aspects of vocabulary knowledge, strategies, or contexts of acquisition. Moreover, Meara recommends the Y/N test and its associated research agenda to other vocabulary researchers:

It is unlikely that such study will get very far, unless we adopt some common standards which might help to make diverse [research] programs relatively compatible. These are: 1) adoption of a week as the basic unit of time;

2) adoption of the T2-T3 transition matrix as the standard datum; 3) adoption of a neutral, minimal vocabulary assessment instrument, based in Meara and Buxton (1987). (Meara, 1989: 73).

Other researchers working within the trait perspective have suggested that other dimensions of the trait also be investigated. For example, Wesche and Paribakht (1993) described the state of research on L2 lexical development:

A problem facing empirical researchers is the lack of sensitive assessment procedures for tracing the development over time of specific vocabulary knowledge, either in terms of stages characterizing how well given words are known, or in terms of the different kinds of knowledge it is possible to have about given words. (Wesche and Paribakht, 1993: 2)

This observation addresses the need to investigate L2 lexical development using methods other than those advocated by Meara in order to construct a theory of L2 vocabulary development that extends beyond a quantitative theory of expanding vocabulary size. However, in doing so, Wesche and Paribakht propose to expand research to other dimensions of the trait rather than to reconceptualize the construct to include strategies and contexts of vocabulary use. A validity study of the word association or Y/N test should investigate their impact on a theory of interlanguage vocabulary development. Having identified the one-dimensional, trait-oriented definition underlying each test, one might make a consequential validity argument against the use of word association and Y/N tests because they have helped to focus theory on one trait dimension while other researchers document the need to understand multiple dimensions of trait. Moreover, as Tarone (Chapter 3, this volume) points out, tests that reflect a trait definition confine the focus of theory to dimensions of knowledge and fundamental processes, causing researchers to overlook the roles of contexts and strategies in performance and acquisition. The perceptions of interlanguage researchers and the nature of the acquisition theory they construct are two of the value implications of the inferences made from the tests chosen for vocabulary research. As I have suggested, however, the impacts of these tests are felt beyond the research community, extending into educational practices, where their social consequences must also be evaluated.

SOCIAL CONSEQUENCES OF INTERLANGUAGE VOCABULARY TESTS

Because much work in applied linguistics is aimed at addressing real language problems and needs, the impact of tests used in applied linguistics research should be expected to extend into classroom settings. Direct impacts might be seen when an SLA study is conducted in a classroom by administering tests to students in their language class. Impacts of research in the classroom also occur when a research test such as the word association test is investigated as a potential proficiency measure for educational use. Kruse et al. (1987) were "concerned with the practical research issue of whether the word association test can indeed be used as a reliable measure of language proficiency" (p. 145). Despite their conclusion that the word association test would not make a good proficiency measure (and might therefore be suitable only for L2 vocabulary research), their study illustrates the blurred distinction between research and classroom in applied linguistics and therefore the potential for today's research tests to appear in tomorrow's classrooms. Even if research tests are not adopted in L2 classrooms, they are likely to influence L2 teaching practices indirectly. For example, from his first reported study of the use of word association tests for vocabulary research, Meara attempted an extension to the classroom:

The production of word associations is not so clearly related to ordinary language activities. My own feeling, however, is that all the various types of language activity are reflections of the same underlying, basic skills, and that if we could develop learning methods that, as a side-effect produced learners with native-like association patterns, we would also be producing learners who were better able to communicate in their foreign language. (Meara 1978: 210–211)

The word association test's successor, the Y/N test, is now claimed to be ideal for educational uses. Meara and Buxton (1987) and Meara (1989) claim the usefulness of the Y/N test despite any apparent limitations:

There are a number of problems with [Y/N vocabulary tests] – notably that they measure passive vocabulary, rather than active vocabulary skills. However, they do have some important practical advantages – ease of construction, simplicity of assessment, time necessary for completion, possibility of large sample rates, and so on – *which seem to outweigh most of the theoretical disadvantages*. (Meara 1989: 72; emphasis added)

According to our current conception of validity, practical advantages do not outweigh "theoretical" disadvantages, such as a test's impact on learners' perceptions of what they should study. One might argue that a Y/N recognition test encourages students to study dictionaries and especially spelling, to the neglect of the interactional abilities that are no less essential for communicative development. Investigation of the social consequences of tests would hypothesize and document these types of testing impacts on students' and instructors' perceptions of language and on their classroom actions (Canale 1987).

Despite the importance of consequences as a facet of validity inquiry, their investigation as a credible mode of validity inquiry has not yet been well developed by educational measurement researchers. The first step in investigating test consequences is to identify the potential intended and unintended consequences of test use. The word association and Y/N tests provide good examples of research tests in applied linguistics with consequences extending beyond a particular research setting. As I suggested earlier, they may affect the perceptions of interlanguage researchers, interlanguage theory, and classroom practices. In examining the values and consequences of these tests, an understanding of their underlying construct definitions was essential. Educational measurement researchers will continue to refine their definition of – and research methods for studying – testing consequences. As this work continues, applied linguists, whose research concerns are situated in classrooms and other contexts of language use, are ideally suited to develop the precedents for consequential validity inquiry.

Implications for SLA and LT research

Current conceptions of construct definition and validity inquiry offer directions and challenges for SLA and LT research. Tests used for both educational and research purposes need to be subjected to the processes of validity inquiry to reveal the quality of any given operational setting for producing the relevant signs and samples of learners' performance. The validation process is ongoing; varieties of justifications pertaining to appropriate test use are continually revisited. This means that there is no "validated test" – one that has been proved valid for all time, and therefore can be picked up and used without further examination. Instead, researchers are at all times responsible for examining construct validity, relevance and utility, value implications, and social consequences. For example, when Kruse et al. (1987) investigated the validity of using a word association test for assessing language proficiency, in addition to the two traditional construct validity methods they used (correlations of the word association test with other language tests and comparison of performance by native and nonnative speakers), other aspects of validity could have also been discussed (e.g., how the use of word associations as a proficiency measure would affect learners' perceptions of proficiency). The eventual impacts of tests in applied linguistics research may even help to prioritize investigation of construct validity inquiry.

Construct definition plays an essential role in rational design and interpretation of validation research. Despite the support in applied linguistics for an interactionalist approach to construct definition, little systematic inquiry has been attempted to better define specific person and context dimensions. Validity researchers, therefore, are challenged to better understand the nature and implications of an interactionalist construct definition because it offers unique dilemmas for each method of construct validity inquiry. Content analysis requires that the person and context sources of learners' performance in the operational setting be hypothesized, but the analytic procedures for making such process-oriented hypotheses have not been developed. Empirical item investigation demands selection of operational variables believed to represent context and person as well as their interaction as sources of difficulty, but the developmental definitions required to make such selections have not been specified. Task analysis investigating the strategies used in operational settings forces all researchers to recognize what Messick (1989) terms the "conundrum of educational measurement" – that strategies can vary across people and tasks even when the same results are achieved. Correlational studies require hypotheses about the strengths of correlations expected among language tests and other tests, but such hypotheses rest on unknown degrees of contribution from the multiple relevant sources of performance consistency. Experimental studies require specification of test method facets that will aid in better understanding the role of theoretical factors in the operational setting, but little theoretical work has addressed questions pertaining to the connection between the two levels of measurement.

An essential step toward substantive progress in these areas is a clear distinction between the measurement data sought from SLA elicitation devices and those from other methods of observation in SLA research. Only when performance consistency is observed do researchers move from fragile, idiosyncratic observations to measurement. As a consequence, estimates of reliability are essential to understanding when data can be summarized to act as dependable indicators of constructs and when construct validity evidence is needed to support construct-related inferences. Although inconsistent performance is interesting in its own right, it cannot be treated as a dependable indicator of a construct. To make progress in understanding the interactionalist construct definition, it is necessary to better understand the nature of operational settings across which consistent performance can be observed.

Teichroew's review of vocabulary research concluded that "it does seem clear that the form of the test has considerable influence on the results gleaned" (1982: 22). Over fifteen years later we can add that the nature of the test also has considerable influence on our implicit construct definitions, which in turn affect the perceptions of researchers, the nature of SLA theory, and classroom practices. As a consequence, validity inquiry informed by current interactionalist construct definition is essential.

References

Abraham, R. G., & C. A. Chapelle. 1992. The meaning of cloze test scores: An item difficulty perspective. *Modern Language Journal, 76,* 468–479.

Aitchison, J. 1987. *Words in the mind: An introduction to the mental lexicon.* New York: Blackwell.

Alderson, J. C. 1993. The relationship between grammar and reading in an EAP test battery. In D. Douglas & C. Chapelle (eds.), *A new decade of language testing research* (pp. 203–219). Arlington, VA: TESOL.

Alderson, J. C., & D. Wall. 1993. Does washback exist? *Applied Linguistics, 14,* 115–129.

Ard, J., & S. Gass. 1987. Lexical constraints on syntactic acquisition. *Studies in Second Language Acquisition, 9,* 233–351.

Arnaud, P. J. L. 1989. Vocabulary and grammar: A multitrait-multimethod investigation. *AILA Review, 6,* 56–65.

Bachman, L. F. 1990. *Fundamental considerations in language testing.* Oxford: Oxford University Press.

Bachman, L. F., F. Davidson, & J. Foulkes. 1993. A comparison of the abilities measured by the Cambridge and Educational Testing Service EFL test batteries. In D. Douglas & C. Chapelle (eds.), *A new decade of language testing research* (pp. 25–45). Arlington, VA: TESOL.

Bachman, L. F., F. Davidson, K. Ryan, & I. Choi. 1995. *An investigation into the comparability of two tests of English as a foreign language: The Cambridge-TOEFL comparability study.* Cambridge: University of Cambridge Local Examinations Syndicate / Cambridge University Press.

Bachman, L. F., A. Kunnan, S.Vanniarajan, & B. Lynch. 1988. Task and ability analysis as a basis for examining content and construct comparability in two EFL proficiency tests. *Language Testing, 5*(2), 128–159.

Bachman, L. F., & A. S. Palmer. 1982. The construct validation of some components of communicative competence. *TESOL Quarterly, 16*(4), 449–465.

Bachman, L. F., & A. S. Palmer. 1996. *Language testing in practice: Designing and developing useful language tests.* Oxford: Oxford University Press.

Bialystok, E. 1981. The role of linguistic knowledge in second language use. *Studies in Second Language Acquisition, 4,* 31–45.

Bialystok, E., & M. Sharwood Smith. 1985. Interlanguage is not a state of mind: An evaluation of the construct for second language acquisition. *Applied Linguistics, 6,* 101–117.

Blum-Kulka, S., & E. Levinson. 1983. Universals of lexical simplification. In C. Faerch & G. Kasper (eds.), *Strategies in interlanguage communication* (pp. 119–139). London: Longman.

Campbell, A. 1961. Some determinants of the difficulty of non-verbal classification items. *Educational and Psychological Measurement, 21,* 899–913.

Campbell, D. T., & D. W. Fiske. 1959. Convergent and discriminant validation by the multitrait-multimethod matrix. *Psychological Bulletin, 56,* 81–105.

Canale, M. 1987. Language assessment: The method is the message. In D. Tannen & J. E. Alatis (eds.), *The interdependence of theory, data, and application* (pp. 249–262). Washington, DC: Georgetown University Press.

Canale, M., & M. Swain. 1980. Theoretical bases of communicative approaches to second language teaching and testing. *Applied Linguistics, 1*(1), 1–47.

Carroll, J. B. 1976. Psychometric tests as cognitive tasks: A new "structure of intellect." In L. B. Resnick (ed.), *The nature of intelligence* (pp. 27–56). Hillsdale, NJ: Lawrence Erlbaum.

Carroll, J. B. 1989. Intellectual abilities and aptitudes. In A. Lesgold & R. Glaser (eds.), *Foundations for a psychology of education* (pp. 137–197). Hillsdale, NJ: Lawrence Erlbaum.

Carroll, J. B. 1993. *Human cognitive abilities: A survey of factor analytic studies.* Cambridge: Cambridge University Press.

Chapelle, C. A. 1994. Are C-tests valid measures for L2 vocabulary research? *Second Language Research, 10*(2), 157–187.

Chapelle, C. A., & R. G. Abraham. 1990. Cloze method: What difference does it make? *Language Testing, 7*(1), 121–146.

Chapelle, C. A., & D. Douglas. 1993. Interpreting L2 performance data. Paper presented at the second Language Research Colloquium, Pittsburgh, PA, March.

Chapelle, C. A., & P. Green. 1992. Field independence/dependence in second language acquisition research. *Language Learning, 42,* 47–83.

Chitiri, H-F., Y. Sun, D. M. Willows, & I. Taylor. 1992. Word recognition in second language reading. In R. J. Harris (ed.), *Cognitive processing in bilinguals* (pp. 283–297). New York: Elsevier.

Cohen, A. 1984. On taking language tests: What the students report. *Language Testing, 1*(1), 70–81.

Cohen, A., & M. Robbins. 1976. Toward assessing interlanguage performance: The relationship between selected errors, learners' characteristics, and the learners' explanations. *Language Learning, 26,* 45–66.

Dollerup, C., E. Glahn, & C. R. Hansen. 1989. Vocabularies in the reading process. *AILA Review, 6,* 21–33.

Douglas, D., & L. Selinker. 1985. Principles for language tests within the "discourse domain" theory of interlanguage: Research, test construction and interpretation. *Language Testing, 2,* 205–226.

Douglas, D., & L. Selinker. 1992. Analyzing oral proficiency test performance in general and specific purpose contexts. *System, 20*(3), 317–328.

Duff, P. 1993. Tasks and interlanguage performance: An SLA perspective. In G. Crookes & S. M. Gass (eds.), *Tasks and language learning: Integrating theory and practice* (pp. 57–95). Philadelphia: Multilingual Matters.

Eckman, F. R. 1994. The competence-performance issue in second-language acquisition theory: A debate. In E. E. Tarone, S. M. Gass, & A. D. Cohen (eds.), *Research methodology in second-language acquisition* (pp. 3–15). Hillsdale, NJ: Lawrence Erlbaum.

Ellis, R. 1989. Sources of intra-learner variability in language use and their relationship to second language acquisition. In S. Gass, C. Madden, D. Preston, & L. Selinker (eds.), *Variation in second language acquisition. Psycholinguistic issues* (Vol. 2, pp. 22–45). Philadelphia: Multilingual Matters.

Embretson, S. 1983. Construct validity: Construct representation versus nomothetic span. *Psychological Bulletin, 93*(1), 179–197.

Faerch, C., & G. Kasper 1983. Plans and strategies in foreign language communication. In C. Faerch & G. Kasper (eds.), *Strategies in interlanguage communication* (pp. 20–60). London: Longman.

Faerch, C., & G. Kasper (eds.). 1987. *Introspection in second language learning.* Clevedon: Multilingual Matters.

Feldmann, U., & B. Stemmer. 1987. Thin_____ aloud a_____ retrospective da_____ in C-te_____ taking: Diffe_____ languages-diff_____ learners-sa_____ approaches? In C. Faerch and G. Kasper (eds.), *Introspection in second language research* (pp. 251–267). Philadelphia: Multilingual Matters.

Frenck-Mestre, C., & J. Vaid. 1992. Language as a factor in the identification of ordinary words and number words. In R. J. Harris (ed.), *Cognitive processing in bilinguals* (pp. 265–282). New York: Elsevier.

Gass, S. 1988. Integrating research areas: A framework for second language studies. *Applied Linguistics, 9*(1), 198–217.

Grotjahn, R. 1986. Test validation and cognitive psychology: Some methodological considerations. *Language Testing, 3*(2), 159–185.

Gulliksen, H. 1950. Intrinsic validity. *American Psychologist, 5*, 511–517.

Gumperz, J. J. 1976. Language, communication and public negotiation. In P. R. Sanday (ed.), *Anthropology and the public interest* (pp. 273–292). New York: Academic Press.

Halliday, M. A. K., & R. Hasan. 1989. *Language, context, and text: Aspects of language in a social-semiotic perspective.* Oxford: Oxford University Press.

Henderson, L. 1985. Toward a psychology of morphemes. In A. W. Ellis (ed.), *Progress in the psychology of language* (Vol. 1, pp. 15–72). London: Lawrence Erlbaum.

Hymes, D. 1967. Models of the interaction of language and the social setting. *Journal of Social Issues, 23*(2), 8–28.

Hymes, D. 1972. *Towards communicative competence.* Philadelphia: Pennsylvania University Press.

Kellerman, E. 1978. Giving learners a break: Native speaker intuitions as a source of predictions about transferability. *Working Papers on Bilingualism, 15*, 59–92.

Kruse, H., J. Pankhurst, & M. Sharwood Smith. 1987. A multiple word association probe in second language acquisition research. *Studies in Second Language Acquisition, 9*, 141–154.

Lantolf, J. P., & W. Frawley. 1988. Proficiency: Understanding the construct. *Studies in Second Language Acquisition, 10*, 181–195.

Laufer, B. 1990. "Sequence" and "order" in the development of L2 lexis: Some evidence from lexical confusions. *Applied Linguistics, 11*(3), 281–296.

Loevinger, J. 1957. Objective tests as instruments of psychological theory. *Psychological Reports, 3*, 635–694.

Luppescu, S., & R. R. Day. 1993. Reading, dictionaries, and vocabulary learning. *Language Learning, 43*(2), 263–287.

Marshalek, B. 1981. Trait and process aspects of vocabulary knowledge and verbal ability. Technical Report No. 15, Aptitude Research Project. AD A102757. Stanford, CA: School of Education, Stanford University.

Marslen-Wilson, W. 1989. Access and integration: Projecting sound onto meaning. In W. Marslen-Wilson (ed.), *Lexical representation and process* (pp. 3–24). Cambridge, MA: MIT Press.

McLaughlin, B. 1990. Restructuring. *Applied Linguistics, 11*(2), 113–128.

Meara, P. 1978. Learners' word associations in French. *Interlanguage Studies Bulletin, 3*, 192–211.

Meara, P. 1984. The study of lexis in interlanguage. In A. Davies, C. Criper, & A. P. R. Howatt (eds.), *Interlanguage* (pp. 225–239). Edinburgh: Edinburgh University Press.

Meara, P. 1989. Matrix models of vocabulary acquisition. *AILA Review, 6*, 66–74.

Meara, P., & B. Buxton. 1987. An alternative to multiple choice vocabulary tests. *Language Testing, 3,* 142–154.

Messick, S. 1981. Constructs and their vicissitudes in educational and psychological measurement. *Psychological Bulletin, 89,* 575–588.

Messick, S. 1989. Validity. In R. L. Linn (ed.), *Educational measurement* (3rd ed., pp. 13–103). New York: Macmillan.

Nation, P. 1993. Using dictionaries to estimate vocabulary size: Essential but rarely followed procedures. *Language Testing, 9,* 27–40.

Nattinger, J., & J. DeCarrico. 1989. Lexical phrases, speech acts, and teaching conversation. *AILA Review, 6,* 118–139.

Olshtain, E. 1987. The acquisition of new word formation processes in second language acquisition. *Studies in Second Language Acquisition, 9,* 221–232.

Palmberg, R. 1987. Patterns of vocabulary development in foreign language learners. *Studies in Second Language Acquisition, 9,* 201–220.

Perkins, K., & S. E. Linnville. 1987. A construct definition study of a standardized ESL vocabulary test. *Language Testing, 4*(2), 126–141.

Sharwood Smith, M. 1984. Discussant: The study of lexis in interlanguage by P. Meara. In A. Davies, C. Criper, & A. P. R. Howatt (eds.), *Interlanguage* (pp. 236–239). Edinburgh: Edinburgh University Press.

Shepard, L. 1993. Evaluating test validity. *Review of Research in Education, 19,* 405–450.

Singleton, D., & D. Little 1991. The second language lexicon: Some evidence from university-level learners of French and German. *Second Language Research, 7,* 62–81.

Skehan, P. 1987. Variability and language testing. In R. Ellis (ed.), *Second language acquisition in context* (pp. 195–206). Englewood Cliffs, NJ: Prentice-Hall.

Soderman, T. 1989. Word associations of foreign language learners and native speakers – a shift in response type and its relevance for a theory of lexical development. *Scandinavian Working Papers on Bilingualism, 8,* 114–121.

Spolsky, B. 1985. The limits of authenticity in language testing. *Language Testing, 2,* 29–40.

Stemmer, B. 1991. What's on a C-test taker's mind? Mental processes in C-test taking. Bochum, Germany: Universitätsverlag Dr. N. Brockmeyer.

Sternberg, R. J. 1977. *Intelligence, information processing, and analogical reasoning: The componential analysis of human abilities.* Hillsdale, NJ: Lawrence Erlbaum.

Sternberger, J. P., & B. MacWhinney. 1988. Are inflected forms stored in the lexicon? In M. Hammond & M. Noonan (eds.), *Theoretical morphology: Approaches in modern linguistics* (pp. 101–116). San Diego, CA: Academic Press.

Swain, M. 1990. Second language testing and second language acquisition: Is there a conflict with traditional psychometrics? In J. Alatis (ed.), *Georgetown University Round Table, 1990* (pp. 401–412). Washington, DC: Georgetown University Press.

Tarone, E. 1988. *Variation in interlanguage.* London: Edward Arnold.

Teichroew, J. M. 1982. A survey of receptive versus productive vocabulary. *Interlanguage Studies Bulletin, 6,* 3–33.

Tryon, W. W. 1979. The test-trait fallacy. *American Psychologist, 34,* 402–406.

Vollmer, H. 1983. The structure of foreign language competence. In A. Hughes

& D. Porter (eds.), *Current developments in language testing* (pp. 3–29). London: Academic Press.

Votaw, M. C. 1992. A functional view of bilingual lexicosemantic organization. In R. J. Harris (ed.), *Cognitive processing in bilinguals* (pp. 299–321). New York: Elsevier.

Wesche, M. B. 1987. Second language performance testing: The Ontario test of ESL as an example. *Language Testing, 4,* 28–47.

Wesche, M., & T. S. Paribakht. 1993. Assessing vocabulary knowledge: Depth versus breadth. Paper presented at the American Association of Applied Linguistics conference, Atlanta, GA, April.

Widdowson, H. 1983. *Learning purpose and language use.* Oxford: Oxford University Press.

Yang, L., & T. Givon. 1993. Tracking the acquisition of L2 vocabulary: The Keki language experiment. Technical Report No. 93–11. Eugene: Institute of Cognitive & Decision Sciences, University of Oregon.

Young, R. 1989. Ends and means: Methods for the study of interlanguage variation. In S. Gass, C. Madden, D. Preston, & L. Selinker (eds.), *Variation in second language acquisition. Psycholinguistic issues* (Vol. 2, pp. 65–90). Philadelphia: Multilingual Matters.

Zuroff, D. C. 1986. Was Gordon Allport a trait theorist? *Journal of Personality and Social Psychology, 51,* 933–1000.

3 Research on interlanguage variation: Implications for language testing

Elaine Tarone

From the inception of research on second language acquisition (SLA), there has been an emphasis on the importance of studying authentic second language (L2) use in context. Selinker (1972) defined *interlanguage* as the linguistic system evidenced when adult second language learners attempted to express meanings in the language being learned. In attempting to model this underlying linguistic system, researchers were urged to use as data only

utterances produced by second-language learners when they were trying to communicate meaning in the target language. The relevant data were clearly *not* learner utterances produced in response to classroom drills and exercises where the learner was focusing attention on grammar rules or target language form. (Tarone 1994: 1717)

Thus, in its original formulation, the construct of "interlanguage" was construed to be the linguistic system revealed when learners were involved in authentic, situated L2 use. Although subsequent research has clearly used a much wider range of data than that originally envisioned by Selinker (1972), much – though not all – research in second language acquisition has continued to focus upon situated second language use. SLA theoreticians (e.g., Brown & Yule 1983a; Widdowson 1983) have provided useful frameworks for the study of contextualized second language use. However, it is important to note that theories of second language acquisition have been proposed that explicitly reject the value of authenticity of situational context for the study of second language acquisition (see Gregg 1990), and a great deal of SLA data has been gathered without particular regard for the influence of situational context (see Tarone 1988 for a discussion of this phenomenon). However, in general, the field of SLA has tended to value the study of authentic learner performance in context.

This focus of most SLA researchers upon the study of authentic, meaningful language use in situational context seemed for many years to contrast with the approach used by most second language testers and assessors, which seemed to rely heavily on the use of decontextualized, grammatically focused classroom drills and exercises as measures. However, recently there has been a growing emphasis in language testing upon the notion of task authenticity (see articles in *Language Testing*, 1985,

71

2,1; and Bachman 1990, 1991; Hoekje & Linnell 1994; Bachman & Palmer 1996). Hoekje and Linnell even state that "it is no longer acceptable to have language tests which are statistically valid and reliable but inauthentic in their tasks" (1994: 122).

Yet, for both SLA researchers and second language testers, the use of authentic, situationally contextualized tasks in eliciting learner language has brought with it a thorny problem: systematic interlanguage variation.[1] Tarone (1979, 1985, 1988, 1997), Ellis (1987, 1994), and others have argued that this systematic L2 variation in reaction to different contextual factors has important theoretical and methodological implications for the field of research on second language acquisition and use.

Researchers in the field of language testing and assessment have also documented evidence that *test method* may cause learner language variation. Bachman states:

> It is widely recognized that the features of the language use context, such as the relationship between the language users, the topic, and the purpose, influence the way we use language. It would thus not be surprising to find that characteristics of the method of testing affect the way individuals perform on tests. Indeed, one of the major findings of language testing research over the past decade is that performance on language tests is affected not only by the ability we are trying to measure but also by the method we use to measure it. (Bachman 1991: 687)

Research on SLA has clearly established that learner language is affected by (varies with) situational context. This chapter documents the phenomenon of interlanguage variation from the point of view of SLA research, and suggests several implications this phenomenon may have for language testing.

Interlanguage variation

An example

A graduate student who was an international teaching assistant at the University of Minnesota took two versions of the SPEAK (Spoken Proficiency English Assessment Kit) test, one of them with general content and

1 Research on L2 use in context (e.g., Dickerson 1975; Schmidt 1980; Tarone 1985, 1988; Smith 1992) shows that the situated language production of L2 learners varies significantly and systematically from one situation to another in terms of its grammatical accuracy and fluency. Tarone (1988) documents existing evidence in the SLA research literature that various factors affect systematic interlanguage variation, among these linguistic context, interlocutor, topic, and social norms. Chapelle (Chapter 2, this volume) defines *systematic variability* as "performance consistency within particular contexts" (p. 39). Particular situational conditions have been shown to correlate predictably with a language learner's production of particular linguistic features, such as third person singular -*s*, article usage, and tense usage.

the other with field-specific content. Here are this student's utterances on two versions of the same sentence completion item:

(1) General   By saving our money, we will be able to buy a house.
(2) Specific   By calibrating your instrument, you should be careful and patient.

(Smith 1989: 162)

Has this student mastered the use of the target syntactic construction? The answer to this question depends on which test version is used to elicit the data. The general content version of the test elicited a sentence that seems to provide evidence that the learner has mastered the structure in question, whereas the specific content version elicited a sentence in which the structure is not used correctly.

Definition

Interlanguage (IL) variation is the tendency for a second language learner's utterances, produced in the attempt to convey meaning, to vary systematically in grammatical and phonological accuracy as specific situational features change. This variation in grammatical accuracy can occur within one time frame, sometimes within minutes, and quite predictably in response to specific changes in features of situational context and task. A shift in grammatical accuracy may occur, as in the example just cited, when the topic of the communication changes. It may also occur in response to the presence or absence of an interlocutor in the data collection situation, a change in the number or identity of interlocutors, the physical location of the data collection, the degree to which the subject is asked to focus on grammatical accuracy as opposed to meaning, or other situational variables.

It is important to distinguish this synchronic, situation-related variation in the use of a second language from individual differences in SLA. The latter have sometimes been referred to as "variation." *Individual difference* refers to the great variety in style of learning and possibly even path of acquisition among learners (see Pienemann, Johnston, & Brindley 1988). Individuals may differ from each other in their acquisition processes – one may acquire structures faster than another, for example, or as Pienemann and others have convincingly argued, one learner may use one set of strategies to acquire the language and another learner may use a different set of strategies.

While it is clear that such individual differences exist, it is proposed here that this sort of difference across individuals should not be called "variation" but rather "individual difference." The term *variation* ought to be reserved to refer to shifts *within* the performance of any given individual and not to differences *across* individuals; the latter would be more consistent with the use of the term *variation* in sociolinguistics.

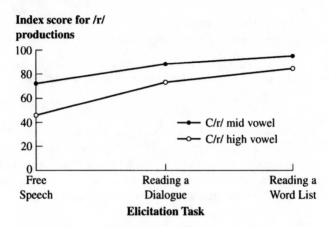

Figure 3.1   Phonological variation in Japanese-English interlanguage (adapted from Dickerson 1975)

Evidence of variation at different linguistic levels

Both Bachman (Appendix, this volume) and Shohamy (Chapter 7, this volume) refer to the fact that much of the research on systematicity and variation within the IL of given learners is related to the observation/elicitation procedure: the way in which subtle changes in task parameters and elicitation procedure can cause relatively major changes in both the degree to which particular IL forms and structures are supplied, and the degree of accuracy of those forms and structures. Research on interlanguage has shown that these shifts in accuracy may occur at any linguistic level: phonological, morphological, syntactic, or lexical.

For example, on the phonological level, Dickerson (1975) found that Japanese learners of English varied in the accuracy of their pronunciation of /r/ in consonant clusters when they were asked to perform three tasks: reading a word list, reading a dialogue, and conversing freely. They were least accurate in free conversation and most accurate on the word list (see Figure 3.1).

On the morphological level, Tarone (1985) found that Japanese and Arabic learners of English supplied the third person singular -s morpheme with variable accuracy on three tasks: a multiple choice grammar test, an oral interview, and an oral narrative. As Figure 3.2 shows, these learners produced the target form most accurately on the grammar test and least accurately on the narrative.

A completely different pattern of variation occurred with another morpheme – the English article. Here, the most accurate production of

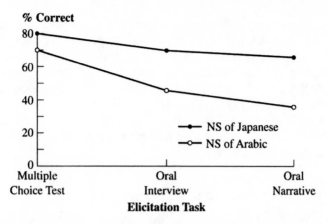

Figure 3.2 Task-related variation in marking of third person singular present tense verbs in ESL (adapted from Tarone 1985)

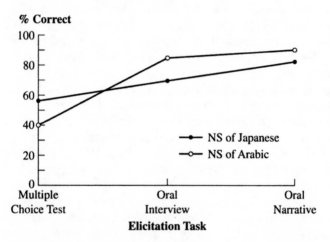

Figure 3.3 Task-related variation in article use in ESL (adapted from Tarone 1985)

the target form occurred on the narrative task, not the multiple choice test (Figure 3.3).

Liu (1991) provides an example of variation on the syntactic level with a study showing contextual variation in production of English questions (see also Tarone & Liu 1995). Liu conducted a longitudinal case study of a 6-year-old Chinese boy acquiring English as a second language in three contexts, each distinguished by the interlocutors with whom the boy was interacting and his role relationships with them. The boy's movement through five developmental stages of question formation in English was affected differentially by these situational contexts. Each new stage of question formation generally appeared first in Situation 1 (interaction with a friendly and interested adult friend during "play sessions" in the boy's home), later in Situation 2 (interactions in the classroom with the boy's peers in desk work), and last (often weeks later) in Situation 3 (interactions with the boy's teacher in class). Thus, at any given time, this boy's use of English questions appeared most advanced in Situation 1 and least advanced in Situation 3.

Contextual variables that influence interlanguage variation

Tarone (1988) summarizes 75 studies in second language acquisition to show, first, that this sort of variation in language production is very common for L2 learners and, second, that shifts in accuracy may be triggered by such contextual factors as shifts in the identity of the interlocutor and the learner's relationship with that interlocutor, topic, degree to which the learner was encouraged to focus on accuracy, and communicative pressure (defined as the speaker's perception of the interlocutor's need for the information being transmitted), among others. There has been much discussion in sociolinguistics about the relative weight of these contextual variables in causing variation; that is, is a shift in topic as influential as a shift in the identity of the interlocutor? Is one of these variables more fundamental or basic than the others? It is probably fair to say that this issue is still open to debate, although Bell (1984) has made a powerful argument for interlocutor effects as causal, underlying other factors such as setting and topic.

These contextual factors are clearly among those that language testers must consider in designing elicitation tasks. Research has shown that interlanguage variation related to topic, interlocutor, and other effects clearly occurs in language testing situations, as predicted by Bachman (1990, 1991).

Several studies have established that different test tasks have different effects on L2 oral proficiency scores (see Henning 1983; Shohamy 1983; Shohamy, Reves, & Bejarano 1986; among others). It now seems noncontroversial to state that test task affects L2 learners' oral performance. Chalhoub-Deville (1995a, b) goes further to argue that the nature of the L2 oral construct itself is context-specific, shifting from task to task (a proposal possibly similar to Tarone's 1983 suggestion that variation is not just a performance factor, but that L2 learners' underlying capability itself may be variable). Chalhoub-Deville supports her proposal by empirically deriving task-specific dimensions of L2 oral proficiency on interview, narration, and read-aloud tasks, and showing that three different rater groups accorded these dimensions differing degrees of importance in learners' performance.

Even when tasks are otherwise held constant, topic can affect interlanguage performance. Smith (1992) found that the pronunciation, grammar, fluency, and overall comprehensibility of many international teaching assistants (ITAs) were all subject to variation in relation to changes in topic, and in relation to particular test tasks. Smith showed that the scores of individual TAs on a SPEAK test could differ strikingly depending on whether they were given a field-specific topic or a general topic for otherwise identical test tasks. For example, some TAs did equally well in terms of their grammatical error ratings on both tests, some did better on the general topic test, and others did better on the field-specific test. The effect of topic, even when extensive attempts were made to keep the elicitation procedures constant in every other respect, was enough to make the difference between passing or failing the SPEAK test for many learners. Overall, it seemed that whether the general topic SPEAK test or the field-specific SPEAK test was used, 12 "passed" and 26 "failed." However, the *same* 12 did not pass both tests: 4 of those who passed the general test failed the field-specific test, and a different 4 who passed the field-specific test failed the general test.

Other research on language testing has also documented the way in which topic (whether related to the learner's field of study or not) can affect learner performance (see Alderson & Urquhart 1985; Hale 1988). An obviously related issue is the influence of topic and field of study on the assessment of vocabulary (Chapelle, Chapter 2, this volume).

Hoekje and Linnell (1994) use Bachman's (1990, 1991) standard of "authenticity" for language testing instruments to evaluate three instruments of spoken language assessment: the SPEAK test, the OPI (Oral Proficiency Interview), and the IP (Interaction Performance) test.[2] A performance test typically asks the student to role-play a situation designed to replicate a target language use context. Hoekje and Linnell demonstrate that these three instruments differ from one another primarily with regard to interlocutor effects. The SPEAK test requires the learner to respond on tape to audiotaped questions; thus, the interlocutor is physically absent and no negotiation between speaker and interlocutor is possible. The OPI has the learner interact with a single interlocutor who controls turn taking and topic. The IP test asks the learner to interact with a group of interlocutors while giving a presentation on a topic in the learner's field of

2 The authors note: "Performance testing in ITA education has usually involved the testing of the examinee's spoken language skills within a (mock) teaching context. The tasks in such tests often include a presentation on a key point or term in the candidate's academic field and a period of answering questions from the audience" (Hoekje & Linnell 1994: 109).

study. The tests vary with regard to whether or not an interlocutor is present, the number of interlocutors present, and the power of the speaker to control turn taking and topic in relation to the interlocutor(s). The authors argue that these three instruments "show substantial differences with regard to the dimensions of language use considered" (p. 121) – those dimensions primarily being the length of learner turn and the learner's use of discourse markers (e.g., "Now to understand that . . ." and "As you can see . . .").[3]

There seems to be ample documentation that when learner language is elicited using different test methods, learner language can vary systematically in accuracy at all levels (phonological, morphological, syntactic, lexical) in tandem with changes in situational variables such as topic and interlocutor, both in SLA research studies and in language testing situations.

Implications of interlanguage variation for language testing

In determining the significance of this IL variation for second language testing, there are several implications to consider:

1. Documentation of systematic effects of context on learners' variable production of language forms
2. Evaluation of SLA theories before use in the testing process
3. Insufficient controls for task-based variation in the formation of an SLA database
4. Failure of some SLA theories to take variation sufficiently into account

Documentation of systematic effects of context on learners' variable production of language forms

The studies cited in the previous section are persuasive in indicating that situational context can have an important effect on learner language; however, at present we know very little about the precise ways in which a learner's interlanguage production can be affected by situational context. For example, though Hoekje and Linnell (1994) show that the three

---

3 It is interesting to an SLA researcher to see that the authors do not examine in any greater detail the language produced by the learner to show to what degree different language features vary across the three measures. This would obviously be an important thing to do in examining the precise interlocutor effects upon the form of learner language; the research cited earlier on variation across all levels of learner language would lead one to expect shifts in lexical, syntactic, morphological, and phonological production across the three instruments examined.

instruments examined have an impact on the learner's length of turn and use of discourse markers, they do not (and perhaps cannot in that article) examine in detail what other aspects of this learner's interlanguage are affected. For example, are other cohesive devices, such as pronominal reference or article use, affected? verb tense? lexicon? If in fact one of the goals of language testing is to establish when a given L2 form has been acquired, and if in fact (as we now know) different "authentic" tasks can result in differential accuracy of production of L2 forms (like questions, articles, and pronouns) at any given time, then we need more information. Ultimately, we need to know what changes in context affect what linguistic forms and in what way. Then we need to develop "a theory of how the context of a particular situation within a broader context of culture constrains the linguistic choices a language user can make during linguistic performance" (Chapelle, this volume, p. 45).

L2 testers and SLA researchers interested in situational context and interlanguage variation might profitably join forces to initiate and carry out a research program. Such a joint research program is in fact most likely to provide the long-term solution to many of the testing problems outlined in the rest of the chapter. In the meantime, before we know precisely how context systematically affects linguistic features in the interlanguage, there will be other implications for language testing, as the following sections outline.

Evaluation of SLA theories before use in the testing process

Before applying SLA theories to the language testing process, testers should carefully consider whether those theories have taken sufficient account of the existence of interlanguage variation. As mentioned earlier, some SLA theories discount the effect of situational context on interlanguage production, holding this phenomenon to be irrelevant to the task of theory building (see Gregg 1990).

INSUFFICIENT CONTROLS FOR TASK-BASED VARIATION IN THE FORMATION OF AN SLA DATABASE

One consideration for testers has to do with evaluating the database supporting research findings, particularly when researchers argue that their findings have applications in testing. For example, testers need to evaluate the claim that SLA researchers have established universals of SLA that can provide a theoretical basis for language testing (e.g., Pienemann 1991, 1992). However, the sort of variation described here as characteristic of the language production of L2 learners makes it very difficult for researchers to obtain good data to support strong claims about universality. Such claims have been made, but often upon too small a database to be relied upon as yet – and often the database that is available does not sufficiently monitor the effects of contextual factors affecting the elicitation of those data.

Pienemann et al. (1988), for example, propose a universal model of SLA. This model was originally developed in a study of the acquisition of German as a second language that focused upon the acquisition of German word order by nonnative speakers. In that study, a developmental sequence for German L2 word order was established in which there were five stages, each one incorporating all previous stages. In Stage X, learners used canonical word order (subject-verb-object for German); in Stage X + 1, learners preposed adverbs but retained SVO word order; in Stage X + 2, they separated verbs ("He must the break have"); in Stage X + 3, they inverted subject and verb when preposing elements; and in Stage X + 4, they moved the finite verb to the end of subordinate clauses. Clahsen (1984) proposed that these stages could be accounted for by various combinations of three basic cognitive strategies; he suggested that these were universal and should apply universally to the acquisition of word order in any L2. This "multidimensional model" is now being extended to the acquisition of ESL, and proposals are being made to use the hypothesized sequence of acquisition of ESL in evaluating learners (see, for example, Brindley, Chapter 5, this volume).

Studies on the accuracy of this model in predicting the acquisition of word order in ESL are still in progress, but Hudson (1993) argues that the claim for universality is premature, citing problems in the methods used for analysis, among others. One must of course question the "universality" of a model for which the primary supporting data are drawn almost exclusively from German L2 learners. Not many data are yet available from learners acquiring target languages whose word order is less rigid than in German and English. And, of course, the sort of systematic task variation described here as essentially characteristic of interlanguage must cause us to demand a kind of rigor and consistency in task design, and in reporting on task design, that has too often been missing but that is essential if we are to have a trustworthy database upon which to build claims of universality. In any case, given the current lack of firm empirical validation for the multidimensional model for ESL, it certainly seems to be premature to use the model as the norm against which to measure individual learners, as proposed in Pienemann (1991), Pienemann et al. (1988), and Brindley (Chapter 5, this volume).

FAILURE OF THE QUANTITATIVE APPROACH AND THE
EMERGENCE APPROACH TO TAKE VARIATION
SUFFICIENTLY INTO ACCOUNT

A related issue here is how to establish when a given L2 form has been acquired by an L2 learner, particularly given the sort of interlanguage variation described earlier. This is a problem central to the larger issue of establishing a more general sequence of acquisition of interlanguage forms. SLA researchers claim that there are universal sequences of acquisition of second languages. Proving that these exist involves establishing sequences of acquisition for individual learners and comparing these to one another. This enterprise requires a method for determining when a given form has been acquired that can be applied equally to all learners – especially in light of interlanguage variation.

There are two ways of trying to do this. One has been referred to by Pienemann (1992) as the quantitative approach – using either an obligatory context or a performance analysis approach to count the use of variants of each variable interlanguage form, as exemplified by Dickerson (1975). For example, a set of tasks may be used to elicit data from a learner at a given point in time, and an array of scores may be established for each task. How can an acquisition point be pulled out of this array of data? Most commonly, an arbitrary percentage of correct answers is set as the acquisition point – 80 percent or 90 percent correct three sessions in a row is a common benchmark. Cazden et al. (1975) used this approach, based on work by Roger Brown (1973). But the Cazden study was relatively simple – no distinction was made between types of task and elicitation situation. All the data from all elicitation tasks were pooled within every session, and it was assumed that the elicitation methodology did not differ from one time to the next (an assumption that now seems naive).[4] The results often showed seemingly erratic changes in grammatical accuracy from one time to the next. When grammatical accuracy apparently shifts dramatically from one week to the next, at what point do we say that the learner has "acquired" the target form? The answer to this question, as in the Cazden study, must be arbitrary.

Pienemann (1992) proposes another solution, which shifts away from this kind of quantitative paradigm: The point at which a new form emerges is its acquisition point. For Pienemann, "acquisition is defined by emergence; and the level of acquisition is therefore defined by the complexity acquired" (1992: 7). In Pienemann's system, "differences in the percentage of rule application are understood as accuracy differences which do not alter the basic nature of the maturity of the IL system" (1992: 7). The old form and the new form are both part of the IL at the same time; rate of production of either form seems to be distinctly secondary in importance in Pienemann's model to the mere fact that both can be used.

Using this system, for example, Pienemann shows that a quantitative analysis of plural -s on a variety of tasks yields substantial variation.

---

4 Researchers more affected by sociolinguistic methodology, like Dickerson, have kept the data from distinct elicitation tasks separate in their longitudinal studies, and have attempted to give the same tasks at each sampling session.

However, because every task contains at least two noun stems with a plural suffix in plural contexts, Pienemann argues that "there is no principle difference between the sub-samples in relation to the plural -*s* marker" (1992: 18). In pragmatic terms, however, it would seem to be very important, both to students and to teachers, not just whether a learner *can* under some circumstance produce a form, but whether a learner *does* produce it, and what the rate of suppliance is across tasks. This is an old issue from the Audiolingual era: If a learner can produce a form in the language laboratory, but never uses it outside the laboratory, the form is not, in a practical sense, acquired. Similarly, from the cognitive transformational-generative era: If a learner can correctly mark sentences containing a form as grammatical and sentences lacking that form as ungrammatical, but if the learner does not consistently produce that form across a set of speaking/writing tasks that require that form, there is a basic sense in which that form has not been acquired.

It is obviously much simpler to sweep this problem of IL variation under the rug – to find ways to simplify the answer to the question of when any given IL form is acquired. Attempts to simplify the problem, however, are usually much less interesting and enlightening. A slower, more detailed approach, which describes the systematic, contextually related variation in all its complexity, will illuminate the interaction between innate psycholinguistic processes and contextually induced sociolinguistic processes, and amass sufficiently reliable and generalizable documentation of the existence of universal sequences of acquisition.

The emergence solution in particular seems to gloss over the basic fact of IL variation: Emergence will occur at different points in time on different tasks. Liu (1991) demonstrates how each new stage of question formation emerged at different points in time in the three situational contexts examined. A new form does not usually emerge simultaneously under all conditions. If we are to compare learners to each other with regard to emergence of a given form, we will have to ensure that the conditions under which that form was elicited are identical for all learners. This identity of tasks would seem to be impossible to establish at present.

I have argued that testers need to be aware that, because of the phenomenon of interlanguage variation, the database supporting many SLA research findings is simply too unreliable to support claims of universality at present, and so does not currently warrant easy applications to the field of language testing and language assessment.

Interlanguage variation and the language testing process

The next two implications of language variation relate to the process of language testing itself. They lead to a recommendation for the use of a *set* of carefully designed tasks in order to arrive at a more comprehensive description of the learner's abilities.

Task design in language testing

One implication of interlanguage variation for the process of language testing is, then, the design of the tasks used to elicit test data. Here we are concerned not with the psycholinguistic factors involved in various tasks (see Bialystok 1991) but rather with the sociolinguistic validity of the tasks. What sort of elicitation procedures should be used in a language test when learners' interlanguage is so sensitive (in quantitative terms) to subtle differences in elicitation procedures? If topic, for example, as Smith (1992) argues, does have a strong effect on many learners' accuracy rates, then tests and SLA research tasks that are claimed to be "identical" in construction but that vary in the topics tested are not in fact the same across learners. In norm-referenced testing, we usually want to compare learners, but we cannot do so if data from different learners are obtained under different conditions.

Bachman (1988; reprinted in the Appendix to this volume) points out that the concern for authenticity in test design has led to the use of a greater variety of tasks in language proficiency tests. However, if Tarone (1979, 1988), Smith (1992), and Ellis (1987) are right in making the point that different tasks can elicit different accuracy rates, or in essence, different "views" of the degree of development of the interlanguage system, there may be serious problems for norm-referenced language testing that uses a greater variety of tasks, as Bachman recommends. How are the different accuracy rates, fluency rates, grammaticality rates, and comprehensibility rates produced on those different tasks to be evaluated in relation to a single abstract norm?

Bachman (1990), Hoekje and Linnell (1994), and others suggest a move away from norm-referenced language testing toward criterion-referenced performance testing: designing elicitation tasks that are more authentic in the sense that the testing situation shares more features in common with particular target language use situations. This is a pragmatic approach in that it authentically measures the learner's ability to function in a specified real-world target situation. Of course, moving toward better validity in this way brings with it a reduction in reliability and generalizability (Hoekje & Linnell 1994); in other words, this approach will not allow us to compare learners to one another when those learners' target use situations differ.[5]

---

5 It might be argued that the ability to compare learners across target language use domains might be possible when we have a better theory and database to use in predicting the systematic relationship between specific contextual variables and specific

But as Bachman (1990) points out, perhaps we do not need to compare subjects to one another across target use situations, as is done in norm-referenced testing. In criterion-referenced testing, a language test consists of tasks either drawn from a particular target language use (TLU) situation, or designed so as to share crucial characteristics with tasks naturally occurring in that TLU situation. Then test results can be interpreted in terms of their relationship with the specific TLU situation or situations upon which the test tasks were based. That is, we look only for generalizability to particular TLU situations – not for generalizability to all TLU situations.

One form of the criterion-referencing solution, then, would give up the attempt to arrive at a single number descriptive of the language proficiency of each learner and comparable to all the other numbers descriptive of all the other learners. Rather, a set of different test scores relating to different TLU criterion situations might be assembled for any given learner. (Obviously, such a record should become part of the research database referred to earlier.)

The crucial factor is careful task design: How can we ensure that test elicitation conditions correspond with the authentic language use conditions that apply in the real-world situation or domain to which we want to generalize? For example, did every speaking task require exchange of real information with a real interlocutor who needed that information for some purpose? Or did some test tasks have speakers addressing an imaginary interlocutor, or even the tester? The presence or absence of an interlocutor who lacks the information being sent and who needs that information for some purpose can have a profound impact upon the degree of suppliance of a form in learner language (Brown & Yule 1983b; Yule 1997). In the testing literature, Shohamy (1994) has made a similar point with regard to the influence of the presence or absence of an interlocutor upon learner production. Brown and Yule (1983b) and Yule (1997) provide an excellent framework for the controlled elicitation of spoken language data within which such variables can be considered, controlled, and consistently reported.

Many current language tests might be improved by more such careful consideration of task design. Pienemann (1992) describes a picture description task used in his Rapid Profile; however, it is not clear whether this task includes a listener who does not have the information being encoded by the speaker or who needs that information for any purpose. If the TLU

language choices. However, proponents of a discourse domain view of interlanguage development (e.g., Selinker & Douglas 1985) might very well argue that a learner's mastery of language use within one discourse domain may proceed fairly independently of mastery in other domains. If this is true, then there may be no principled way to predict a learner's performance in domains other than those upon which criterion-referenced testing was based.

situation involves an interlocutor who needs the information a speaker is supplying for some purpose, then the testing task should include such an interlocutor. It is imperative that when a variety of test tasks is used, the elicitation conditions operative for each task that might have affected variation must be carefully specified and controlled so as to match the corresponding TLU situation as precisely as possible. The Hoekje and Linnell (1994) study provides a good beginning model for such an approach.

Interpretation of test results

Another implication of interlanguage variation for the language testing process itself has to do with interpreting test data. If, for example, testers want to compare learners but are, as we have shown, at present unable in principle to completely equalize elicitation procedures for all learners, they will need to take this fact into account in drawing implications from their test results. The most obvious point here is that testers will need to interpret their test results as applying to very restricted TLU situations and testing conditions. They are comparing learners who in fact cannot be compared *exactly*, because their TLU situations may be different and because test elicitation conditions may be different.

When we follow Bachman's suggestion that a variety of tasks be used, how is differing performance on these different tasks to be interpreted? Do any of the test tasks provide a "better" or "more accurate" picture of the state of the learner's interlanguage (i.e., of that learner's proficiency)? The position taken in criterion-referenced testing must be that none of the tasks provides a universally "better" picture than any other: Different test tasks simply relate more or less authentically to different TLU situations. To view the situation another way, following Chalhoub-Deville (1995b), the nature of the L2 oral construct itself may be viewed as context-specific, shifting from task to task; task-specific dimensions of that construct may be identified empirically for purposes of interpretation using techniques being perfected by Chalhoub-Deville and others.

How, then, are such different scores on different tasks to be viewed? How are we to conceive of a context-specific oral language proficiency; and how might this relate to a more traditional unitary measure of language proficiency? One possibility is to avoid a single unitary measure. One might rather identify those dimensions of oral proficiency that are most relevant to the various tasks used. Or, in studying the development of syntax in interlanguage, one might record and chart, over time, a learner's accuracy rate on a set of tasks, in order to show those contexts in which acquisition occurs first, second, third, and so on. If we are to use Pienemann's emergence schema, we might note the conditions under which a new form progressively emerges: A new form does not usually emerge simultaneously under all elicitation conditions. A close examination of those conditions under which a learner uses and does not use a given grammatical form can be most enlightening. The systematic progress over time in the emergence of new linguistic forms across tasks and TLU situations is, both theoretically and practically, interesting and useful information to chart.

Summary

It has been argued that research on interlanguage variation has shown that it is common for the language production of second language learners to vary systematically in grammatical accuracy and fluency (among other characteristics) in response to contextual changes. Such systematic variation, it was argued, has important implications for language testing. For example, researchers in language testing may be interested in joint research projects with SLA researchers to establish exactly what situational features tend to be related to what sorts of systematic variation in particular interlanguage forms, or to what dimensions of language proficiency. An understanding of this relationship should provide the best long-term solution to the problem of interlanguage variation, as it would enable testers to systematically manipulate situational features with a clear understanding of the sorts of choices those manipulations offer learners. (Chapelle, in Chapter 2 of this volume, makes an eloquent case for a similar solution.)

Another implication is that many current SLA research findings must be viewed with some skepticism, since few studies currently control carefully for the sort of interlanguage variation described here, or allow for the implications of this variation when drawing conclusions. Of particular concern here is the claim of some researchers to have evidence of universals of second language acquisition. Although such universals probably do exist, documentation of their existence must allow and control for the existence of sociolinguistic forces in data elicitation situations as well. Another implication is that, because of interlanguage variation, it is in principle impossible for test tasks to be identical in their impact upon second language learners, and therefore upon their language production. Thus, norm-referenced testing is severely compromised. One possible solution to this problem is to relate testing more directly to the uses of those tests in the real world – that is, to move toward criterion-referenced performance testing. This solution might avoid trying to arrive at a single number descriptive of the proficiency of each learner and comparable with the numbers descriptive of other learners. Rather, each learner would be described by a set of scores obtained on several clearly defined tasks, themselves relatable in clear ways to target use situations.

A final implication is that when comparisons between such learners must be made, they should be strongly tempered by the awareness that the scores are approximations only. It is difficult to compare learners exactly because at present we so poorly understand the effects of situational factors on learners' test performance.

References

Alderson, J. C., & A. H. Urquhart. 1985. The effect of students' academic discipline on their performance on ESP reading tests. *Language Testing, 2*(2), 192–204.

Bachman, L. 1988. Language testing–SLA research interfaces. *Annual Review of Applied Linguistics, 9,* 193–209.

Bachman, L. F. 1990. *Fundamental considerations in language testing.* Oxford: Oxford University Press.

Bachman, L. F. 1991. What does language testing have to offer? *TESOL Quarterly, 25*(4), 671–704.

Bachman, L. F., & A. S. Palmer. 1996. *Language testing in practice: Designing and developing useful language tests.* Oxford: Oxford University Press.

Bell, A. 1984. Language style as audience design. *Language in Society, 13,* 145–204.

Bialystok, E. 1991. Achieving proficiency in a second language: A processing description. In R. Phillipson, E. Kellerman, L. Selinker, M. Sharwood Smith, & M. Swain (eds.), *Foreign/second language pedagogy research* (pp.63–78). Clevedon: Multilingual Matters.

Brown, G., & G. Yule. 1983a. *Discourse analysis.* Cambridge: Cambridge University Press.

Brown, G., & G. Yule. 1983b. *Teaching the spoken language.* Cambridge: Cambridge University Press.

Brown, R. 1973. *A first language: The early stages.* Cambridge, MA: Harvard University Press.

Cazden, C., E. Cancino, E. Rosansky, & J. Schumann. 1975. Second language acquisition sequences in children, adolescents and adults. Final report submitted to the National Institute of Education, Washington, DC.

Chalhoub-Deville, M. 1995a. Deriving oral assessment scales across different tests and rater groups. *Language Testing, 12*(1), 16–33.

Chalhoub-Deville, M. 1995b. A contextualized approach to describing oral language proficiency. *Language Learning, 45*(2), 251–281.

Clahsen, H. 1984. The acquisition of German word order: A test case for cognitive approaches to L2 development. In R. Andersen (ed.), *Second language: A crosslinguistic perspective* (pp. 219–242). Rowley, MA: Newbury House.

Dickerson, L. 1975. The learner's interlanguage as a system of variable rules. *TESOL Quarterly, 9,* 401–407.

Ellis, R. 1987. *Second language acquisition in context.* London: Prentice-Hall.

Ellis, R. 1994. *The study of second language acquisition.* Oxford: Oxford University Press.

Gregg, K. 1990. The variable competence model of second language acquisition and why it isn't. *Applied Linguistics,11*(4), 364–383.

Hale, G. 1988. Student major field and text content: Interactive effects on reading comprehension in the Test of English as a Foreign Language. *Language Testing, 5*(1), 49–61.

Henning, G. 1983. Oral proficiency testing: Comparative validities of interview, imitation, and completion methods. *Language Learning, 33,* 315–332.

Hoekje, B., & K. Linnell. 1994. "Authenticity" in language testing: Evaluating spoken language tests for international teaching assistants. *TESOL Quarterly, 28*(1), 103–126.

Hudson, T. 1993. Nothing does not equal zero: Problems with applying developmental sequence findings to assessment and pedagogy. *Studies in Second Language Acquisition, 15*(4), 461–493.

Liu, G. 1991. Interaction and second language acquisition: A case study of a Chinese child's acquisition of English as a second language. Doctoral dissertation, La Trobe University, Melbourne, Australia.

Pienemann, M. 1991. Report: COALA, a computational system for interlanguage analysis. *Second Language Research, 8,* 59–92.

Pienemann, M. 1992. Assessing second language acquisition through Rapid Profile. Paper presented at the American Association for Applied Linguistics Conference, Seattle.

Pienemann, M., M. Johnston, & G. Brindley. 1988. Constructing an acquisition-based procedure for second language assessment. *Studies in Second Language Acquisition, 10*(2), 217–243.

Schmidt, M. 1980. Coordinate structures and language universals in interlanguage. *Language Learning, 30*(2), 397–416.

Selinker, L. 1972. Interlanguage. *International Review of Applied Linguistics, 10,* 209–241.

Selinker, L., & D. Douglas. 1985. Wrestling with "context" in interlanguage theory. *Applied Linguistics, 6,* 190–204.

Shohamy, E. 1983. The stability of the oral proficiency trait on the Oral Interview Speaking Test. *Language Learning, 33,* 527–540.

Shohamy, E. 1994. The validity of direct versus semi-direct oral tests. *Language Testing, 11*(2), 99–124.

Shohamy, E., T. Reves, & Y. Bejarano. 1986. Introducing a new comprehensive test of oral proficiency. *English Language Teaching Journal, 40,* 212–222.

Smith, J. 1989. Topic and variation in ITA oral proficiency: SPEAK and field-specific tests. *English for Specific Purposes, 8,* 155–167.

Smith, J. 1992. Topic and variation in the oral proficiency of international teaching assistants. Doctoral dissertation, Department of Linguistics, University of Minnesota.

Tarone, E. 1979. Interlanguage as chameleon. *Language Learning, 29,* 181–191.

Tarone, E. 1983. On the variability of interlanguage systems. *Applied Linguistics, 4*(2), 142–163.

Tarone, E. 1985. Variability in interlanguage use: A study of style-shifting in morphology and syntax. *Language Learning, 35*(3), 373–404.

Tarone, E. 1988. *Variation in interlanguage.* London: Edward Arnold.

Tarone, E. 1994. Interlanguage. In *The Encyclopedia of Language and Linguistics* (Vol. 4, pp. 1715–1719). Oxford: Pergamon Press.

Tarone, E. 1997. Analyzing IL in natural settings: A sociolinguistic perspective on second language acquisition. *Communication and Cognition, 30,* 137–149.

Tarone, E., & G. Liu. 1995. Situational context, variation and second language acquisition theory. In G. Cook & B. Seidlhofer (eds.), *Principles and prac-*

tice in the study of language and learning: A Festschrift for H. G. Widdowson (pp. 107–124). Oxford: Oxford University Press.

Widdowson, H. G. 1983. *Learning purpose and language use.* Oxford: Oxford University Press.

Yule, G. 1997. *Referential communication tasks.* Mahwah, NJ: Lawrence Erlbaum.

4 Strategies and processes in test taking and SLA

Andrew D. Cohen

A process approach to test taking

One of first requests that more attention be paid to the processes of respondents in giving answers on language tests was issued by Bormuth
(1970):

There are no studies, known to the author, which have attempted to analyze
the strategies students use to derive correct answers to a class of items. The
custom has been to accept the test author's claims about what underlying
processes were tested by an item. And, since there were no operational
methods for defining classes of items, it was not scientifically very useful
to present empirical challenges to the test author's claims. (p. 72)

Bormuth's book outlines the objectives and major components of a theory
for writing items for achievement tests, drawing on structural linguistics,
semantics, and logic. Subsequently, studies began to appear that entailed
observation and description of how learners at different age levels actually accomplish first language (L1) testing tasks. For example, with respect
to a teacher's oral questioning of young children, it has been suggested that
"the interrogator and respondent work together to jointly compose the
'social fact' we call an answer-to-a-question" (Mehan 1974: 44). On the
basis of his research efforts, Mehan indicated that it may be misguided to
conclude "that a wrong answer is due to a lack of understanding, for the
answer may come from an *alternative,* equally valid interpretation."

Since the late 1970s, interest has slowly begun to grow in approaching second language (L2) testing from the point of view of the strategies
used by respondents going through the process of taking the test (e.g.,
Cohen & Aphek 1979; Homburg & Spaan 1981; Cohen 1984; MacLean
& d'Anglejan 1986; Gordon 1987; Anderson 1989; Nevo 1989). By the
1990s, L2 testing textbooks acknowledged this concern as a possible
source of insights concerning test reliability and validity (Bachman 1990;
Cohen 1994a).

I wish to acknowledge Lyle F. Bachman, Elaine Tarone, and an anonymous reviewer to
Cambridge University Press for their helpful comments in the revision of this chapter.
Some sections of this chapter are based on Cohen (1994a).

Tests that are relied upon to indicate the comprehension level of readers may produce misleading results because of numerous test-wise techniques that readers have developed for obtaining correct answers on such tests without fully or even partially understanding the text. As Fransson (1984) put it, respondents may not proceed via the text but rather around it. In effect, then, there are presumptions held by test constructors and administrators as to what is being tested, and there are the actual processes that test takers go through to produce answers to questions and tasks. The two may not necessarily be one and the same. Students may get an item wrong for the right reasons or right for the wrong reasons. Discovering that a respondent used poor logic in attempting to answer a reading comprehension item may be of little interest to the test constructors if the problem resides solely with the respondent. However, if the poor logic was precipitated by an overly ambiguous text passage or by an ambiguous question, then the test constructor may wish to edit the text or revise the question.

Even if the problem resides exclusively with the test taker, a concerned test developer and test administrator may wish to have more information about the items that provide such illogical responses or about the test-taking strategies that result in incorrect answers. Respondents may be consistently using certain strategies that are detrimental to their performance on certain types of items or on an entire test. For example, respondents may plod laboriously through a text only to find that once they reach the multiple choice questions, they have forgotten most of what they read or have failed to focus adequately on those elements being tested. In such a case, the strategy of studying the questions carefully before reading the text might have been more beneficial.

The intent of this chapter is to describe test-taking strategy data emerging from studies of respondents taking different kinds of tests, and to discuss the role these data can and do play in second language acquisition (SLA) research. Traditionally, the difference has been relatively clear-cut between language tasks intended for SLA research purposes and language tests constructed for assessing language achievement. An SLA measure (e.g., a communication task such as relaying directions from a map) is not intended for gate-keeping purposes. In fact, such tasks may purposely encourage risk taking by putting the respondents in a situation where they do not have the vocabulary or other language forms needed to complete the task, so that researchers can determine the strategies that they use. The respondents are usually in a low anxiety situation because their performance would not normally have implications for their lives.

In a traditional achievement testing situation, the testers usually check for control of language that the respondents have been taught. The respondents know that there is a premium put on better performance. Whereas in SLA research tasks the respondents can get points for communication in spite of inaccuracies, and their performance does not usually affect their grade in a language course, in instructional achievement testing the respondents must perform accurately, often under time constraints, and are held accountable for their responses.

In recent years, the distinction between assessment for the purposes of SLA research versus assessment for instructional purposes has lessened somewhat. More and more tasks and tests are being used interchangeably. As language tests have become a greater part of SLA research, there has been a growing concern for the reliability and validity of such measures. While there is nothing new in pointing out that certain instruments used in SLA research are lacking in validity, it is a relatively new undertaking to use data on test-taking strategies in order to validate such tests. This chapter mentions efforts in this direction, drawing on insights from both L1 and L2 testing.

Let us start by looking at the purpose for considering the processes involved in test taking. The main purpose is to determine the effects of test input upon the test taker – specifically, the processes that the test taker makes use of in order to produce acceptable answers to questions and tasks. There is a concomitant concern to determine the respondent's perceptions about tests before, during, and after test taking.

What is meant by test-taking strategies?

Language use strategies are mental operations or processes that learners consciously select when accomplishing language tasks. These strategies also constitute *test-taking strategies* when they are applied to tasks in language tests. For the purposes of this discussion, test-taking strategies will be viewed as those test-taking processes that the respondents have selected and of which they are conscious, at least to some degree. In other words, the notion of strategy implies an element of selection. Otherwise, the processes would not be considered strategies.

Strategies vary according to context. One strategy is to *opt out* of the language task at hand (e.g., through a surface matching of identical information in the passage and in one of the response choices). Another is to use shortcuts to arrive at answers (e.g., not reading the text as instructed but simply looking immediately for the answers to the given reading comprehension questions). In such cases, the respondents may be using test-wiseness to circumvent the need to tap their actual language knowledge or lack of it, consistent with Fransson's (1984) assertion that respondents may not proceed via the text but rather around it. In some cases, quite the contrary holds true. One Hebrew second language respondent in a study of test-taking strategies in Israel determined that he had to produce a written translation of a text before he could respond to questions dealing with that text (Cohen & Aphek 1979).

At times, the use of a limited number of strategies in a response to an item may indicate genuine control over the item, assuming that these strategies are well-chosen and are used effectively. At other times, true control requires the use of a host of strategies. It is best not to assume that any test-taking strategy is a good or a poor choice for a given task. That evaluation depends on how individual test takers – with their particular cognitive style profile and degree of cognitive flexibility, their language knowledge, and their repertoire of test-taking strategies – employ the strategies at a given moment on a given task. Some respondents may get by with using a limited number of strategies, and using them well for the most part. Others may be aware of an extensive number of strategies but may use few, if any, of them, effectively. So, for example, while a particular skimming strategy (such as paying attention to subheadings) may provide adequate preparation for one test taker on a recall task, the same strategy may *not* work well on a *different* text that lacks reader-friendly subheadings. In addition, the strategy, while successful for one respondent, may not work well for another respondent.

The ability of learners to use language strategies has been referred to as their *strategic competence* – a component of communicative language use (Canale & Swain 1980). This model puts the emphasis on "compensatory" strategies – that is, strategies used to compensate for or remediate a lack in some language area. Bachman (1990) provided a broader theoretical model for viewing strategic competence. Bachman and Palmer (1996) refined the Bachman (1990) categories somewhat. Their current framework includes an *assessment component*, whereby the respondents (in the case of language testing) assess which communicative goals are achievable and what linguistic resources are needed; a *goal-setting component*, wherein the respondents identify the specific tasks to be performed; and a *planning component*, whereby the respondents retrieve the relevant items from their language knowledge and formulate a plan for their use in a response.

Despite the theoretical shift away from a primary focus on compensatory strategies, it may still be the case that a fair number of test-taking strategies are, in fact, compensatory. When put on the spot, respondents often omit material because they do not know it, or produce different material from what they would like with the hope that it will be acceptable in the given context. They may use lexical avoidance, simplification, or approximation when the exact word escapes them under the pressure of the test situation or because they simply do not know the word well or at all.

Thus, in keeping with the Bachman and Palmer model, when respondents are given a situation in which to perform an oral role play, they may assess the situation and identify the information that is needed in that context. They may also set their general goals. They may plan their specific response and go about retrieving from their language knowledge the grammatical, discourse, and sociocultural features needed for the role play. Then at some point they execute the role play. After they have finished, they may again perform an assessment to evaluate the extent to which the communicative goal was achieved.

As is the case with any theoretical model, test takers may make differential use of the components of this model when performing specific testing tasks. Hence, there are respondents who might not assess the situation before starting the role play. This approach may be successful, or it may lead to the violation of certain sociocultural conventions. For example, a respondent in a Japanese L2 role play may neglect to take into account the older age and higher status of the interlocutor, and may select language forms that are not adequately respectful. In addition, there are respondents who may set general goals for an utterance or string of utterances in the Japanese L2 role play without making a detailed plan of their utterances before producing them. Again, this may work well, or it may lead to ineffective utterances that lack grammatical fine tuning.

By the same token, role-play respondents may also plan specifics without having general goals in mind. In such cases, the respondents may produce one or more L2 utterances that have been carefully monitored for grammatical accuracy but that do not fit into the overall discourse and, hence, come across as incoherent. There may be still other respondents who begin talking without first determining either general goals or a detailed plan. Indeed, the same respondent may assume one or another of these response patterns at different moments during a given test-taking situation and/or in different test-taking situations.

Recent research involving the use of verbal report directly after the performance of oral role-play interaction is just beginning to yield results regarding the extent of assessment and planning that actually takes place before the execution of speech acts, such as apologies, complaints, and requests (Cohen & Olshtain 1993). Clearly, more such work is needed in order to understand how respondents arrive at utterances in complex speech situations.

The use of verbal report in identifying test-taking strategies

The field of research methods has supplied us with suggested approaches for looking at test taking. One means is through observation of what respondents do during tests. Another means is through designing items that are assumed to require the use of certain strategies (e.g., cloze items calling for *anaphoric reference*) and adding up the correct responses as an indicator of strategy use. A third approach is through the use of *verbal report,* while the items are being answered, immediately afterward, or some time later on.

Verbal report techniques have constituted a major tool in the gathering of data on test-taking strategies. Such techniques were initially developed in first language and then second language acquisition research in order to study the processes of reading and writing. Verbal reports have helped determine how respondents actually take tests of various kinds (Nickerson 1989; Norris 1989). Moreover, innovative research on test taking has helped to refine the research methodology for tapping such test-taking strategies. For example, studies have found that it is possible to collect introspective and retrospective data from students just after they have answered each item on a multiple choice reading test. Several such studies are described in this section. Earlier work reported on approaches that involved at most a request of respondents to reflect back on the strategies they used in arriving at answers to a subtest or group of items, producing data of more questionable reliability and validity (Cohen 1984).

Just as there is a keen interest in using verbal report methods to improve the reliability and validity of assessment instruments, there needs to be an ongoing concern for assuring the reliability and validity of the very verbal report methods that are being used to collect test-taking strategy data. They cannot be immune from such scrutiny.[1] A recent article by the author deals extensively with the issue of improving the reliability and validity of verbal reports (Cohen, in press), especially concerns about the appropriate use of such measures and the nature of reports that include the findings from the use of such measures. The issues discussed include the effects of the immediacy of the verbal report, the potential value of having the respondents themselves interpret the data, the benefits of prompting for specifics in verbal report, the advantages of providing guidance in how to produce verbal report, and the effects of verbal report on task performance.

The article concludes by focusing on what needs to be included in the write-ups so that others will understand fully what was done, enabling comparisons with other studies and replication of the study. The following areas are addressed: (1) the subjects' characteristics, (2) the characteristics of the materials, (3) the nature of the criterion task, (4) the extent of guidance in verbal reporting, (5) the methods of analysis used, (6) the

---

1 Discussions of reliability and validity of verbal reports can be found in Ericsson and Simon (1984) and, with respect to SLA research, in Grotjahn (1987) and Haastrup (1987). Extensive discussions of reliability and validity in qualitative research can be found in Kirk and Miller (1986), Miles and Huberman (1994), and Denzin and Lincoln (1994).

categories used to score verbal report protocols, (7) the results of inter-rater reliability checks, (8) the criteria for selecting verbal report excerpts for inclusion in research reports, and (9) any theories used in framing the verbal report study. Care in the write-up can help to dispel arguments that such methodological approaches are not adequately rigorous. Since the use of verbal report techniques is becoming more prevalent in investigating test-taking strategies, there is a need to provide greater systematicity both in the collection of such data and in the reporting of such studies in the research literature.

Because verbal report techniques can be said to have emanated in part from literacy studies within the field of SLA – that is, studies eliciting strategies from writers as to how they plan, generate, and revise their text – it can be said that SLA research methods have provided the testing field with a means for validating not only nontesting tasks but testing tasks as well. By the same token, experts in the field of testing in turn contribute to SLA research by reminding researchers of the need to validate their research instruments.

Strategies for taking tests of reading and writing

In considering strategies on tests of reading and writing skills, I focus first on two more indirect testing formats, multiple choice and cloze, and on strategies for three more direct formats, namely, summarization tasks, open-ended questions, and compositions. The chapter closes with several suggestions that may lead to more effective test taking. Unless it is specified that the activity constituted a research task, the tasks and tests for which the respondents reported strategy use contributed to their course grades in language classes.[2]

Indirect testing formats

Indirect formats for testing – in other words, those formats that do not reflect real-world tasks – may prompt the use of strategies solely for the purpose of coping with the test format. Let us look at two such formats, multiple choice and cloze, and at some of the research findings regarding strategies used in taking such tests.

MULTIPLE CHOICE TEST FORMATS

Investigating a standardized test of English L1 reading (the Cooperative Primary Test, Form 12 A) by sitting down with individual first grade

---

2 I make this point because it is possible that respondents to a research task would use different strategies from those used when the results "count" toward a grade.

Figure 4.1

learners and going over each item separately after the testing session, MacKay (1974) found that learners did not necessarily link the stem and the answer in the same way that the test constructor assumed was correct. MacKay determined that the test had a somewhat arbitrary frame of reference and offered no concrete information as to how children reasoned. For example, pictures were sometimes ambiguous. In an item requiring the student to link the expression "The bird built his own house" to a picture, a student chose a nest of twigs with eggs in the middle over a wooden birdhouse because he claimed that some big birds could not fit in the hole of the birdhouse. MacKay noted that the student chose the right picture for the wrong reason. The student missed the element that people, not birds, are responsible for building wooden birdhouses with perches.

A test constructor receiving such feedback might wish to alter the item a bit, requiring, for example, that the respondents give their rationale for choosing one alternative over another. Naturally, there would be constraints on such an approach – the natural constraints of group testing, the age and ability of the respondents to provide this extra information, and so on. It would also be interesting to know whether this is just one isolated anecdote or whether this faulty logic is shared by other respondents as well.

MacKay also gave an example of an item missed for the wrong reasons. The statement "The cat has been out in the rain again" had to be linked to one of three pictures, which looked roughly like those in Figure 4.1. The student perceived the dotted wallpaper as snow and decided that this picture was of the exterior of the house. Thus, he gave the dripping raincoat as the correct answer. Once the child had perceived the wallpaper as snow and thus had eliminated the third picture, his selection of the first picture, the dripping raincoat, rather than the second, was perfectly reasonable – even though cats do not wear raincoats. If this kind of logic was shared by numerous respondents, it might suggest the need to improve the pictures in order to eliminate any ambiguities in them.

Haney and Scott (1987) found patterns similar to those reported by MacKay with regard to the sometimes dubious fit between elementary school children getting the L1 language arts item right or wrong and their verbal report as to whether they had applied the skill meant to be tested. For example, they found unusual and perceptive interpretations of questions. The interpretations resulted in the wrong answer in the item "Which needs least water?" (followed by pictures of a cactus, a potted plant, and a cabbage). The respondent answered "cabbage" because it had been picked and therefore needed no water at all, whereas the expected correct answer was "cactus." The interpretation resulted in the right answer in an item asking why Eva likes to watch TV. The respondent reported personalizing the item and responding according to why he liked to watch TV, in this case producing the correct answer without relating to Eva at all.

With respect to older respondents, the patterns are relatively similar, as in a study of 40 college ESL respondents that used retrospective verbal report to gain insights about test-taking strategies (Larson 1981, in Cohen 1984). As a research task, the students were requested to describe how they arrived at answers to a 10-item multiple choice test based on a 400-word reading passage. This formed part of the midterm for the advanced ESL course. Seventeen students met with the author of the test in groups of two or three within 24 hours after the test, while 23 students met in groups of five or six 4 days after taking the test. The investigator found that the respondents used the following strategies: (1) they stopped reading alternatives when they got to the one that seemed correct to them, (2) they matched material from the passage with material in the item stem and in the alternatives (e.g., when the answer was in the same sentence with the material used to write the stem), and (3) they preferred a surface-structure reading of the test items to one that called for more in-depth reading and inferencing (Larson 1981, in Cohen 1984). This superficial matching would sometimes result in the right answer. One example was as follows:

5) The fact that there is only one university in Filanthropia might be used to show why . . .
   a) education is compulsory through age 13.
   b) many people work in the fishing industry.
   c) 20 percent of the population is illiterate.
   d) the people are relatively happy and peaceful.

Students were able to identify (c) as the correct answer by noticing that this information appeared earlier in the same sentence with the information that reappeared in the item stem:

The investigating travel agency researchers discovered that the illiteracy rate of the people is 20 percent, which is perhaps reflective of the fact that there is only one university in Filanthropia, and that education is compulsory, or required, only through age 10.

They assumed that this was the correct answer without understanding the item or the word *illiterate*. They were right.

In another example, students did not have to look in the text for surface matches. They were able to match directly between the stem and the correct alternative:

2) The increased foreign awareness of Filanthropia has . . .
   a) resulted in its relative poverty.
   b) led to a tourist bureau investigation.
   c) created the main population centers.
   d) caused its extreme isolation.

Students associated *foreign* in the stem with *tourist* in option (b), without understanding the test item.

It was also found that more reasoned analysis of the alternatives – for example, making calculated inferences about vocabulary items – would lead to incorrect answers, as in the following item:

4) The most highly developed industry in Filanthropia is . . .
   a) oil.
   b) fishing.
   c) timber.
   d) none of the above.

This item referred to the following portion of the text:

. . . most [dollars] are earned in the fishing industry. . . . In spite of the fact that there are resources other than fish, such as timber in the forest of the foothills, agriculture on the upland plateaus, and, of course, oil, these latter are highly underdeveloped.

One student read the stem phrase "most highly developed industry" and reasoned that this meant "technologically developed" and so referred to the "oil industry." He was relying on expectations based on general knowledge rather than on a careful reading of the text. His was a reasoned guess rather than a surface match, as in the previous example.

It needs to be stressed that the Larson study was a student course project and therefore limited in scope. If the test were to be used widely, then it would be advisable to conduct a series of such investigations to determine both the reliability and the validity of the verbal report techniques used to elicit the information, as well as the generalizability of the findings across a range of different students.

In an effort to investigate the extent to which multiple choice questions are answered on the basis of prior knowledge of the topic and general vocabulary knowledge, 32 intermediate and 25 advanced Israeli EFL students were given as a research task the title and the first paragraph of a passage appearing on the previous year's exemption examination. They were then asked to answer 12 questions dealing with the portion of text not provided. Two weeks later they were given the text in full along with the questions, and once again were asked to respond (Israel 1982, in Cohen 1984). The rate of success on the multiple choice items was surprisingly high the first time – 49 percent for the advanced group and 41 percent for the intermediates. These results were far better than the 25 percent success rate that would be expected on the basis of chance alone.[3] When the students were given the test with the complete passage and questions two weeks later, the advanced group scored 77 percent and the intermediates 62 percent. The score necessary for exemption from further EFL study was 60 percent. The fact that the average performance on the test was low even when the passage was provided makes the results without the passage that much more striking.

In a research study with 30 tenth grade EFL students – 15 high proficiency readers and 15 low proficiency readers – respondents were asked to verbalize thoughts while finding answers to open-ended and multiple choice questions (Gordon 1987). The researcher found that answers to test questions did not necessarily reflect comprehension of the text. Both types of reading comprehension questions were regarded by the respondents as "mini" reading comprehension tests. With respect to test-taking strategies, the low proficiency students tended to process information at the local (sentence/word) level, not relating isolated bits of information to the whole text. They used individual word-centered strategies like matching words in alternatives to text, copying words from the text, translating word for word, or formulating global impressions of text content on the basis of key words or isolated lexical items in text or test questions. The high proficiency students, on the other hand, were seen to comprehend the text at a global level – predicting information accurately in context and using lexical and structural knowledge to cope with linguistic difficulties.

In an effort to provide immediate verbal report data, Nevo (1989) designed a testing format that would allow for immediate feedback after each item. She developed a response strategy checklist, based on the test-taking strategies that have been described in the literature and on her intuitions about strategies respondents were likely to select. A pilot study had shown that it was difficult to obtain useful feedback on an item-by-item basis without a checklist to jog the respondents' memory as to possible strategies.

Nevo's checklist included fifteen strategies, each appearing with a brief description and a label meant to promote rapid processing of the check-

---

3 These results are also consistent with those for native English readers, where the results were far better than chance (Tuinman 1973–4; Fowler & Kroll 1978).

list. As a research task, she administered a multiple choice reading comprehension test in Hebrew L1 and French as a foreign language to 42 tenth graders, and requested that they indicate for each of the ten questions on each test the strategy that was most instrumental and second most instrumental in arriving at their answer. The responses were kept anonymous so as to encourage the students to report exactly what they did, rather than what they thought they were supposed to do.

It was found that students were able to record the two strategies that were most instrumental in obtaining each answer. The study indicated that respondents transferred test-taking strategies from their first language to the foreign language. The researcher also identified whether the selected strategies aided in choosing the correct answer. The selection of strategies that did not promote choice of the correct answer was more prevalent in the foreign language than in the first language test. The main finding in this study was that it was possible to obtain feedback from respondents on their strategy use after each item on a test if a checklist was provided for quick labeling of the processing strategies utilized. Furthermore, the respondents reported benefiting greatly from the opportunity to become aware of how they took reading tests, having been largely unaware of their strategies prior to this study.

Another study of test-taking strategies among nonnatives (Anderson et al. 1991) revealed that respondents used certain strategies differently, depending on the type of question that was being asked. For example, the strategies of "trying to match the stem with the text" and "guessing" were reported more frequently for inference questions than for direct statement and main idea question types. The strategy of "paraphrasing" was reported to occur more in responding to direct statement items than with inference and main idea question types.

Anderson et al.'s study originated as a doctoral dissertation in which 28 native speakers of Spanish studying at an intensive ESL language school in Austin, Texas, took as research tasks three measures of reading comprehension: a reading comprehension subtest from a test of language skills, a measure of ability to read college-level textbook prose (Textbook Reading Profile, Segal 1986), and a second form of the standardized reading comprehension test (Anderson 1989). After the first two tasks, the participants provided retrospective think-aloud protocols describing the strategies they used while reading the textbook material and answering the comprehension questions. The respondents also provided think-aloud protocols along with the final test. The data were categorized into a list of 47 processing strategies.

In the follow-up phase of the research, data from the participants' retrospective think-aloud protocols of their reading and test-taking strategies were combined with data from a content analysis and an item analysis to obtain a truly convergent measure of test validation (Anderson et al. 1991). The content analysis of the reading comprehension passages and questions was comprised of the test designer's analysis and one based on an outside taxonomy, and the item performance data included item difficulty and discrimination. This study marked perhaps the first time that both think-aloud protocols and more commonly used types of information on test content and test performance were combined in the same study in order to examine the validation of the test in a convergent manner.

Another recent study corroborated earlier test-taking strategy research in finding that examinees focused on the search for answers to test questions. The English L1 respondents in the study paid little attention to strategies that provided an overall understanding of the native language passage (Farr, Pritchard, & Smitten 1990: 223). The investigators concluded that a reading comprehension test is a special kind of reading task, in which skilled examinees contemplate answer choices, use background knowledge, weigh choices, skim and reread portions of the reading selection, and refrain from making choices until they feel confident about an answer. They suggested that the types of questions following the passage will determine whether the reading focuses only on the surface meaning of the text.

Emerging from these various studies on multiple choice tests of reading comprehension is a series of strategies that respondents may utilize at one point or another in order to arrive at answers to the test questions. Whether these strategies are of benefit depends to a large extent upon when they are used and how effectively they are used. Table 4.1 presents a composite list of some of the more salient test-taking strategies appearing in one or more of the studies mentioned here. There is probably not a single strategy on this list that has not been written up in the testing literature somewhere; the innovation is to pinpoint who uses such strategies, when they use them, why they use them, and (ideally) their relative success at using them. This last issue is perhaps the most difficult to ascertain.

In recent years some attention has been focused on explicit training for ESL respondents in test-wiseness. For example, Allan (1992) developed a test of test-wiseness that included stem option cues, in which it was possible to match information from the stem with information in the correct option; grammatical cues, where only one alternative matched the stem grammatically; similar option cues, where several distractors could be eliminated because they essentially said the same thing; and item giveaway, where another item already gave away the information. In preliminary validation work, Allan tested three groups of students ($N = 51$), having one group write a brief explanation of how they selected their answers. Even though the items were meant to be content-free, it turned out that prior knowledge and guessing were still possible. The reliabilities for

TABLE 4.1. STRATEGIES FOR TAKING A MULTIPLE CHOICE
READING COMPREHENSION TEST

1. Read the text passage first and make a mental note of where different kinds of information are located.
2. Read the questions a second time for clarification.
3. Return to the text passage to look for the answer.
4. Find the portion of the text that the question refers to and then look for clues to the answer.
5. Look for answers to questions in chronological order in the text.
6. Read the questions first so that the reading of the text is directed at finding answers to those questions.
7. Try to produce your own answer to the question before you look at the options that are provided in the test.
8. Use the process of elimination – i.e., select a choice not because you are sure that it is the correct answer, but because the other choices do not seem reasonable, because they seem similar or overlapping, or because their meaning is not clear to you.
9. Choose an option that seems to deviate from the others, is special, is different, or conspicuous.
10. Select a choice that is longer/shorter than the others.
11. Take advantage of clues appearing in other items in order to answer the item under consideration.
12. Take into consideration the position of the option among the choices (first, second, etc.).
13. Select the option because it appears to have a word or phrase from the passage in it – possibly a key word.
14. Select the option because it has a word or phrase that also appears in the question.
15. Postpone dealing with an item or selecting a given option until later.
16. Make an educated guess – e.g., use background knowledge or extratextual knowledge in making the guess.
17. Budget your time wisely on this test.
18. Change your responses as appropriate – e.g., you may discover new clues in another item.

Note: The order in which the strategies are listed does not constitute a hierarchy of importance, nor does it reflect the frequency with which the given strategies have been found to occur.

the stem option and similar option items were low, suggesting that these cues were only sometimes recognized by respondents or that only some of the items in the subscales were measuring those test-wise phenomena.

CLOZE TEST FORMATS

Research regarding strategies for taking cloze tests is of interest in that it has helped to determine whether such tests actually measure global reading skills, as they are commonly purported to do. As more studies have been undertaken on the cloze test, it has become clearer that the instrument elicits more local, word-level reading than it does macro- or discourse-level reading (Klein-Braley 1981; Alderson 1983; Lado 1986), contrary to the claims of its early supporters, who have maintained that cloze assesses global reading (see, e.g., Chihara et al. 1977; Chávez-Oller et al. 1985). In the following excerpt from a cloze passage, items 1 and 3 can be answered on a microlevel, whereas item 2 would call for macro- or discourse-level comprehension:

People today are quite astonished by the rapid improvements in medicine. Doctors (1) _____ becoming more specialized, and (2) _____ drugs are appearing on (3) _____ market daily. (based on Cohen 1994a: 234)

That is, the local context provides the answer to (1), "are." The answer to (2), "new," depends on an understanding of the opening sentence, so this would be a discourse-level response. Once item (2) is filled in, item (3) is simply a local response based on the immediate context of that phrase. More proficient readers are more skilled at correctly completing cloze items such as (2), which assess discourse-level reading, whether reading in the native or in a foreign language (Bachman 1985).

Studies on strategies for taking cloze tests have shown that perhaps only a quarter of nonnative respondents read the entire EFL cloze passage before responding (Emanuel 1982 and Hashkes & Koffman 1982, in Cohen 1984). A case study shed some light on the issue of reading the text before completing an L1 cloze test (Kleiman et al. 1986). Verbal protocol data provided by a seventh grade Brazilian girl filling in two cloze passages – one as a warm-up and the other as an exercise in Portuguese L1 – indicated that the respondent was preoccupied with local clues from isolated elements of text. What emerged was that she did not use global clues until she had completed a substantial number of blanks on the cloze. In other words, it is easier to read the cloze passage once it has been partially completed and the respondent has some idea of what it is about, much as a child may have an easier time of connecting numbered dots once the picture that the dots are forming becomes clearer.

One of the early studies of strategy use in completing a cloze passage involved indirect assessment of strategies used. The researchers administered a rational deletion cloze with 23 blanks to 39 EFL subjects from three levels (Homburg & Spaan 1981). One of four strategies was hypothesized to be necessary in finding a correct word for each of the blanks: recognition of parallelism, sentence-bound reading, forward reading, or backward reading. Success at items calling for "forward reading" *(cataphora)* was significantly associated with success at understanding the main idea. In verbal report studies, it was found that nearly 20 percent of the respondents did not use the preceding or following sentence for clues to blanks but rather guessed on the basis of the immediate context (Emanuel 1982 and Hashkes & Koffman 1982, in Cohen 1984).

The picture regarding the taking of cloze tests in a native language does not appear to be much different. One study, for example, involved 18 fifth graders at three levels of reading (high, intermediate, low) who were given a rational deletion cloze test in Hebrew L1 and were asked to think aloud as they completed it (Kesar 1990). An analysis of the verbal report protocols yielded at least 26 different strategies, which were grouped into seven categories: word level/part of sentence; sentence level; and five categories at the level of discourse-intersentential, whole-text level, extratextual level, metacognitive level, and "other." The results demonstrated that although the better readers were more likely to use macro-level schemata and strategies in completing the cloze and also did better on the completion task as a whole, all respondents favored micro-level reading at the sentence level.

Thus, the research on strategies in taking cloze tests would suggest that such tests assess local-level reading more than they measure global reading ability. Furthermore, such tests are more likely to test for local-level reading when they are in a foreign language (see, e.g., MacLean & d'Anglejan 1986).

More direct formats

SUMMARIZATION TASKS

Whereas more direct formats for testing, such as text summarization, are less likely than indirect formats to elicit test-taking strategies that take the place of genuine language use strategies, responses to such measures are still influenced by test-wiseness. As long as the task is part of a test, students are likely to use strategies that they would not use under non-test conditions. In the case of a summary task, the respondent is invariably summarizing a text for a reader who already has a notion of what the summary should look like; therefore, the respondent is reacting to a set of perceived and real expectations on the part of the reader. In the real world, we usually summarize a text for our own future use or for the benefit of someone who has not read it, in which case the set of expectations of the summarizer may be quite different.

Case study research concerning the strategies used in producing summaries in Portuguese L1 on a test of EFL texts has suggested that respondents might use various shortcut measures (Cohen 1994b). One strategy was to summarize by lifting material directly from the passage rather than restating it at a higher level of abstraction or generality, in the hope that the raters' ambiguity over whether the respondent understood the material would work in the respondent's favor. Furthermore, when respondents were in doubt about whether to include or exclude material, they might be prone to include it (as in the case of one less proficient student), assuming that a longer summary would probably be preferred by the raters to one that is too terse. The case study found that the respondents spent more time on their strategies for reading the texts to be summarized than they did on the production of their summaries, so – not surprisingly – the summaries were not particularly coherent or polished.

OPEN-ENDED QUESTIONS AND COMPOSITIONS

Like summarization tasks, open-ended tasks allow respondents to copy material directly from a text in their response, so that raters cannot tell whether the respondent in fact understands the material. Such copying may produce linguistically awkward responses. For example, in a study of 19 college-level learners of Hebrew L2 that involved a retrospective verbal report one week after the learners took their final exam, it was found that students lifted material intact from an item stimulus or from a text passage for use in their written responses (Cohen & Aphek 1979). Results included verb forms incorrectly inflected for person, number, gender, or tense; verbs reflecting the correct root but an incorrect conjugation; and so forth. Various strategies were observed for producing a verb form when the rules for production had not been learned. If students did not know the correct verb form, they would use the infinitive, take a form from a tense that they knew, take one inflectional ending and generalize it across person and gender, take an inappropriate tense from the stimulus and simply add the prefix for person, and so on.

Another strategy that the learners in the Cohen and Aphek (1979) study used in their writing was to introduce prepackaged, unanalyzed material and combine it with analyzed forms. For example, given that Hebrew prepositions like *mi* ("from") can be prefixed to the object of the preposition through elision (*mi* + *tsad* "side" = *mitsad*), one student learned this form as one word and then affixed another preposition to it on an exam: *bemitsad* "on from a side" intending "on a side."

The interpretation of essay topics is a problem that is related to inadequate attention to instructions. Usually, an essay topic is presented in the form of a minitext that the respondent needs to understand and operationalize. Ruth and Murphy (1984) note cases where English L1 students misinterpreted words in the prompt, such as confusing the words *profit* and *prophet*, thus shifting the meaning of the topic entirely. Perhaps of greater consequence are the strategies the respondents have to evaluate the nature of the task. Ruth and Murphy give the example of a supposedly friendly letter topic wherein what the raters of the "letter" will actually value is a response at a higher level of formality than might be reflected in an authentic friendly letter. The guideline, then, for respondents in writing tasks is to be especially careful in interpreting the gen-uine intention of instructions for completing testing tasks.

Conclusion

This chapter has examined process approaches to language testing, which have usually entailed the use of verbal report techniques to bet-ter understand these processes and the test-taking strategies that respon-dents use. There are not yet abundant data linking the specific use of test-taking strategies with success or failure on language tests.[4] On the other hand, the use of qualitative methodologies such as verbal report provides a valuable source of information – perhaps the most focused possible – on the strategies respondents used in their responses and why they did so. Verbal report can help us see what items are actually test-ing, aiding us in making decisions about which items to keep and which to throw out. One could go so far as to say that it is now close to es-sential to have verbal report as part of pretesting/piloting. If a respon-dent has legitimate reasons for marking an item wrong, then the item needs to be rewritten.

The emphasis in this chapter has been on the relationship between the characteristics of the test task and the strategies used, and on the con-nection between testing methods and SLA research – especially on the types of investigations needed to provide information as to which testing methods would be potentially more or less reliable and valid for SLA re-search. For example, we already know that the multiple choice format poses problems. It has come under strong criticism in recent years, as pointed out in Hughes (1989: 60–62), who includes the following in his list of shortcomings:

1. Items meant to assess just grammar may also test for lexical knowl-edge as well.

---

4 Studies are beginning to appear that link the selection of a given strategy with rated success at performance in a foreign language. A study by Cohen, Weaver, and Li (1996), on intermediate college learners of French and Norwegian, for example, identified a link between the frequency of use of a given strategy and performance on the speaking task for which that strategy was chosen. It was found that an increase in certain preparatory strategies (e.g., translating specific words, writing out sentences, and practicing the pronunciation of words) and monitoring strategies (e.g., monitor-ing for grammar, paying attention to the pronunciation of words, and analyzing a story for its key elements) related to an increase in ratings by outside raters on one or more of the rating scales – self-confidence, grammar, vocabulary, and identifying and ordering elements in a story. A recent study by Purpura (1996), discussed by Bach-man and Cohen in this volume (Chapter 1), provides an example of a quantitative approach to investigating the relationships among cognitive and metacognitive strategies reported by test takers and their scores on an English L2 test.

2. Distractors may be eliminated as being absurd.
3. Correct responses may be common knowledge.

It would appear that the test-taking strategy research can be utilized to substantiate or refute claims about multiple choice items, at least with respect to a given test in a given testing situation with given respondents. In other words, criticisms of the multiple choice format are not new and did not originate with qualitative investigations. However, qualitative investigations can help us to move beyond superficial pronouncements to determine how decisions are actually made. So, for example, a study could be designed whereby students need to indicate through retrospective verbal reports the process whereby they arrived at answers to multiple choice grammar items. The intention would be to determine if it was actually grammatical knowledge that was being tapped in each item or whether the deciding element was, for example, control of one or another vocabulary word in the stem or in the distractors.

The results of test-taking strategy studies on cloze tests would also appear to provide crucial information regarding what those tests actually measure. The various types of cloze tests have been subjected to careful scrutiny in recent years, and, of the studies carried out, those that deal with response strategies are perhaps among some of the most insightful. Thus, while the reliability of a given cloze test may be high because the individual items are interrelated, the validity as a measure of global reading ability could be questioned if the respondents indicate that they answered most of the items by means of local micro-level strategies.

It would appear that the nature of test-taking strategies with respect to the more open-ended formats, such as summarization, open-ended responses to questions, and essays, has yet to be fully investigated. Since the assessment of summaries and essays depends on judgments made by raters, there is a concomitant need for research on strategies used in doing the ratings, such as the work conducted by Hamp-Lyons (1989), Vaughan (1991), Connor and Carrell (1993), and Cushing Weigle (1994).

Given the results from test-taking strategy research, however embryonic they may be at present, SLA researchers would probably want to consider validating the testing measures that they use through triangulation, which would include the collection of test-taking strategy data on subsamples of respondents, as in the Anderson et al. (1991) study. Even though the field of test-taking strategy research is a fledgling one, and even though these techniques are still in need of refinement, researchers can find useful descriptions in the literature of techniques for identifying the strategies used by respondents. Consideration of the findings from this growing research area will undoubtedly prove beneficial at all points in constructing, administering, and interpreting language tests.

References

Alderson, J. C. 1983. The cloze procedure and proficiency in English as a foreign language. In J. W. Oller, Jr. (ed.), *Issues in language testing research* (pp. 205–228). Rowley, MA: Newbury House.

Allan, A. 1992. Development and validation of a scale to measure test-wiseness in EFL/ESL reading test takers. *Language Testing, 9*(2), 101–122.

Anderson, N. J. 1989. Reading comprehension tests versus academic reading: What are second language readers doing? Doctoral dissertation, University of Texas, Austin.

Anderson, N. J., L. Bachman, K. Perkins, & A. Cohen. 1991. An exploratory study into the construct validity of a reading comprehension test: Triangulation of data sources. *Language Testing, 8*(1), 41–66.

Bachman, L. F. 1985. Performance on cloze tests with fixed-ratio and rational deletions. *TESOL Quarterly, 19*(3), 535–556.

Bachman, L. F. 1990. *Fundamental considerations in language testing.* Oxford: Oxford University Press.

Bachman, L. F., & A. S. Palmer. 1996. *Language testing in practice: Designing and developing useful language tests.* Oxford: Oxford University Press.

Bormuth, J. R. 1970. *On the theory of achievement test items.* Chicago: University of Chicago Press.

Canale, M., & M. Swain. 1980. Theoretical bases of communicative approaches to second language teaching and testing. *Applied Linguistics, 1*(1), 1–47.

Chávez-Oller, M. A., T. Chihara, K. A. Weaver, & J. W. Oller, Jr. 1985. When are cloze items sensitive to constraints across sentences? *Language Learning, 35*(2), 181–206.

Chihara, T., J. W. Oller, Jr., K. Weaver, & M. A. Chávez-Oller. 1977. Are cloze items sensitive to constraints across sentences? *Language Learning, 27*(1), 63–73.

Cohen, A. D. 1984. On taking language tests: What the students report. *Language Testing, 1*(1), 70–81.

Cohen, A. D. 1994a. *Assessing language ability in the classroom* (2nd ed.). Boston: Newbury House/Heinle & Heinle.

Cohen, A. D. 1994b. English for academic purposes in Brazil: The use of summary tasks. In C. Hill & K. Parry (eds.), *From testing to assessment: English as an international language* (pp. 174–204). London: Longman.

Cohen, A. D. In press. Exploring the strategies that respondents use in test taking. In G. Ekbatani & H. Pierson (eds.), *Learner-directed assessment in ESL.* Mahwah, NJ: Lawrence Erlbaum.

Cohen, A. D., & E. Aphek. 1979. Easifying second language learning. Research report under the auspices of Brandeis University and submitted to the Jacob Hiatt Institute, Jerusalem. ERIC Document ED 163753.

Cohen, A. D., & E. Olshtain. 1993. The production of speech acts by EFL learners. *TESOL Quarterly, 27*(1), 33–56.

Cohen, A. D., S. J. Weaver, & T-Y. Li. 1996. *The impact of strategies-based instruction on speaking a foreign language.* CARLA Working Paper Series No. 4. Minneapolis: Center for Advanced Research on Language Acquisition, University of Minnesota.

Connor, U. M., & P. L. Carrell. 1993. The interpretation of tasks by writers and readers in holistically rated direct assessment of writing. In J. G. Carson &

I. Leki (eds.),, *Reading in the composition classroom: Second language perspectives* (pp.141–160). Boston: Heinle & Heinle.

Cushing Weigle, S. 1994. Effects of training on raters of ESL compositions. *Language Testing, 11*(2), 197–223.

Denzin, N. K., & Y. S. Lincoln. 1994. *Handbook of qualitative research.* Newbury Park, CA: Sage.

Emanuel, E. 1982. The use of the cloze technique – regular cloze and discourse cloze – in the teaching of Hebrew as a mother tongue. Course paper (in Hebrew), School of Education, Hebrew University of Jerusalem, Jerusalem, Israel.

Ericsson, K. A., & H. A. Simon. 1993. *Protocol analysis: Verbal reports as data* (rev. ed.). Cambridge, MA: MIT Press.

Farr, R., R. Pritchard, & B. Smitten. 1990. A description of what happens when an examinee takes a multiple-choice reading comprehension test. *Journal of Educational Measurement, 27*(3), 209–226.

Fowler, B., & B. M. Kroll. 1978. Verbal skills as factors in the passageless validation of reading comprehension tests. *Perceptual and Motor Skills, 47,* 335–338.

Fransson, A. 1984. Cramming or understanding? Effects of intrinsic and extrinsic motivation on approach to learning and test performance. In J. C. Alderson & A. H. Urquhart (eds.), *Reading in a foreign language* (pp. 86–121). London: Longman.

Gordon, C. 1987. The effect of testing method on achievement in reading comprehension tests in English as a foreign language. Master's thesis, School of Education, Tel Aviv University, Tel Aviv, Israel.

Grotjahn, R. 1987. On the methodological basis of introspective methods. In C. Faerch & G. Kasper (eds.), *Introspection in second language research* (pp. 54–81). Clevedon: Multilingual Matters.

Haastrup, K. 1987. Using thinking aloud and retrospection to uncover learners' lexical inferencing procedures. In C. Faerch & G. Kasper (eds.), *Introspection in second language research* (pp. 197–212). Clevedon: Multilingual Matters.

Hamp-Lyons, L. 1989. Raters respond to rhetoric in writing. In H. W. Dechert & M. Raupach (eds.), *Interlingual processes* (pp. 229–244). Tübingen: Gunter Narr.

Haney, W., & L. Scott. 1987. Talking with children about tests: An exploratory study of test item ambiguity. In R. O. Freedle & R. P. Duran (eds.), *Cognitive and linguistic analyses of test performance* (pp. 298–368). Norwood, NJ: Ablex.

Hashkes, B., & N. Koffman. 1982. Strategies used in a cloze test. Course paper, School of Education, Hebrew University of Jerusalem, Jerusalem, Israel.

Homburg, T. J., & M. C. Spaan. 1981. ESL Reading proficiency assessment: Testing strategies. In M. Hines & W. Rutherford (eds.), *On TESOL '81* (pp. 25–33). Washington, DC: TESOL.

Hughes, A. 1989. *Testing for language teachers.* Cambridge: Cambridge University Press.

Israel, A. 1982. The effect of guessing in multiple-choice language tests. Course paper, School of Education, Hebrew University of Jerusalem, Jerusalem, Israel.

Kesar, O. 1990. Identification and analysis of reading moves in completing a rational deletion cloze. Master's thesis (in Hebrew), School of Education, Hebrew University of Jerusalem, Jerusalem, Israel.

Kirk, J., & M. L. Miller. 1986. *Reliability and validity in qualitative research.* Newbury Park, CA: Sage.

Kleiman, A. B., M. C. Cavalcanti, S. B. Terzi, & I. Ratto. 1986. Percepçao do léxico e sua funçao discursiva: Algums fatores condicionantes. Unpublished manuscript, Department of Applied Linguistics, Universidade Estadual de Campinas, Campinas, Brazil.

Klein-Braley, C. 1981. Empirical investigation of cloze tests: An examination of the validity of cloze tests as tests of general language proficiency in English for German university students. Doctoral dissertation, University of Duisburg, Duisburg, West Germany.

Lado, R. 1986. Analysis of native speaker performance on a cloze test. *Language Testing, 3*(2), 130–146.

Larson, K. 1981. A study of student test-taking strategies and difficulties. Unpublished manuscript, ESL Section, University of California, Los Angeles.

MacKay, R. 1974. Standardized tests: Objectives/objectified measures of "competence." In A. V. Cicourel et al. (eds.), *Language use and school performance* (pp. 218–247). New York: Academic Press.

MacLean, M., & A. d'Anglejan. 1986. Rational cloze and retrospection: Insights into first and second language reading comprehension. *Canadian Modern Language Review, 42*(4), 814–826.

Mehan, H. 1974. Ethnomethodology and education. In D. O'Shea (ed.), *The sociology of the school and schooling* (pp. 141–198). Washington, DC: National Institute of Education.

Miles, M. B., & M. Huberman. 1994. *Qualitative data analysis* (2nd ed.). Newbury Park, CA: Sage.

Nevo, N. 1989. Test-taking strategies on a multiple-choice test of reading comprehension. *Language Testing, 6*(2), 199–215.

Nickerson, R. S. 1989. New directions in educational assessment. *Educational Researcher, 18*(9), 3–7.

Norris, S. P. 1989. Can we test validly for critical thinking? *Educational Researcher, 18*(9), 21–26.

Purpura, J. 1996. Modeling the relationships between test takers' reported cognitive and metacognitive strategy use and performance on language tests. Doctoral dissertation, University of California, Los Angeles.

Ruth, L., & S. Murphy. 1984. Designing topics for writing assessment: Problems of meaning. *College Composition and Communication, 35*(4), 410–422.

Segal, K. W. 1986. Does a standardized reading comprehension test predict textbook prose reading proficiency of a linguistically heterogeneous college population? Doctoral dissertation, University of Texas, Austin.

Tuinman, J. J. 1973–4. Determining the passage dependency of comprehension questions in five major tests. *Reading Research Quarterly, 9*, 206–23.

Vaughan, C. 1991. Holistic assessment: What goes on in the raters' minds? In L. Hamp-Lyons (ed.), *Assessing second language writing in academic contexts* (pp. 111–125). Norwood, NJ: Ablex.

5 Describing language development? Rating scales and SLA

Geoff Brindley

Over the last decade or so, rating scales describing different levels of language proficiency or achievement have been widely adopted in language learning programs throughout the world as a means of assessing individual learner attainment and reporting program outcomes. Such scales have tended to be of two main types. The first type of scale is behaviourally based and is exemplified by instruments such as the American Council on the Teaching of Foreign Languages Proficiency Guidelines (ACTFL 1986), which seek to define language ability globally in terms of features of "real-life" performance and thus describe specific contexts of language use. Although behavioural scales have generally met with widespread acceptance within the language teaching fraternity, their theoretical foundations have been questioned (e.g., Bachman & Savignon 1986; Lantolf & Frawley 1988). Their validity as indicators of language ability has also been challenged on the basis that the scales fail to distinguish between the ability being assessed and the elicitation procedures used, thus limiting the generalizability of score interpretation (Bachman 1990). Their usefulness for diagnostic and achievement testing has also been questioned, in that they fail to provide specific information on different components of language ability (Bachman & Palmer 1996). As a result, proposals have been put forward for a second type of rating scale, one that is defined independently of content and context, that is derived from a theoretical model of the ability construct being assessed, and that provides analytic ratings of the various components of language ability that may be of interest to stake holders (Bachman 1988, 1990; Bachman & Palmer, 1996).

Of the two types of scale, it is probably the former which has had the most influence on testing practice until now. Significant decisions affecting individuals' future are routinely made on the basis of proficiency ratings derived from behaviourally based scales. In the United States, instruments such as the ACTFL guidelines and the Interagency Language Roundtable scale (ILR 1985) have been used for some time in order to certify the proficiency of foreign language majors and government employees. In Europe, a wide variety of behavioural scales have been developed in conjunction with formal language examinations and are now being built into

112

national language standards (e.g., Languages Lead Body 1993). At the same time, the need for a common framework for describing language progress and attainment across different language learning populations has led to proposals for a "scale of scales" which would permit equivalences to be drawn between different qualifications (Scharer & North 1992). Rating scales have also played an important role in immigrant education in Australia, where language proficiency scales have been used to determine access of adult immigrants to government-funded labour market training programs (Mawer 1992) and to describe and assess the progress of ESL school learners (National Languages and Literacy Institute of Australia 1994).

Given the high stakes associated with the use of behavioural rating scales, it is important to examine the extent to which the descriptions of language performance which they embody can be justified in terms of what is known about second language acquisition (SLA). The purpose of this chapter is therefore to examine the construct validity of such scales from an SLA perspective. Rather than focussing on the measurement properties of rating scales, however, as others have done (e.g., North 1993), I propose to look more specifically at the nature and status of the verbal descriptors which define different levels of ability. The first section of the chapter briefly describes the nature and purpose of behavioural rating scales and considers the extent to which these can be said to characterize SLA. The second section examines the evidence for the text, task, and skill hierarchies which are typically described in such scales, drawing on research findings from both language testing (LT) and SLA. In the third and final section I suggest ways in which information and insights from various branches of both SLA and LT research might be drawn on to assist in the construction and validation of rating scales for a variety of purposes and audiences.

Rating scales and SLA

The nature and purpose of behavioural rating scales

Behavioural rating scales usually consist of a series of descriptions of stages or ranges of language behaviour in one or more language skill areas along some kind of continuum of increasing ability, which usually ranges from "zero" to "nativelike". The level definitions typically describe the kinds of tasks and texts that learners can handle at different ability levels and the degree of skill with which they can achieve various communicative goals. In this context, it is important to note that although they describe performance, most behavioural rating scales claim to be measures of underlying competence. Performance, in other words, is interpreted as an indirect indicator of ability (Ingram 1984; Lowe 1988; Griffin & McKay 1992).

Ratings are assigned by eliciting a sample of language performance under test conditions. With speaking and writing, this is usually done by having trained raters compare learner's observed performance with the descriptions on the scale. Listening and reading ratings may be administered by asking learners to carry out tasks as part of an oral interview or by administering tests based on the descriptions and converting test scores to a rating.

The level descriptors used in behavioural scales vary in their content and organization, according to their purpose and audience. Some are very brief and seek only to give fairly general indications of overall communicative ability, as in the following definition of Level 7 from the English Speaking Union yardstick scale of overall English language proficiency (Carroll & West 1989: 21):

Uses language effectively and in most situations, except the very complex and difficult. A few lapses in accuracy, fluency, appropriacy and organisation but communication is effective and consistent, with only a few uncertainties in conveying or comprehending the content of the message.

Other scales include quite detailed descriptions of particular features of language use typical of each level, as in this description of Speaking Level 1+ from the Australian Second Language Proficiency Rating Scale (ASLPR) (Ingram & Wylie 1984):

Able to satisfy all survival needs and limited social needs. Developing flexibility in a range of circumstances beyond immediate survival needs. Shows some spontaneity in language production but fluency is very uneven. Can initiate and sustain a general conversation but has little understanding of the social conventions of conversation; grammatical errors still frequently cause misunderstandings. Limited vocabulary range necessitates much hesitation and circumlocution. The commoner tense forms occur but errors are frequent in formation and selection. Can use most question forms. While basic word order is established, errors still occur in more complex patterns. Cannot sustain coherent structures in longer utterances or unfamiliar situations. Ability to describe and give precise information is limited by still tentative emergence of modification devices. Aware of basic cohesive features (e.g., pronouns, verb inflections), but many are unreliable, especially if less immediate in reference. Simple discourse markers are used relating to closely contiguous parts of the text, but extended discourse is largely a series of discrete utterances. Articulation is reasonably comprehensible to native speakers, can combine with most phonemes with reasonable comprehensibility, but still has difficulty in producing certain sounds, in certain positions, or in certain combinations, and speech may be laboured. Stress and intonation patterns are not native-like and may interfere with communication. Still has to repeat utterances frequently to be understood by the general public. Has very limited register flexibility, though, where a specialist register has been experienced, may have acquired some features of it.

Different scales focus on different aspects of language use and hence use different criteria for describing levels. The ACTFL guidelines, for example, use the categories of *global tasks/functions, context, content, accuracy,* and *text type* as a framework for describing levels (North 1993: 25), while the Royal Society of Arts (RSA) Certificate in Communicative Skills in English (CCSE) defines levels in terms of *complexity, range, speed, flexibility* and *independence* (University of Cambridge Local Examinations Syndicate 1990: 12). Scales describing particular skills will often employ specific criteria related to the skill in question, such as *fluency, intelligibility, grammar,* or *vocabulary* in the case of oral language proficiency.

Rating scales are used for a variety of purposes. In this regard, Alderson (1991b: 72–74) makes a useful distinction between three functions that scales can serve: the *user-oriented* function, where the scales provide information on the meaning of the levels to test users; the *assessor-oriented* function, where they are used as rating criteria to assess the quality of a performance; and the *constructor-oriented* function, where they provide guidance to test constructors. Pollitt and Murray (1996) add a fourth *diagnosis-oriented* purpose, where the scales are used to provide diagnostic information to teachers and learners.

Alderson (1991b: 74) points out that the writers of rating scales need to be very clear about the purpose which scales are meant to serve. He gives examples of a range of problems that can arise when a scale designed for one purpose is used for another. In particular, he demonstrates how the validity of scale descriptors as indicators of ability may be brought into question in circumstances where the performances described are not actually those that are elicited in the test.

Do rating scales describe SLA? The claims

It is difficult to know to what extent behavioural rating scales are intended to operationalize SLA processes, since scale developers do not always reveal the theoretical basis of their level descriptors or make explicit claims concerning the universality of the developmental phenomena described in the scales. Dandonoli and Henning (1990: 12), for example, in discussing the validity of the ACTFL guidelines, state that "ACTFL has never claimed that the Guidelines reflect a particular second-language acquisition model". Whether this means that the scales cannot be interpreted in any sense as descriptions of SLA is not clear, however.

Dandonoli (1987: 93) adopts an even more equivocal position:

While this content domain (language proficiency) may also ultimately reflect concepts in the literature on the nature and sequence of language acquisition (Byrnes, this volume), or may be underpinned by aspects of a theory of language behaviour including various constructs, it is useful for pragmatic purposes as it stands, whether or not it does. It is only later, as the tests are studied for their construct validity and as we attempt to build a theory of language proficiency, that we become concerned with the guidelines in this regard.

On the other hand, some authors appear to make strong claims concerning the ACFTL guidelines. Liskin-Gasparro (1984: 37), for example, quotes a comment from Omaggio to the effect that "knowing what competencies lie at the next level will help us sequence materials to conform to natural developmental patterns in adult second language learners and prepare them for making progress". Through semantic slippage the implication here seems to be that the ACTFL levels describe "natural developmental patterns". In a similar vein, Byrnes (1987: 116) claims that the ACTFL guidelines are "built on a hierarchy of task universals". At the same time, Galloway (1987: 37) refers to the guidelines as describing "learner performance expectancies at various positioned stages of evolution". This would seem to suggest that the ACTFL level descriptions are referenced to learner norms and thus can be interpreted as a picture of universal developmental patterns.

Elsewhere in the literature on rating scales one frequently finds the notion of "language proficiency" confounded with "language development" and/or "language acquisition". As Pienemann and Mackey (1992: 136) comment, this is consistent with a commonsense understanding of "proficiency development". It would seem reasonable enough to assume that learning a language consists of an evolution through progressive levels of mastery, each approximating more closely to the target, and that a cross-sectional description of typical behaviours at each level would by definition constitute a picture of the developmental process over time. Thus, Griffin and Nix (1991: 182) refer to scales of reading proficiency as "language acquisition scales", while Graham (1993: 6) asserts that the development of the Ontario provincial language standards is based on language outcomes which are "described in terms of knowledge, skills, and values that are consistent with the developmental stages of language acquisition". A similar implication is found in the account of the development of the ASLPR by Ingram (1984: 17), who states that the scale indicates "where the learner's proficiency falls along the developmental path from zero to native-like". The fact that scales such as the ASLPR give examples of specific features of interlanguage which are characteristic of each level might further lead the reader to believe that the scales aimed to describe acquisitional processes.

To what extent, then, can behavioural rating scales be interpreted as descriptions of SLA? In order to answer this question, we need to know whether the scales are intended to describe what people *ought* to be able to do or what they actually *do* do – that is, whether they reflect desired curriculum goals for particular groups in particular instructional contexts or whether they aim to present a picture of second language development based on the actual performance of language learners as they behave in the real world. Unfortunately, these two purposes are sometimes hard to disentangle, since some rating scales are used to guide curriculum development as well as to assess and report proficiency. Nevertheless, the accounts of scale development summarized here suggest that some widely used scales are presented as generalizable descriptions of what learners are thought to do as their language develops in the direction of the target. For example, Galloway (1987) refers to the ACTFL guidelines as describing "expectancies of performance". But expectancies in relation to what? Since learners cannot be expected to behave like native speakers, the descriptions of the expected performance standards can be referenced only to learner norms. In this sense it is difficult to avoid the conclusion that the scales are descriptions of SLA.

The empirical basis of rating scales: Where do they come from?

As various writers have noted (e.g., de Jong 1988; Pienemann, Johnston, & Brindley 1988; North 1993), it is often difficult to find explicit information on how the descriptors used in some high profile rating scales were arrived at. Liskin-Gasparro (1984: 37), for example, states that the ACTFL guidelines

were developed empirically, that is by observing how second language learners progress in the functions they can express or comprehend, the topic areas they can deal with, and the accuracy with which they receive or convey a message. The guidelines then, are descriptive rather than prescriptive, based on experience rather than theory.

No specific research evidence is provided, however, to support these claims.

A similar claim is found in the account of the development of the ASLPR by Ingram (1984: 7):

Drawing on the FSI scale, psycholinguistic studies of second language development, and the intuitions of many years of experience teaching English, French and Italian as second or foreign languages, Elaine Wylie and the present writer sought to describe language behaviour at nine proficiency levels along the developmental path from zero to native-like.

As with the ACTFL development process, very little precise information is provided on the origins of the scale. We are not told which specific psycholinguistic studies have been drawn on, or what these studies tell us about the regularities of SLA. Nor are we told how the findings from such studies are reflected in the scale.

Some scale developers, however, do provide quite detailed information on the development process. Examples can be found in recent accounts of a number of rating scales which aim to describe English as a second language development in the school context in Australia (Griffin 1990; Griffin & Nix 1991; Griffin & McKay 1992). These scales were built up by collecting and analyzing practitioners' observations of key indicators of learner behaviour. Following progressive refinement through consultation with teachers, input from specialists, and trialling, these indicators were calibrated using the Rasch model and sorted into bands according to their position on the scale.[1]

However, while systematic observation and documentation of learners performance clearly provide a useful starting point for scale development, such an approach is essentially theory-free. In other words, there is no linguistic basis for positing the proposed hierarchies in the scale. The levels are arrived at on the basis of the fit of particular tasks or items to the Rasch model. For this reason, some scales developed using this method have been subjected to criticism on the basis that they fail to reflect the complexity and multidimensionality of language learning and use. In addition, there are a number of dangers in basing scale descriptors on practitioner observation. These are acknowledged by Griffin and McKay (1992: 20):

Limitations of this approach include the difficulties involved in obtaining appropriate descriptions of language behaviour from practitioners. It is often the case that practitioners' observations are limited by a lack of knowledge of theoretical models, by inadequate observation skills and/or an inability to articulate descriptions of independent student language behaviour. The developer of the scales has to make decisions about the need to use the imprecise language of the practitioner, and perhaps lose part of the definitive nature of the theoretical model, or to use a specialist terminology and run the risk of practitioner misinterpretation and rejection.

They emphasize the need for scales to be informed by a theoretical framework and stress the importance of checking the behavioural indicators against "theoretical research and other published data" as part of the development and validation process (p. 21).

Ability levels and difficulty hierarchies in rating scales

Rating scales conventionally express ability levels in terms of texts, tasks, and skills, as noted earlier. In the case of reading and listening, the pro-

---

1 The Rasch model is a mathematical measurement model which assumes that all the items on a test, or in the case of rating scales, all the bands on a rating scale, assess a single, unidimensional underlying construct, or trait. If this assumption of unidimensionality is met, the model can provide estimates of candidates' "true ability score" that are independent of the particular samples of items or tasks and test takers upon which they are based. If, however, this assumption of unidimensionality is not met (e.g., if the construct is multidimensional), then the data do not fit the model, and inferences about ability based on the analyses may not be valid.

cessing strategies used at different levels are sometimes described as well. One of the main concerns, then, in validating rating scales would be to investigate the claims made concerning the hierarchy of texts, tasks, or skills defined in the descriptors and to establish the extent to which an implicational relationship can be shown to exist. As Lee and Musumeci (1988: 173) comment in relation to the ACTFL definition of reading proficiency:

By the definition of hierarchy, high level skills and text types subsume low ones so that readers demonstrating high levels of reading proficiency should be able to interact with texts and be able to demonstrate the reading skills characteristic of low levels of reading proficiency. Conversely, readers at low levels of the proficiency scale should neither be able to demonstrate high level skills nor interact with high level texts.

There have been relatively few published studies of such hierarchies in rating scales, however, and the research that has been carried out has produced mixed results. One such study was undertaken by Dandonoli and Henning (1990) in response to criticisms that the ACTFL guidelines confound language ability and test method factors (Bachman & Savignon 1986). It included a multitrait-multimethod (MTMM) analysis of the data provided by tests of speaking, listening, reading, and writing in French and ESL which were based on the ACTFL guidelines, along with Rasch analyses of the relationship between proficiency levels and test item difficulty. MTMM analysis involves the comparison of correlations between two or more tests of the same traits using two or more different methods, in order to establish the extent to which the variance in test scores can be attributed to differences in underlying ability as opposed to the test method used. Evidence for *convergent validity* would be provided by high positive correlations between different measures of the same trait, whereas evidence for *discriminant validity* would be indicated by low or zero correlations between measures of different traits using different methods (Bachman 1990).

According to the researchers, an examination of the MTMM correlation matrix generated by the tests of the different skills revealed that "in both English and French, all four skills exhibited convergent validity by the MTMM criteria" (Dandonoli & Henning 1990: 14). Speaking and reading in ESL demonstrated discriminant validity in all required comparisons, writing in 11 out of 12 comparisons, and listening in 9 out of 12. In French, speaking, writing, and reading exhibited discriminant validity in all comparisons, but the listening test met only 4 of the required 13 comparisons, prompting the authors to call for "greater attention to listening text characteristics and selection criteria" at the test development stage (p. 20).

In order to investigate the extent to which the test results reflected the task and text difficulty hierarchies proposed in the ACTFL guidelines,

Rasch analysis of item difficulty and person ability estimates associated with particular proficiency levels was undertaken. Here the researchers found that "with a few exceptions, there was adequate progression in the appropriate direction on the latent ability and difficulty continua associated with the descriptors provided in the Guidelines" (p. 20).

A study conducted by Lee and Musumeci (1988) also set out to examine the task and text hierarchies proposed in the ACTFL guidelines, but came to somewhat different conclusions. In this case, reading texts were identified which were characteristic of the different levels of proficiency described in the guidelines. Questions were then developed for each text that were aimed at tapping the reading skills which defined the levels. On the basis of an analysis of reader performance on different text types and reading skills, they concluded:

The results of the study raise serious doubts about the validity of the model. Text type one was as difficult as text types three and five. Skill two was more difficult than skills one, three and four. Only four percent separates the highest percentage of correct responses from the lowest. We find *no* evidence for:
• the proposed hierarchy of text types;
• the proposed hierarchy of reading skills;
• performance on higher proficiency tasks subsuming lower ones;
• a developmental pattern such that second-year students comprehend better than first-year students.

(Lee & Musumeci 1988: 180).

Leaving aside some of the methodological questions which could be posed about this study (we are not told, for example, how semester level is presumed to relate to any independent measures of language proficiency), it still raises a number of concerns in relation to validation studies of rating scales which are carried out through parallel test construction. One is the essential circularity of attempting to validate proficiency descriptors through constructing tasks or tests based on those descriptors. This is illustrated by the Dandonoli and Henning study. If the results of the tests do not conform to the predicted task/text hierarchies, it is not clear whether this is because the tests are just poorly constructed or because the descriptors themselves are inadequate, although Dunkel, Henning, and Chaudron (1992) seem to be of the view that if the tests demonstrate high internal reliability, then the fault may lie with the scale descriptors. These difficulties are further compounded by the fact that it is hard to see how the kind of impressionistic terminology which is typically used in the ACTFL guidelines could be translated directly into test specifications or items; subjective judgement would still have to play a major role. On what basis, for example, would test designers decide what is a "linguistically noncomplex text" (Intermediate-Mid Reading) or write items testing "emerging awareness of culturally implied meanings beyond the surface meanings of the text" (Advanced-Plus Listening)? And how would negatively defined descriptors such as "Listener is aware of cohesive devices but may not be able to use them to follow the sequence of thought in an oral text" (Advanced Listening) be translated into items?

Since the item statistics cited in the Dandonoli and Henning study indicate that the mean item difficulties show a progression of difficulty in the desired direction, one assumes that the test constructors were able to broadly agree on the assignment of passages and items to proficiency levels. However, this agreement could merely indicate an "in-house" understanding of what constitutes text and task difficulty within the ACTFL system (in this regard, North 1993: 8 observes that "it is indeed surprising the extent to which proficiency is defined in the ACTFL literature as that which is tested in the Oral Proficiency Interview"). Since no information is given on the relationship between test scores and the level descriptors, there is no way of knowing to what extent people who are classified by the tests at a particular level can in fact do the things specified at that level and not those above it. Unless there is independent evidence to demonstrate that candidates at particular levels can indeed handle the tasks and texts and demonstrate the skills specified as accompanying that level, it cannot be assumed that the verbal descriptions in the ACTFL guidelines describe the skills used in test performance. As Alderson (1991b: 74) points out, if descriptors are to be meaningful characterizations of ability, then they should be able to be related to actual performance.

Two other recent studies have also investigated task difficulty in relation to the ACTFL guidelines. Kenyon and Stansfield (1992) discovered a close correspondence between foreign language teachers' ratings of speaking task difficulty and the ACTFL task hierarchy. In a similar vein, a study by Kenyon (1995) found that foreign language learner's perceptions of the amount of ability required to perform different speaking tasks were highly consistent and that their self-assessments of task difficulty generally supported the difficulty hierarchy in the ACTFL scale. Kenyon (1995: 11) concludes, "This provides some additional evidence to support the validity of the Guidelines, at least to the extent that foreign language students validate the assumption that more foreign language proficiency is required to carry out certain speaking tasks than others".

However, even though teacher or learner *perceptions* of task difficulty may be in agreement with the ordering of task difficulty in a scale, such agreement cannot be taken as validating the scale descriptors until such time as it can be demonstrated that the predicted order is also reflected in actual test performance. It cannot automatically be assumed that self-assessed difficulty will match task difficulty under actual test conditions. This is exemplified in a study of essay prompt difficulty by Hamp-Lyons and Mathias (1994). Although there was a high degree of consensus by judges on prompt difficulty, the researchers found that judges' predictions of difficulty were almost totally the reverse of the scoring patterns revealed in the test data. The researchers conclude: "It seems that, in this context at least, 'expert judges' are mistaken in believing they can predict which prompts will result in high or low scores for ESL writers" (1994: 59). This finding suggests that a good deal of further research into writers' actual test-taking processes will be necessary before it is possible to describe with any degree of confidence levels of writing ability in terms of a hierarchy of tasks.

Skill separability and skill hierarchies

The question of the relationship between test performance and level descriptors raises a number of other important issues concerning the nature and status of the underlying skills which are conventionally described in rating scales. Scales often incorporate the assumption that "higher-order" and "lower-order" skills involved in language use can be identified and that the former subsume the latter.

Whether test items which tap higher-order skills should be more difficult is a matter of debate in the language testing literature (Weir, Hughes, & Porter 1990; Alderson 1991a). In this regard, Alderson notes a widespread belief amongst practitioners that "'higher order' items will be more demanding – which must relate in some way to difficulty – and secondly that we should teach and test lower order skills first" (p. 601). This implicit hierarchy is frequently found in rating scale descriptors, where skills such as "identifying key words" are associated with beginner levels and skills such as "inferencing" conventionally only appear at the upper ends of the scale.

However, there is evidence from a number of studies to suggest that expert judges may disagree, firstly about the nature of the subskills involved in language ability, secondly about the extent to which different items are tapping particular skills, and thirdly about the difficulty level of items and tasks (Alderson & Lukmani 1989; Alderson 1990a; Buck 1990, 1991).

Alderson (1990a: 436) found that judges were unable to agree on which skills were being tapped by particular items in EAP tests or on the level of a particular skill or a particular item. He notes that one possible explanation for this lack of agreement may be that there are serious reasons for doubting whether a skill can be said to be "higher" or "lower" than another skill in the hierarchy that implies relative difficulty or some differential stage of acquisition (at least for ESL readers).

Similar findings were reported by Hudson (1993b), who was unable to find evidence for separable reading skills "at any but the lowest ability level" in a study of item difficulty in tests of English for Science and Technology. A factor analysis of a reading test for German elementary school pupils by Rost (1993) also failed to establish either separately identifiable subskills or hierarchical relationships between skills.

Studies of listening comprehension have also failed to reveal clear hierarchies of skill difficulty. Buck (1990) investigated whether it was possible to operationalize lower-level processing (requiring understanding of clearly stated information) and higher-level processing (requiring inferencing) in listening test items. He also sought to establish whether expert judges could agree on which of these levels of processing the items were measuring and whether the performance of the higher-level items differed from that of the lower-level ones. Buck found the raters agreed on which level items were measuring in 27 out of 33 cases. However, there was little agreement between raters on processing level when they were asked to rate the relative difficulty of items. Buck also found no difference between the mean difficulties of lower-level and higher-level items, although lower-level items were easier when item preview was allowed. He concludes that "the fact that the higher-level items are not significantly more difficult than the lower-level items suggests that there is no implicational scale of difficulty such that a listener needs to be proficient in lower-level processing before being able to progress to higher-level processing" (1990: 417). Item analysis also revealed that higher-level items failed to show better discrimination than lower-level ones. Buck suggests that this may be because they not only are dependent on language ability but also measure general knowledge or reasoning.

Findings such as these would suggest, then, that the descriptions of task and skill hierarchies which figure in rating scales are open to question, firstly because of the lack of clear evidence to support the existence of separately identifiable subskills, and secondly because of the failure of many of the studies cited here to show implicational relationships between skills. It should be noted, however, that the methodology used by Alderson (1990a) has been criticised by Weir et al. (1990), who argue, *inter alia,* that the key notions of higher-order and lower-order skills are inadequately defined in the study. Weir et al. also contend that since Alderson did not train judges to make reliable judgements, their lack of agreement was hardly surprising. Lumley (1993), in a partial replication of Alderson's study, reports that following intensive briefing and discussion, he was able to achieve substantial levels of agreement among judges who were asked to rate the difficulty of subskills in an EAP reading test. Alderson (1991a), however, in a reply to Weir et al., argues that training judges is inappropriate if one wishes to establish the extent to which they share a common understanding of skills and item difficulty. If judges disagree, then "this surely tells the researcher something important about their judgements or their understanding of the concepts on which the judgements are based" (Alderson 1991a: 600).

Language skills and test tasks

Establishing the extent to which task or item difficulty can be related either to hypothesized processing difficulty or sequences of skill acquisition remains problematic, since it is very difficult to separate language skills from test-taking strategies. Lumley (1993: 230) points out that what makes a reading test item hard may be related to the test task itself rather than to the reading skill a reader would have to use in everyday life. This effect of test task is supported by evidence from a study by Pollitt, Hutchinson, Entwhistle, and deLuca (1985), who found that the demands of test questions were significant factors in determining the difficulty of a test:

It is clear that some of the variables identified, concerned as they are with the wording of questions, their syntax and their relationship with the text, are those which control the candidate's access both to the task and to the meaning of the passage, by providing him with supports or putting hurdles in his way. (1985: 71)

There remains the possibility, then, that attempts to investigate skills hierarchies will be contaminated by test method effect. At the same time, as Lumley points out, the skills may not be stable across all learners, depending as they do on a range of factors such as background knowledge, cultural background, and cognitive style. One person's "inference" may thus be another's "knowledge". This makes operationalization of the level descriptors extremely difficult.

Text type and task demands

Ability levels on rating scales are frequently distinguished according to text and task type. Yet, as various authors point out, there is little research evidence to justify grouping of texts and tasks together at a particular level (van Ek 1987; Lee & Musumeci 1988; Buck 1990; Pollitt 1993).

There have been few investigations of the effect of text type in language testing. However, research conducted by Pollitt and Hutchinson (1987) and by Shohamy and Inbar (1991) indicates that it may well be a significant factor in determining task difficulty. In an investigation of learner performance on a range of different writing tasks in a Scottish secondary school, Pollitt and Hutchinson (1987) found a strong relationship between three components of writing competence – appropriacy, ideas, and expression – but very low correlations between tasks. They note that text type could be one way of explaining the empirical task hierarchy established, but point out that "any genre effect will be overlaid by a task specific effect caused by both the task demands and the supports provided" (p. 88).

Shohamy and Inbar (1991) investigated the effects of texts and question types on EFL listening test scores. They found that different types of texts resulted in different performances, depending on the extent to which they contained various features of "oral" as opposed to "literate" discourse. Because the texts seemed to involve different degrees of "listenability", they conclude with a recommendation that listening tests should include a variety of texts, tasks, and interactions.

SLA researchers have also looked at the demands of different task types from a developmental perspective. Snow, Cancino, de Temple, and Schley (1991) carried out a large-scale study of the development of the skill of giving formal definitions in bilingual schoolchildren. The study was also intended to explore the hypothesis that "different language tasks call upon different language skills, and that proficiency in one task (e.g. giving formal definitions) should be unrelated to proficiency in tasks which make rather different kinds of demands (e.g. providing communicatively adequate descriptions of the meaning of a word)" (Snow et al. 1991: 101). Snow and her co-researchers found that global levels of performance differed markedly across tasks and concluded that this emphasized the need to analyze specific contexts for acquisition. These findings recall those of the Pollitt and Hutchinson (1987) study, which also established that different writing tasks made different demands on learners and invoked different criteria for competence.

Bialystok (1991a: 75) advances a psycholinguistic explanation for these differences in ability, arguing that proficiency is a function of the processing skills required by the task:

Language proficiency is not a single achievement marking some quantitative level of progress with language learning. Rather it is the ability to apply specific processing skills to problems bearing identifiable cognitive demands. Proficiency in a domain, or in a task, is evident when the demands of the task are not in excess of the demands of the language learner. Thus, language learners with a particular configuration of skill component development will in fact exhibit a range of proficiency with the language that is determined by the impact of the task demands on the processing abilities of the learner.

In the light of these research findings, which have consistently found variations in proficiency according to task demands, the psycholinguistic validity of scale descriptors which group specific texts and tasks together to form a single ability level must remain open to question.

Validating rating scales: Research directions

Thus far I have examined some of the assumptions about SLA which are made in behavioural rating scales and looked at the status of these assumptions in the light of SLA and LT research. The paucity of evidence to support the claimed task and text hierarchies would seem to indicate that a good deal of further work needs to be done before it can be argued that the stages of proficiency development typically described in scales correspond to the realities of language acquisition and use. To this end, I want to consider in the final section of this chapter how various branches of both SLA and LT research might be drawn on in order to contribute to such a research agenda.

Content analysis

Since the empirical status of the task–skills hierarchies described in rating scale descriptors remains unconfirmed, further research is clearly required to establish the extent to which it is possible to link scale descriptors directly to test performance. Such research is particularly important in the case of listening and reading comprehension skills which are not amenable to direct observation.

A number of studies have attempted to establish task–skills hierarchies empirically by mapping the relationship between test content and item difficulty onto a Rasch scale (e.g., Mossenson, Hill, & Masters 1987; Griffin & Nix 1991; Brown, Elder, Lumley, McNamara, & McQueen 1992; Lumley 1993; Pollitt 1993). In this way, the relationship between person ability, item difficulty, and the skills being tested by the test items can be examined. If it can be shown that items or tasks which are testing the same skills tend to "cluster" at the same difficulty level, then scale descriptors based on these skills can be developed. It is important, however, as Brown et al. (1992: 64) note, that the nature of the skills and the way in which they are operationalized in items be discussed and clarified before the test is administered.

Lumley (1993) investigated the extent to which EAP reading test items deemed by teachers to be tapping the same skill could be grouped together at the same level on a Rasch scale. He found a significant correlation between item difficulty and teacher ratings, with the items at each skill level falling into broad but overlapping bands. Lumley concludes that these results give some empirical support to the validity of teachers' perceptions, since teachers were able to identify elements common to groups of items, "or at least part of what makes one item more difficult than another" (p. 45).

Pollitt (1993) also used Rasch analysis to examine student performance on reading comprehension tests in Scottish schools. Using the order of difficulty of the items as a starting point, he analyzed the characteristics of each question and established a difficulty hierarchy based on the task demands. This enabled test-specific grade descriptors to be generated. Pollitt concludes, however, that "the difficulty of each item was the result of its own particular set of influences" (1993: 11) and warns that generalized grade descriptors which do not mention specific texts or text types may be inadequate as indicators of reading ability.

The procedure of mapping skills from test content into bands of increasing difficulty is promising. As Pollitt (1993: 2) comments, one of the advantages of the approach is that it enables many tests to be calibrated onto the same scale, thus building up a more secure base for the description of skills at different levels. However, it is also extremely resource-intensive. In this regard, North (1993: 41) comments that the process of validating test content through independent analysis "implies a doctoral thesis per test". Nevertheless it appears to be one of the few ways available of validating skill and band descriptors in a noncircular way.

Introspective/retrospective research

The psycholinguistic validity of rating scale descriptors depends on the extent to which it can be shown that the skills described in the scale at a given level of ability are those that the test taker uses to respond to tasks or items. Teacher judgement alone, even if obtained after exhaustive discussion, cannot, as Lumley (1993: 230) points out, tell us what is happening inside learners' heads. In order to establish the extent to which given tasks or items are tapping particular skills, it is also necessary to examine the process that test takers go through when responding to test items (Alderson 1990a: 437). Recently a variety of introspective or retrospective studies have been carried out into the way in which language is processed in tests of reading and listening comprehension (e.g., Alderson 1990b; Buck 1990, 1991; Ross 1997; Cohen, Chapter 4, this volume).

Alderson (1990b) used think-aloud protocols based on self-observation to investigate the test-taking processes of two learners in a test of academic reading. Although the study was limited in scope, the results revealed discrepancies between the skills which judges and test constructors thought were being tested and the skills that learners actually used to respond. He also found that incorrect item responses did not always indicate that a learner lacked the skill necessary to answer it. Alderson (1990b: 478) concludes that the evidence for clearly definable skills and for a skills hierarchy is not overwhelming and calls for further research in order to validate theories of reading and their operationalization in tests.

Buck (1991) used verbal reports to examine processes in listening test performance. He found that items intended to operationalize the distinction between "lower-level" and "higher-level" processing did not function as intended because of the wide range of responses that were possible with a short-answer format and that "the same item could be testing the ability to understand clearly stated information for one testee and inferencing ability for another" (1991: 76). This once again highlights the difficulties of attempting to tie particular skills to items.

Ross (1997) used 40 ESL listeners' introspective accounts of listening test-taking processes to investigate the psychological dimensionality of listening test items, concentrating particularly on items which showed misfit to the Rasch model. He identified a number of aural processing stages associated with particular strategies but found some deviations from these strategies due to background knowledge and test-taking strategies. Interestingly, Ross found that a single "key word" processing stage was common to both the ten highest- and the ten lowest-proficiency listeners in the sample. This once again calls into question the association of particular processing strategies with proficiency levels in rating scales (see also Anderson 1991).

As Ross (1997) comments, introspective analysis of test performance can yield important information on the cognitive processes which underlie test performance and provide a valuable supplement to analysis of item response patterns, thus enabling better understanding of why some items "work" and others do not. Such research can also play a useful role in the validation of rating scales by investigating the extent to which the descriptions of processing strategies which conventionally figure in scales of reading and listening ability correspond to those which appear to be deployed by test takers.

Task analysis

The arbitrariness with which tasks are grouped into a level has been identified as a major problem with rating scales. If a scale is to constitute a fair measurement of ability, then information about the relative difficulty of different kinds of language tasks is essential. In this regard, the advent of the many-faceted Rasch analysis and its accompanying software package, *Facets* (Linacre 1989), has provided language testers with a useful means of investigating the measurement characteristics of test tasks and the effect of different facets of the test situation on task performance (e.g., Wigglesworth 1993). However, measurement tools do not in themselves provide any linguistically based hypotheses which would explain why one task is more difficult than another.

Bialystok (1988a, 1991a, b, 1994) suggests a way of addressing this question from a psycholinguistic perspective. She identifies two skill components which are involved in language acquisition and use, *analysis of linguistic knowledge* and *control of linguistic processing*. She points out that different tasks tap these skills in different ways and suggests that the proficiency of learners "can be described more specifically by reference to their mastery of each of the skill components". Bialystok proposes a framework for analysing task demands and demonstrates how specific tasks in different domains of language use can be mapped on to these two dimensions: "It should be possible to predict how a language learner will perform on a given task if there is an assessment of the language learner's level of analysis and control and a task analysis of the levels required by the problem" (Bialystok 1994: 161). Bialystok's framework, which she reports has already been applied successfully to reading tasks (Bialystok

1988b), could provide a useful starting point for investigating the processing demands of different language tasks.

Recent studies by Robinson (1995) and Robinson, Ting, and Urwin (1995) have also investigated the demands imposed by different kinds of second language tasks along a number of dimensions, including cognitive load, prior information, planning time, and displaced versus "here-and-now" reference. Although this line of research is still in its infancy, it has already generated useful information regarding the interaction of task demands, task types, and task conditions and may in time provide an empirical basis for describing the productive demands of tasks at different levels of complexity.

Text analysis

A variety of graded text type hierarchies have been proposed in rating scales (see, e.g., Child 1987). Yet, as we have seen, these have not been unequivocally supported by research evidence. In order to gather evidence that would assist in classifying texts, a two-pronged approach is needed. On the one hand, research into the linguistic features of texts is required; on the other, we need to know how texts are processed and produced.

Genre-based approaches to language teaching and assessment offer one way of analyzing the characteristics of spoken and written texts (Mincham 1995). The genre-based approach is derived from systemic-functional linguistic theory (Halliday 1985) and is concerned with exploring the way in which language is used to realize a variety of social purposes. The genre-based approach to text analysis involves specifying the discourse structure and particular linguistic features of text types which are relevant to the target population (e.g., *argument* or *reporting a process* in the case of secondary school learners). It thus offers testable hypotheses concerning the specific linguistic features which need to be controlled in order for certain tasks to be carried out; and these features can, in turn, serve as criteria for determining task achievement.

Genre-based approaches suggest a number of research strategies which might be adopted in order to explore the question of text/task difficulty. One of these would be to classify a range of commonly recurring text types according to their "spoken" and "written" features and to investigate the interaction between text type and task difficulty, along the lines of studies such as that conducted by Shohamy and Inbar (1991). If a systematic relationship between text and task difficulty and the presence or absence of particular linguistic features could be demonstrated, then this could provide a useful set of linguistic criteria which would assist in establishing text hierarchies.

From an SLA perspective, however, one of the problems with this approach is that the descriptions of genres and the resulting assessment criteria have conventionally been derived from native speaker performance. Thus, while genre analysis might assist in specifying criterial features of the desired target performance, it will not provide any information about the types of performance that might be expected from people at different levels of development towards the target. Text analysis would therefore need to be supplemented by research into the cognitive demands of particular tasks or activities on second language learners.

An additional factor to be considered is the available database of descriptions of texts. Establishing text typologies relies on the availability of very comprehensive descriptions of different oral and written genres. However, as Murray (1994) points out, "full descriptions of the structures of most oral and written genres have yet to be developed."

Other approaches to text description could also be drawn on in attempting to classify text types and examine their relative difficulty. Biber (1986), for example, using two large-scale corpora of over a million words, has identified three textual dimensions which underlie speech and writing in English – *Interactive versus Edited Text, Abstract versus Situated Content,* and *Reported versus Immediate Style.* These dimensions provide another useful framework for investigating text complexity.

Developmental sequences

Commenting on the process of developing scale descriptors, de Jong (1988: 74) notes, that "What we need to know if we want to develop good scales is not linguistic knowledge of how language is structured, what all the features of language are; we need to know how somebody acquires language, that is, what the developmental stages in language acquisition are".

The multidimensional model

One approach which has attempted to link teaching and assessment to developmental stages in a principled way is exemplified in the model of SLA developed by Manfred Pienemann and his colleagues (Meisel, Clahsen, & Pienemann 1981; Pienemann et al. 1988; Pienemann 1985, 1989; Pienemann & Mackey 1992). Based on the analysis of a large body of longitudinal and cross-sectional data collected from learners of German and English as a second language, these researchers have posited the existence of an invariant developmental sequence in syntax and morphology which can be explained in terms of speech processing constraints. While some features in what has come to be known as the multidimensional model (MM) are said to be subject to an invariant sequence of development, other features not involving cognitive operations of any complexity, known as variational features, have also been identified. According to Pienemann and Johnston (1987), the existence of two independent dimensions of development and variation shows how gains in accuracy do not necessarily mean gains in development and vice-versa. This has led Pienemann and Johnston (1987) to distinguish between *development* and *proficiency*. They see the latter as a fuzzy and relational concept to such an extent that "assessments of communicative competence can only be properly interpreted as a mapping of behaviours – that of testers on the one hand and testees on the other" (Pienemann & Johnston (1987: 68). Pienemann and Johnston argue that language assessment should be carried out "within a framework which takes the formal properties of language into account" (p. 91) and suggest ways in which the developmental and variational dimensions of the MM might be used to predict learner's proficiency.

The MM applied to assessment

The MM has been applied to language assessment in a practical way through the development of a computer-based procedure for assessing learner's developmental stage known as Rapid Profile (Pienemann & Mackey 1992). This procedure, based on profile analysis techniques developed in speech pathology, involves first the collection of a sample of interlanguage production through the administration of a task-based procedure. This is followed by an analysis of the learner's output using computer software containing an expert system which matches the structures produced against the stages of acquisition described in the MM.

Although the theoretical status of the MM continues to be hotly debated (see, e.g., Larsen-Freeman & Long 1991; Hulstijn 1992; Hudson 1993a; Cook 1993; Pienemann, Johnston, & Meisel 1993; Tarone, Chapter 3, this volume), a number of arguments can be advanced to support the principle of including procedures for assessing the state of a learner's interlanguage development in language assessment, particularly in the context of achievement and diagnostic testing. In outlining these arguments, however, it should be emphasized that the assessment of a learner's developmental stage has never been proposed as a replacement for proficiency testing (Pienemann et al. 1988: 220). The purpose of this procedure is to obtain a sample of a learner's interlanguage grammar and identify his or her position on the acquisitional map provided by the MM. This is quite separate from the process of assessing proficiency, which involves a much more comprehensive assessment of a wide range of components of language in use (Pienemann & Mackey 1992). According to Pienemann and Mackey (1992: 135), one of the main reasons for assessing a learner's developmental stage is that it enables the teacher not only to obtain an overview of the learner's grammatical development at a particular point in time but also to predict which grammatical structures will be learnable next.

Information on learners' stage of grammatical development could also help to provide a principled basis for selecting the grammatical elements that are to be assessed as part of achievement testing. A number of recent research studies have indicated that form-focussed instruction can contribute positively to SLA (White 1991; White, Spada, Lightbown, & Ranta 1991; Spada & Lightbown 1993), and there is currently a return to activities in language teaching which are aimed at drawing learners' attention in various ways to the structural regularities of the language (Sharwood Smith 1993). In such a climate, information of the kind provided by Rapid Profile can assist teachers in setting realistic criteria for assessing grammar as an enabling skill. This is not to suggest a return to discrete point testing, however – it is merely a recognition of the fact that assessment of "structural proficiency" will remain a part of teachers' armory of procedures for assessing ongoing attainment at the level of the classroom (Brindley 1989).

At the same time, information on learners' grammatical profile is of relevance in the context of task-based learning and assessment. The fact that the elicitation procedures used in Rapid Profile are in the form of tasks means that developmental stage and proficiency level can be rated using the same language sample. This should enable the relationship between the two, which is far from clear at the moment (Pienemann & Mackey (1992: 182), to be investigated more fully. If learners can be rated according to differing sets of grammatical and communicative criteria, then the relationship between task fulfilment and grammatical "enabling skills" can be investigated. This should assist in clarifying the rather murky relationship between form and function which has bedevilled syllabus designers seeking a principled basis for grading, sequencing, and assessing tasks (Long & Crookes 1993). One of the key questions about task-based assessment, as with rating scale descriptors, is the extent to which skills can be generalized across different tasks and contexts. The information generated by Rapid Profile should be of assistance in addressing this important question.

A number of potentially interesting research questions remain to be addressed concerning applications of the MM to assessment. As Hulstijn (1992) notes, the notion of "processing constraints" in the MM applies to production and not to comprehension, and it remains unclear whether a similar developmental order would be found using comprehension tasks. One way of investigating this relationship would be to construct and administer tests of reading and listening containing developmentally sensitive items and to establish the extent to which the same implicational ordering could be found (see Brindley & Singh 1982 for an early attempt to devise a procedure along these lines using dictation in the absence of a theoretical framework such as the MM). Another fruitful area for investigation concerns the relationship between accuracy and developmental stage. One of the critiques of the MM is that use of the "emergence" criterion to determine stages of acquisition glosses over the concerns of testers with accuracy (Tarone, Chapter 3, this volume). Since Rapid Profile records an accuracy measure for each of the targetted grammatical structures, it is now possible to determine the accuracy of suppliance within a given developmental stage. As the database built up by Pienemann and his associates expands, useful information on the evolution of grammatical accuracy over time will become available.

As far as the application of the MM to rating scales is concerned, data on learners' grammatical output of the type generated by Rapid Profile would provide a useful supplement to the proficiency information yielded by proficiency assessment using rating scales, thus enabling detailed diagnostic profiles to be built up. Systematic comparison of the state of learners' developmental grammars and their proficiency ratings may yield hypotheses concerning the expectations of production at different levels of proficiency. At the same time, since they are based on an explicit theory of processing complexity, the stages proposed in the MM could provide a concrete reference point for investigating the processing demands of different task types, a necessary part of the validation of scale desciptors.

Conclusion

In discussing the limitations of behavioral rating scales, North (1993: 7) suggests that they are primarily practical tools intended for people to use and as such represent operational rather than theoretical models. If this is so, it could be argued that it is inappropriate to evaluate scales on theoretical grounds. Nevertheless, the simple fact is that rating scales make very explicit claims that people can use language to achieve various communicative goals at different levels of proficiency, and these claims are presumably believed by various audiences. At the same time, we have seen that the progressions described in some general proficiency scales could appear to present a picture of universal patterns of second language development. It is important therefore that the status of the descriptors which define the levels is examined. Validation becomes particularly important when significant decisions may hinge on the ratings or scores which are assigned on the basis of the level definitions.

Unfortunately, however, it can be rather difficult to validate the descriptors in some scales since there is no way in which they can be related directly to test tasks – that is, as Pollitt (1991: 87–88) points out, they do not describe the qualities of a performance (see also Turner & Upshur 1995: 6). One can always try to create tests based on the descriptors, but this runs the risk of circularity. If the aim of the validation exercise is to determine whether people are in fact capable of doing the things described in the level definitions, the descriptors need to be accompanied by specifications which spell out systematically the range of tasks (stimuli), settings, and performances (responses) (Haertel 1985). As Davies (1992: 14) remarks, "descriptors which are usable in an objective sense are test items".

This is not to suggest that behavioural scales are of no value in themselves. The various stakeholders involved in language programs will continue to require the information that they provide, particularly for purposes of reporting outcomes, and validation studies of scales will still be needed. To this end, performances of learners classified at different levels of ability on different scales will need to be analyzed along a number of psychological and textual dimensions, as suggested in this chapter. However, although they may be helpful for various practical purposes, the generalized descriptions of levels or stages of language proficiency which figure in rating scales represent an inevitable and possibly misleading oversimplification of the language learning process. Language performance is now recognized by both SLA and LT researchers as being highly complex, multidimensional, and variable according to a variety of social and contextual factors (Bachman 1990; Henning & Cascallar 1992; Swain 1993; Tarone, Chapter 3, this volume; Douglas, Chapter 6, this volume). This complexity cannot be captured in a single level descriptor or rating (Spolsky 1995: 358). Language testers have accordingly begun to recognize that proficiency and achievement will no longer be able to be assessed using single ratings or scores and that a wide variety of performances will need to be sampled across a range of different contexts. As Wolf, Bixby, Glann, and Gardner (1991: 63–64) note in the context of general education:

We will have to break step by step with the drive to arrive at single, summary statistics for student performance. In line with more diversified notions of intelligence, it is critical to develop ways of looking at student profiles, both within and across domains. . . . Unless we develop these kinds of differentiated portraits of student performance within a domain, it is difficult to envision student assessment ever informing, rather than merely measuring the educational process.

This trend is also evident in language learning with the increasing adoption of different forms of qualitative assessment and reporting, such as portfolios, profiles, and structured observation, which aim to reflect complex performances of individual second language learners over time. Rather than continuing to proliferate scales which use generalized and empirically unsubstantiated descriptors, therefore, it would perhaps be more profitable to draw on SLA and LT research to develop more specific empirically derived and diagnostically oriented scales of task performance which are relevant to particular purposes of language use in particular contexts and to investigate the extent to which performance on these tasks taps common components of competence (Pollitt & Hutchinson 1987;

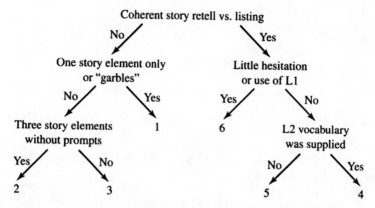

Figure 5.1 Rating scale for communicative effectiveness. From Turner, C. and J. Upshur 1995. Constructing rating scales for second language tests. ELT Journal, 49(1), 1: 3–12.

Chalhoub-Deville 1995; Turner & Upshur 1995). An example of how scale descriptors can be derived from analysis of learner performance is provided by Turner and Upshur (1995), who describe a procedure for developing scales which require the rater to make a series of binary choices concerning key features which distinguish between score levels. (Figure 5.1 shows one of their sample scales for assessing communicative effectiveness in a story-retell task.) Through continuing practical efforts of this kind, supplemented by further theoretically motivated research into generalizable dimensions of task and text complexity, it might eventually be possible not only to develop a better understanding of task performance in context but also to gain deeper insights into the complex linguistic and cognitive skills which go to make up language proficiency.

References

Alderson, J. C. 1990a. Testing reading comprehension skills (Part 1). *Reading in a Foreign Language*, 6(2), 425–438.

Alderson, J. C. 1990b. Testing reading comprehension skills (Part 2). *Reading in a Foreign Language*, 7(1), 465–503.

Alderson, J. C. 1991a. Letter to the editor. *Reading in a Foreign Language*, 7(2), 599–603.

Alderson, J. C. 1991b. Bands and scores. In J. C. Alderson & B. North (eds.), *Language testing in the 1990s* (pp. 71–86). London: Macmillan.

Alderson, J. C., & Y. Lukmani. 1989. Cognition and reading: Cognitive levels as embodied in test questions. *Reading in a Foreign Language*, 5(2), 253–270.

American Council on the Teaching of Foreign Languages. 1986. *ACTFL proficiency guidelines*. Hastings-on-Hudson, NY: ACTFL.

Anderson, N. 1991. Individual differences in strategy use in second language reading and testing. *Modern Language Journal, 75*(4), 460–472.

Bachman, L. F. 1988. Problems in examining the validity of the ACTFL oral proficiency interview. *Studies in Second Language Acquisition, 10*(2), 149–164.

Bachman, L. F. 1990. *Fundamental considerations in language testing.* Oxford: Oxford University Press.

Bachman, L. F., & A. S. Palmer. 1996. *Language testing in practice: Designing and developing useful language tests.* Oxford: Oxford University Press.

Bachman, L. F., & S. Savignon. 1986. The evaluation of communicative language proficiency: A critique of the ACTFL oral interview. *Modern Language Journal, 70*(4), 380–390.

Bialystok, E. 1988a. Psycholinguistic dimensions of second language proficiency. In W. Rutherford & M. Sharwood Smith (eds.), *Grammar and second language teaching* (pp. 31–50). New York: Newbury House.

Bialystok, E. 1988b. Aspects of linguistic awareness in reading comprehension. *Applied Psycholinguistics, 9*, 123–139.

Bialystok, E. 1991a. Achieving proficiency in a second language: A processing description. In R. Phillipson, E. Kellerman, L. Selinker, M. Sharwood Smith, & M. Swain (eds.), *Foreign/second language pedagogy research* (pp. 113–140). Clevedon: Multilingual Matters.

Bialystok, E. 1991b. Metalinguistic dimensions of bilingual language proficiency. In E. Bialystok (ed.), *Language processing in bilingual children* (pp. 113–140). Cambridge: Cambridge University Press.

Bialystok, E. 1994. Analysis and control in the development of second language proficiency. *Studies in Second Language Acquisition, 16*(2), 157–168.

Biber, D. 1986. Spoken and written textual dimensions in English: Resolving the contradictory findings. *Language, 62*(2), 384–414.

Brindley, G. 1989. *Assessing achievement in the learner-centred curriculum.* Sydney: National Centre for English Language Teaching and Research, Macquarie University.

Brindley, G., & K. Singh. 1982. The use of second language learning research in ESL proficiency assessment. *Australian Review of Applied Linguistics, 5*(1), 84–111.

Brown, A., C. Elder, T. Lumley, T. McNamara, & J. McQueen. 1992. Mapping abilities and skill levels using Rasch techniques. *Melbourne Papers in Language Testing, 1*(1), 28–52.

Buck, G. 1990. The testing of second language listening comprehension. Doctoral dissertation, University of Lancaster, Lancaster, England.

Buck, G. 1991. The testing of listening comprehension: An introspective study. *Language Testing, 8*(1), 67–91.

Byrnes, H. 1987. Second language acquisition: Insights from a proficiency orientation. In H. Byrnes & M. Canale (eds.), *Defining and developing proficiency: Guidelines, implementations and concepts* (pp. 107–131). Lincolnwood, IL: National Textbook Co.

Carroll, B. J., & R. West. 1989. *ESU framework.* London: Longman.

Chalhoub-Deville, M. 1995. Deriving oral assessment scales across different tests and rater groups. *Language Testing, 12*(1), 16–33.

Child, J. 1987. Language proficiency levels and the typology of texts. In H. Byrnes & M. Canale (eds.), *Defining and developing proficiency: Guidelines, im-*

plementations and concepts (pp. 97–106). Lincolnwood, IL: National Textbook Co.

Cook, V. 1993. *Linguistics and second language acquisition.* London: Macmillan.

Dandonoli, P. 1987. ACTFL's current research in proficiency testing. In H. Byrnes & M. Canale (eds.), *Defining and developing proficiency: Guidelines, implementations and concepts* (pp.75–96). Lincolnwood, IL: National Textbook Co.

Dandonoli, P., & G. Henning. 1990. An investigation of the construct validity of the ACTFL proficiency guidelines and oral interview procedure. *Foreign Language Annals, 23*(1): 11–22.

Davies, A. 1992. Is proficiency always achievement? *Melbourne Papers in Language Testing, 1*(1), 1–16.

de Jong, J. 1988. Rating scales and listening comprehension. *Australian Review of Applied Linguistics, 11*(2), 73–87.

Dunkel, P., G. Henning, & C. Chaudron. 1992. The assessment of an L2 listening comprehension construct: A tentative model for computer-adaptive test development. *Modern Language Journal, 77,* 180–191.

Galloway, V. 1987. From defining to developing proficiency: A look at the decisions. In H. Byrnes & M. Canale (eds.), *Defining and developing proficiency: Guidelines, implementations and concepts* (pp. 25–74). Lincolnwood, IL: National Textbook Co.

Graham, N. 1993. From curriculum to outcomes-based education. *Orbit, 24*(2): 5–8.

Griffin, P. 1990. Profiling literacy development: Monitoring the accumulation of reading skills. *Australian Journal of Education, 34*(3), 290–311.

Griffin, P., & P. McKay. 1992. Assessment and reporting in the ESL Language and Literacy in Schools Project. In National Languages and Literacy Institute of Australia, *ESL Development: Language and Literacy in Schools Project. Documents on bandscale development and language acquisition* (Vol. 2). Canberra: National Languages and Literacy Institute of Australia.

Griffin, P., & P. Nix. 1991. *Educational assessment and reporting.* Sydney: Harcourt Brace Jovanovich.

Haertel, E. 1985. Construct validity and criterion-referenced testing. *Review of Educational Research, 55*(1), 23–46.

Halliday, M. A. K. 1985. *An introduction to functional grammar.* London: Edward Arnold.

Hamp-Lyons, L., & S. P. Mathias. 1994. Examining expert judgements of task difficulty on essay tasks. *Journal of Second Language Writing, 3*(1), 49–68.

Henning, G., & E. Cascallar. 1992. *A preliminary study of the nature of communicative competence.* Princeton, NJ: Educational Testing Service.

Hudson, T. 1993a. Nothing does not equal zero: Problems with applying developmental sequence findings to assessment and pedagogy. *Studies in Second Language Acquisition, 15*(4), 461–493.

Hudson, T. 1993b. Testing the specificity of ESP reading skills. In D. Douglas & C. Chapelle (eds.), *A new decade of language testing research* (pp. 58–82). Alexandria, VA: TESOL.

Hulstijn, J. 1992. Onset or development of grammatical features? Comments on Pienemann's approach to acquisition orders. Unpublished manuscript, Free University, Amsterdam.

Ingram, D. E. 1984. Introduction to the ASLPR. In Commonwealth of Australia, Department of Immigration and Ethnic Affairs, *Australian Second Language Proficiency Ratings* (pp. 1–29). Canberra: Australian Government Publishing Service.

Ingram, D. E., & E. Wylie. 1984. Australian Second Language Proficiency Ratings. In Commonwealth of Australia, Department of Immigration and Ethnic Affairs, *Australian Second Language Proficiency Ratings* (pp. 31–55). Canberra: Australian Government Publishing Service.

Interagency Round Table. 1985. *ILR skill level descriptions.* Washington, DC: IRT.

Kenyon, D. M. 1995. An investigation of the validity of the demands of tasks on performance-based tests of oral proficiency. Paper presented at the 16th annual Language Testing Research Colloquium, Long Beach, CA.

Kenyon, D. M., & C. Stansfield. 1992. Examining the validity of a scale used in a performance assessment from many angles using the many-facet Rasch model. Paper presented at the annual meeting of the American Educational Research Association, San Francisco, CA. ERIC Document ED 343442.

Languages Lead Body. 1993. *Introduction to the National Language Standards.* London: Languages Lead Body.

Lantolf, J., & W. Frawley. 1988. Proficiency: Understanding the construct. *Studies in Second Language Acquisition, 10*(2), 181–195.

Larsen-Freeman, D., & M. Long. 1991. *An introduction to second language acquisition research.* London: Longman.

Lee, J., & D. Musumeci. 1988. On hierarchies of reading skills and text types. *Modern Language Journal, 72*(2), 173–187.

Linacre, J. M. 1989. *Many-faceted Rasch measurement.* Chicago: MESA Press.

Liskin-Gasparro, J. 1984. The ACTFL guidelines: A historical perspective. In T. V. Higgs (ed.), *Teaching for proficiency: The organizing principle* (pp. 11–42). Lincolnwood, IL: National Textbook Co.

Long, M., & G. Crookes. 1993. Units of analysis in syllabus design. In G. Crookes & S. Gass (eds.), *Tasks in a pedagogical context.* Clevedon: Multilingual Matters.

Lowe, P. 1988. The unassimilated history. In P. Lowe & C. Stansfield (eds.), *Second language proficiency assessment: Current issues* (pp. 11–51). Englewood Cliffs, NJ: Prentice Hall/Regents.

Lumley, T. 1993. The notion of subskills in reading comprehenion tests: An EAP example. *Language Testing, 10*(3), 211–235.

Mawer, G. 1992. *Language audits in industry.* Sydney: National Centre for English Language Teaching and Research, Macquarie University.

Meisel, J., H. Clahsen, & M. Pienemann. 1981. On determining developmental stages in natural second language acquisition. *Studies in Second Language Acquisition, 3*(2), 109–135.

Mincham, L. 1995. ESL student needs procedures: An approach to language assessment in primary and secondary school contexts. In G. Brindley (ed.), *Language assessment in action* (pp. 65–92). Sydney: National Centre for English Language Teaching and Research, Macquarie University.

Moss, P. 1992. Shifting conceptions of validity in educational measurement: Implications for performance assessment. *Review of Educational Research, 62*(3), 229–258.

Mossensen, L., P. Hill, & G. Masters. 1987. *TORCH: Tests of Reading Comprehension.* Hawthorn, Victoria: Australian Council for Educational Research.

Murray, D. 1994. Using portfolios to assess writing. *Prospect, 9*(2), 56–65.

National Languages and Literacy Institute of Australia. 1994. *ESL Development: Language and Literacy in Schools Project. Teachers' Manual* (Vol.1, 2nd ed.). Canberra: National Languages and Literacy Institute of Australia.

North, B. 1993. *The development of descriptors on scales of language proficiency.* Washington, DC: National Foreign Language Center.

Pienemann, M. 1989. Is language teachable? Psychycholinguistic experiments and hypotheses. *Applied Linguistics, 10*(1), 52–79.

Pienemann, M., & M. Johnston. 1987. Factors influencing the development of second language proficiency. In D. Nunan (ed.), *Applying second language acquisition research* (pp. 45–141). Adelaide: National Curriculum Resource Centre.

Pienemann, M., M. Johnston, & G. Brindley. 1988. Constructing an acquisition-based procedure for second language assessment. *Studies in Second Language Acquisition, 10*(2), 217–243.

Pienemann, M., M. Johnston, & J. Meisel. 1993. The multi-dimensional model, linguistic profiling and related issues: A reply to Hudson. *Studies in Second Language Acquisition, 15*(4), 495–503.

Pienemann, M., & A. Mackey. 1992. An empirical study of children's ESL development and *Rapid Profile.* Sydney: NLLIA Language Acquisition Research Centre, University of Sydney.

Pollitt, A. 1991. Response to Charles Alderson's paper: "Bands and scores." In J. C. Alderson & B. North (eds.), *Language testing in the 1990s* (pp. 87–94). London: Macmillan.

Pollitt, A. 1993. Reporting test results in grades. Paper presented at the Language Testing Research Colloquium, Cambridge, England, August 1–3.

Pollitt, A., & C. Hutchinson. 1987. Calibrating graded assessments: Rasch partial credit analysis of performance in writing. *Language Testing, 4*(1), 72–92.

Pollitt, A., C. Hutchinson, N. Entwhistle, & C. de Luca. 1985. *What makes exam questions difficult?* Edinburgh: Scottish Academic Press.

Pollitt, A., & N. Murray. 1996. What raters really pay attention to. In M. Milahovic and N. Saville (eds.), *Performance testing, cognition, and assessment.* Cambridge: University of Cambridge Local Examinations Syndicate/ Cambridge University Press.

Robinson, P. 1995. Task complexity and second language narrative discourse. *Language Learning, 45*(1), 99–140.

Robinson, P., S. C-C. Ting, & J. Urwin. 1995. Investigating second language task complexity. *RELC Journal, 26.*

Ross, S. 1997. An introspective approach to understanding inference in a second language listening test. In G. Kasper (ed.), *Communication strategies: Psycholinguistic and sociolinguistic perspectives.* London: Longman.

Rost, D. 1993. Assessing different components of reading comprehension: Fact or fiction? *Language Testing, 10*(1), 79–92.

Scharer, R., & B. North. 1992. *Towards a common framework for reporting language competency.* Washington, DC: National Foreign Language Center.

Sharwood Smith, M. 1993. Input enhancement in instructed SLA. *Studies in Second Language Acquisition, 15*(2), 165–179.

Shohamy, E., & O. Inbar. 1991. Construct validation of listening comprehension tests: The effect of text and question type. *Language Testing, 8*(1), 23–40.

Snow, C. E., H. Cancino, J. de Temple, & S. Schley. 1991. Giving formal definitions: A linguistic or metalinguistic skill. In E. Bialystok (ed.), *Language processing in bilingual children* (pp. 90–112). Cambridge: Cambridge University Press.

Spada, N., & P. Lightbown. 1993. Instruction and the development of questions in L2 classrooms. *Studies in Second Language Acquisition, 15*(2), 205–224.

Spolsky, B. 1995. *Measured words.* Oxford: Oxford University Press.

Swain, M. 1993. Second language testing and second language acquisition: Is there a conflict with traditional psychometrics? *Language Testing, 10*(2), 193–207.

Turner, C., & J. Upshur. 1995. Constructing rating scales for second language tests. *ELT Journal, 49*(1), 3–12.

University of Cambridge Local Examinations Syndicate (UCLES). 1990. *Certificates in Communicative Skills in English.* Cambridge: UCLES/RSA.

van Ek, J. 1987. *Objectives for foreign language learning. Levels* (Vol. 2). Strasbourg: Council for Cultural Co-operation.

Weir, C. J. 1983. Identifying the language problems of overseas students in tertiary education in the U.K. Doctoral dissertation, Institute of Education, University of London.

Weir, C. J., A. Hughes, & D. Porter. 1990. Reading skills: Hierarchies, implicational relationships and identifiability. *Reading in a Foreign Language, 7*(1), 505–510.

White, L. 1991. Adverb placement in second language acquisition: Some effects of positive and negative evidence in the classroom. *Second Language Research, 7*(2), 133–161.

White, L., N. Spada, P. Lightbown, & L. Ranta. 1991. Input enhancement and L2 question formation. *Applied Linguistics, 12*(4), 416–432.

Wolf, D., J. Bixby, J. Glenn, & H. Gardner. 1991. To use their minds well: New forms of student assessment. *Review of Research in Education, 17*, 31–74.

Wigglesworth, G. 1993. Exploring bias analysis as a tool for improving rater consistency in assessing oral interaction. *Language Testing, 10*(3), 305–336.

6 Testing methods in context-based second language research

Dan Douglas

In an important paper published over a quarter of a century ago, J. B. Carroll (1968) articulated very succinctly, albeit unintentionally, the relationship between language testing (LT) and second language acquisition (SLA) research by defining a test as "a procedure designed to elicit certain behavior from which one can make inferences about certain characteristics of an individual" (p. 6). If some of the "characteristics" include the linguistic (as they do), then the link between LT and SLA is clear: A language test is an SLA elicitation device. However, it has largely been the case that language testing concerns and SLA concerns have tended to develop in their separate ways. Part of the impetus for the present volume is the recognition that SLA and LT researchers have much to say to each other, and that insights and methods from both fields (and others within applied linguistics) are mutually beneficial.

In a discussion of mutual influences between SLA research and language testing, Bachman (1989; reprinted in the Appendix, this volume) notes a growing consensus among language testing researchers that language ability consists of a number of distinct but related component abilities. This multicomponential view of language ability, Bachman suggests, raises complex issues for SLA researchers, including the effect of context of language use on the development of different components of language proficiency. In this chapter I first consider the range of applications of the notion of "context" in LT and SLA research; second, I will argue that what really matters in investigating the effect of context in SLA and language testing is the learner's own construction and interpretation of contextual variables, and that, consequently, we may never know with any precision what the salient features of context are in any given communicative situation; and finally, I suggest how, in spite of this fundamental uncertainty, aspects of testing methods can be manipulated in LT and SLA research to engage the learner's internal construct of context in the elicitation of interlanguage.

141

Wrestling with "context" in LT and SLA research

Since the early 1980s, a recurring theme in second language acquisition studies has been the role of context both in the acquisition of the language code itself and in the development of communicative ability (for discussion see Ellis & Roberts 1987; Larsen-Freeman & Long 1991). *Context* has been defined in various ways by researchers, and has been associated with such notions as "situation," "setting," "domain," "environment," "task," "content," "topic," "schema," "frame," "script," and "background knowledge." Traditionally, context has been seen as containing both linguistic and extralinguistic elements, and both types of elements may be analyzed at a micro or a macro level. For example, a micro-linguistic analysis might focus on subjects' ability to supply plural morphemes in obligatory contexts, such as "There are two _____ in the nest," whereas a macro-linguistic analysis might focus on the discourse structure of an interaction and its effect on syntactic choice. A micro-situational analysis might be concerned with lexical choice with different interlocutors, whereas a macro-situational analysis might study learning in classrooms versus learning in "natural" settings. For the purposes of this discussion, I will collapse the distinction between linguistic and situational context as irrelevant to the main thesis, which is that context is a social-psychological construct that results from attention to a variety of external and internal factors.

There is no doubt that context does play a role in influencing language choice and acquisition; the problem has been arriving at a common understanding of the nature of context and what constitutes it, and then determining specifically how various contextual features influence language use and development. A confounding factor in achieving more specificity in the study of context and SLA has been a concomitant uncertainty about the nature of language knowledge itself. As has become clear in recent years through empirical studies conducted by language testers and others, language proficiency is multicomponential (see, e.g., Canale 1983; Sang, Schmitz, Vollmer, Baumert, & Roeder 1986; Bachman, 1990); however, what is extremely unclear is precisely what those components may be and how they interact in actual language use. There is a paradox here, in that in LT and SLA research, we are attempting to test something that we do not really have a firm understanding of. One is reminded of the so-called Apostle Principle articulated by Bruner (1978): "to learn something about a domain requires that you already know something about the domain" (p. 243). It seems clear that we are engaged in a boot-strapping exercise, wherein theory drives research, which informs theory, and so on.

The term *communicative competence* has been invoked since the early 1970s to encompass the notion that language competence involves more than Chomsky's (1965) rather narrowly defined "linguistic competence."

Hymes, with whose name communicative competence is most often associated, has pointed out that as the term came into general use in the various subdisciplines of linguistics, its meaning became somewhat fuzzy as a theoretical, technical term (Hymes 1985). As Hymes (1972) originally formulated the concept, communicative competence involves judgments about what is systemically possible, psycholinguistically feasible, and socioculturally appropriate, and about what is entailed in the actual accomplishment of a particular linguistic event. This latter point is of particular interest since it involves not only conscious and unconscious judgments within the control of the language user about how particular language tasks may be accomplished, but also includes events not within the user's control, thus bringing into the equation of language proficiency many situational and interactional factors that we normally think of as chance or serendipity but that form a part of the context of language acquisition and use (see Hornberger 1989 for a cogent discussion of this point). It is important to remember, too, that for Hymes, "competence" is more than grammatical knowledge; it has to do with rules for use: "Competence is dependent upon both [tacit] *knowledge* and [ability for] *use*" (Hymes 1972: 282; brackets and emphasis in original). Hymes's notion of competence is not an enhanced Chomskian competence; rather, it is a different species altogether: "Social life has affected not merely outward performance, but inner competence itself" (Hymes 1972: 274).

In considering the various aspects of context, scholars have listed a number of features, such as those in Hymes's own SPEAKING mnemonic:

Situation: physical and temporal setting, psychological and cultural scene
Participants: speaker/sender, addressor, hearer/receiver/audience, addressee
Ends: outcomes, goals
Act sequence: message form and message content
Key: tone, manner
Instrumentalities: channels, codes
Norms: norms of interaction, norms of interpretation
Genres: categories of speech events

(Hymes 1974)

Brown and Fraser (1979) offer a framework that divides situation into "scene," which consists of setting and purpose, and "participants," which looks at the relationship between the participants, who are seen both as individuals and as members of social categories. It seems clear that such situational factors as those set out by Hymes and Brown and Fraser derive from a number of different sources: societal and community values, social situations, role relationships, personal interactions, and linguistic resources. I have listed them here as a reminder that the notion of context is grounded in a complex interaction among physical, social, and psychological factors. In an article that presents a complex challenge to LT and SLA researchers, Hornberger (1989) describes an extended speech event in which she was a participant, involving her attempts to obtain a duplicate driving license, using her English/Spanish interlanguage. She employs Hymes's framework in her analysis, and refers to a number of situational variables that many would find irrelevant to language acquisition and use: the altitude of the Peruvian city she was in, the location of offices (e.g., on the roof of a building), an electrical blackout, the closing of a bank, a driver's license obtained eight years previously, the theft of the license at a religious festival, ongoing transportation strikes, and the presence of terrorists. However, Hornberger argues that the point of her analysis is that "the very essence of a communicative event [is] that it is situated in a real, physical, cultural, historical, and socio-economic context" (p. 228), and that these features all figured in the advancement of the acquisition of her own communicative competence in Spanish.

Context as a social-psychological construct

A context is not simply a collection of features imposed upon the learner/ user; it is also constructed by the participants in the communicative event. A salient feature of context is that it is dynamic, constantly changing, as a result of negotiation between and among the interactants as they construct it, turn by turn. It must be constantly borne in mind that context is not an object, but a dynamic social-psychological accomplishment, and that therefore, as Erickson and Shultz (1981) put it, in a paper instructively titled "When is a context?": "The production of appropriate social behavior from moment to moment requires knowing what context one is in and when contexts change *as well as* knowing what behavior is considered appropriate in each of those contexts" (p. 147; emphasis added). In the study of context and its effect upon second language acquisition and use, then, it is important to take account of those features of *external context* that participants attend to in constructing an *internal context* (with the proviso that we may never be able to know with any precision what those features are because such assessment is dynamic, internal, highly personal, and to some degree unconscious). Gumperz (1976) has referred to "contextualization cues" – changes in voice tone, pitch, tempo, rhythm, code, topic, style, posture, gaze, and facial expression – which are culturally conventional, highly redundant signals that interactants attend to in their mutual construction of context. For example, a study of contextualization cues used, and not used, by an elementary school teacher suggested that the pupils attended to the teacher's use of explicit formulations, paralinguistic shifts in speech rate and volume, and framing words, and that when the teacher employed such cues (largely unconsciously), the transition from context to context occurred smoothly (Dorr-Bremme 1990). However, in the instances where the cues were absent, the context remained unestablished for some period and the interactions were marked by uncertainty, confusion, and chaos on the part of the children and the teacher. Though researchers can analyze communicative events of groups with respect to certain contextualization cues to see what effect the presence or absence of the cues seems to have upon the development of the discourse, it remains true, owing to individual variation in attention and schematic expectations and to redundancy in the cuing system, that we can never be sure that individuals are all attending to the same cues, or that the absence of one type of cue is the factor that leads to particular observed twists and turns of discourse.

It is worth reconsidering the issue of redundancy in contextualization cues. Erickson and Shultz (1981) suggest that redundancy makes it more likely that interactants will "get the message" that something new is happening, in spite of "differences in interactional competence, whether due to difference in culture, to personality, or to level of acquisition of competence . . . and despite differences in individual variation in focus of attention at any given moment" (p. 150). Quite apart from the obvious LT/SLA research area concerning acquisition of an ability to recognize and act upon contextualization cues in a second language, there are two other issues relevant to LT and SLA research here. First, it needs to be investigated whether redundancy in contextualization cues does in fact tend to mask learner differences, as Erickson and Schultz claim. This is an important research issue, since learner differences are what researchers in LT and SLA are attempting to investigate in the first place. If natural language is so highly redundant that learners will "get the message," then the use of natural, or authentic, language in research might not allow for the teasing out of particular aspects of interlanguage competence researchers require. One is reminded of Widdowson's (1990) suggestion that the most authentic language may not be the most useful for learning and that the language used in the classroom, rather than conforming to a criterion of natural language use, might rather conform to a criterion of natural processes of language learning derivable from SLA research. Certainly, questions concerning the effect of natural/authentic language on, and its effectiveness in, LT and SLA research are themselves researchable, and part of the purpose of this chapter is to call for such research. Experimental methods could be used to investigate whether learners of varying levels of second language acquisition can recognize changes in context in natural communicative situations, and whether natural redundancy in contextualization cues does in fact wash out individual variation.

Second, the redundancy in contextual cues means it will be difficult to determine exactly what features of a context are critical; there is probably a "threshold," a cumulative effect of cues, that determines for an individual what is going on, and this will vary both from individual to individual and from time to time. One aspect of this issue, and a crucial one, is that if what "counts" in the complex of contextualization cues is which of them the interactant attends to, then what really "counts" in the analyst's consideration of context is how the interactant *interprets* it. Thus, we are compelled, it seems, toward an internal view of context as a cognitive construct created by language users for the interpretation and production of language.

Discourse domains

Selinker and Douglas (1985) proposed the notion of discourse domain to clearly distinguish the idea of external features of context from the *internal interpretation* of them in the learner. More recently they have defined discourse domain as a cognitive construct created by a language learner as a context for interlanguage development and use (Douglas & Selinker 1989, 1995). This notion embodies the ideas presented earlier that what we need information about is what features of external context "count" for the learners as they proceed with the tasks of analysis and synthesis in the acquisition process.

In an article on principles for language tests within the discourse domains theory, Douglas and Selinker (1985) hypothesized that language test takers create intelligibility in language tests either by engaging already-existing discourse domains or by creating temporary domains for the purpose of "making sense" of a test item. This notion is related to a long-held suspicion that test takers may not be interpreting the test items in the way intended by the test constructors. Cohen (Chapter 4, this volume) provides numerous examples of test takers getting an item wrong for the right reasons or right for the wrong reasons, and presents a strong case for the use of verbal reports in the understanding of test-taking strategies. A number of studies (Douglas & Pettinari 1983; Selinker & Douglas 1985; Rounds 1987; Douglas & Selinker 1989, 1991, 1993) have employed a related approach based upon ethnomethodology and subject-specialist informant procedures (see Selinker & Douglas, 1989; Douglas & Selinker 1994) to investigate context-based interlanguage use and development.

Discourse domains, then, establish for the language user what the external context "counts as" and then serve as input to goal-setting and planning processes in which the components of language competence required to deal with the situation are brought into play. The interactions among the components are weighted differentially on a continuum of "domain strength," which is established by familiarity, depth of knowledge, affective factors, personality variables, and probably a number of other currently unspecified factors.

It is worth a short excursus to place the notion of discourse domain in the larger context of other hypotheses about interpreting and responding to context, namely, those involving strategic competence (e.g., Canale & Swain 1980; Canale 1983; Bachman 1990). The description of strategies in Faerch and Kasper (1983) concerns communicative strategies. Faerch and Kasper talk about setting communicative goals and carrying out communicative plans. Clearly, this is an important set of strategies for second language acquisition researchers to take note of. Assessment procedures use basic cognitive processes to access the language knowledge needed to comprehend the communicative situation and identify the appropriate discourse domain. The subject's discourse domain, which may or may not be in concert with what an interlocutor or researcher intended, affects subsequent strategies. It is used by the goal-setting process, which determines the *communicative goal:* what the person's communicative objective will be. The goal may be either production or comprehension. The communicative goal is the input for the planning procedure, which constructs a *communicative plan* for accomplishing the goal. That plan is carried out by an execution procedure, which will result in either comprehension of linguistic input or production of linguistic output, depending on the goal. The subject must then control the execution of the plan (Bialystok 1990) by making a *communicative response:* retrieving appropriate knowledge, organizing it, and employing appropriate psychophysiological mechanisms (Bachman 1990). Whether the result is comprehended meanings or produced language, it serves as additional input to the assessment procedure, which will update its assessment of the situation. Thus, discourse domain is seen to be a part of the strategic component of communicative language ability. (This discussion may be found in more detail in Chapelle & Douglas 1993.)

This formulation leads to a hypothesis of individual variation in interpretation; that is, language learners/users might respond to features of external context differentially, and, from the point of view of "language community" or "native speaker," perhaps erroneously. The result might be, for example, interpreting an approach by a colleague as a bid to engage in "work talk" when in fact the colleague had in mind a casual conversation of a more social nature. This mismatch in domains might lead to serious misunderstanding, frustration, hurt feelings, or simply a difficult time getting the conversation off the ground. An example of this sort of miscommunication can be found in the field manual for the study of second language acquisition by adult immigrants (Perdue 1984). In a role-played interview between a prospective employer and an Asian industrial trainee, the following exchange took place:

Interviewer: Can you tell me about the welding that you learnt?
Trainee: Yes, there is a – acetylene welding, acetylene gas welding and electronic welding.
Interviewer: hm – sorry – and – what?

(Perdue 1984: 77)

The interviewer was attempting to find out what the trainee himself had learned about welding and specifically what experience he had had. The trainee interpreted the question as a sort of examination question and formed his answer in that genre. In other words, the interlocutors did not agree on an interpretation of the context, and this led to a communication breakdown.

Another source of variation, it can be hypothesized, would be in making the link between the discourse domain and units of communicative competence. Once a language learner/user had settled upon an interpretation, relevant aspects of communicative competence would be brought to bear in response, whether for comprehension or for production. In Hymes's terms, the interpretation of the context would interact with judgments of what was formally possible, feasible, and appropriate and what the accomplishment of the communicative event would entail. A learner might not possess the grammatical, psycholinguistic, or sociolinguistic "wherewithal" to carry out the linguistic task, or be able to employ effective strategies for dealing with the situation. An example comes from the SPEAK test, based on the Test of Spoken English (Educational Testing Service 1983). A Chinese test taker, responding to the instruction to "describe a bicycle in as much detail as you can," produced the following answer:

A bicycle consist of a – two wheels – one by – and a one triangle – and two pedals – a chain – and a seat – in in China – most of a – bicycle – have a ring – on the bar (Fagundes 1989: 71)

In this case, the learner knew what was required in the situation but lacked the linguistic knowledge – lexis, for the most part – to carry it out. Thus, he offers "one by [one]" for *one in front of the other,* "a one triangle" for *triangular frame,* "ring" for *bell,* and "bar" for *handlebar.*

It is also possible, given Hymes's notion that competence includes both "knowledge" and "ability," for the units of competence to be present, but for the learner/user to lack the ability to employ them. As Widdowson (1989) suggests, an individual might possess knowledge of, say, appropriacy, but lack the ability to *be appropriate.* This notion is related, too, to the distinction between competence and control made by Bialystok and Sharwood Smith (1985).

With regard to the link between the discourse domain and communicative competence, there is a kind of affective factor that can influence the outcome, as well. The effectiveness and accuracy of comprehension and production would reflect the variable interaction among the components of competence, which in turn would be determined by "domain strength," or, we might say, by how comfortable, knowledgeable, and in control the language user felt about the interpretation. A result of discomfort might be rhetorical/grammatical inaccuracy, a sociolinguistically inappropriate response, a lack of precision, or a lack of cohesion. On the other hand, a high degree of comfort with the interpretation could produce more accuracy, precision, and so on, even (and this is crucial) if the interpretation were "wrong." It is quite common for a language learner/user to "get the wrong end of the stick," as we say, and rattle along for quite a while under a deviant set of assumptions about what the context is. Oller (1979) cites examples of this sort of problem in dictation test data (e.g., "person in facts" for "pertinent facts").

Testing methods in context-based second language research

I wish to conclude this discussion with suggestions for how to manipulate testing methods in LT and SLA research to engage the learner's internal discourse domain in the elicitation of interlanguage. I have argued that this is important in LT and SLA research because tests, as defined by Carroll (1968) in the passage quoted at the beginning of this chapter, represent an important part of our common research methodology. Furthermore, the effect of context, as defined in the body of this chapter, on the development and use of second language is a central issue in current LT and SLA research.

Douglas and Selinker (1991, 1993) have explored this area in two empirical studies in which the goal was to investigate the effect of manipulating test method facets (Bachman 1990) – such as the instructions, vocabulary, contextualization, distribution of information, level of abstraction, topic, and genre – on outcomes. Briefly, it was found that a different combination of contextual features in mathematics and chemistry versions of a speaking test produced not only measurement results different from those produced by a "general" test, but differences in the rhetorical structure of candidates' responses as well. It is important to note in this regard that Douglas and Selinker did *not* find that language performances on the context-based tests were necessarily more complex or targetlike than those on the more general tests. That is, when performing a language test task in their own field of study, examinees will not necessarily produce "better" language – but they will produce *different* language, allowing score users to make a more useful interpretation of the performance in terms of a candidate's language ability for the specific purposes they are interested in. Continuing with the findings of Douglas and Selinker, raters of the speech protocols seemed to be rating a category of "rhetorical complexity" but calling it "grammar," since this was the only relevant category available. This was evident only in subsequent rhetorical/grammatical interlanguage analyses. Finally, evidence was found (albeit inconclusively) that the field-specific tests provided a measurement advantage over the general test in predicting judges' ratings of candidates' suitability for assignment to teaching duties, using the results of a performance test as a criterion. Perhaps the most important outcome of this research has been the realization that the job of producing contextualized language tests that present relevant features of context to engage discourse domains in test takers is going to be punishingly difficult.

A number of other empirical studies in recent years have also explored the interaction between aspects of context and interlanguage proficiency, though from different perspectives. In an investigation of the effect of learners' field of study on reading comprehension, Alderson and Urquhart (1985) found that their subjects were disadvantaged in responding to "overview" questions (e.g., "Which sentence best summarizes the passage?") when they were not familiar with the content area of the passage. In a study of a similar nature on the TOEFL reading subtest, Hale (1988) found a significant but small effect of background knowledge on test performance. Finally, in another large-scale study of the effect of background knowledge, Clapham (1996) found a significant interaction between test performance and background knowledge *when the reading passages were sufficiently field specific,* and *when subjects' level of reading proficiency was sufficiently high to be able to respond to the content.*

In the area of speaking tests, Smith (1992) found a significant difference in performance on a general test and a mathematics field-specific test, in favor of the mathematics test, although, at the same time, she found no differences between performance on the general test and either chemistry or physics field-specific tests. She speculates that this finding may be due to a somewhat higher overall English proficiency level among the mathematics subjects, a notion that is in concert with Clapham's findings. Zuengler and Bent (1991) investigated patterns of conversational participation between native (NS) and nonnative (NNS) speaker interlocutors, and found that relative control of content knowledge had a significant influence on conversational involvement. They conclude that "relative content knowledge should be recognized as an important dynamic affecting many NS-NNS conversations" (p. 410).

With regard to writing assessment, Read (1990) found that "experience" writing tasks, in which learners were given the opportunity to study relevant content material before producing their writing, did not result in significantly superior writing over traditional "free composition" tasks. Read's subjects, though, were not familiar with the content area before the "experience" task was begun. A study by Tedick (1990), however, was designed to explore whether writing tasks related to subjects' field of study would produce superior writing when compared with general writing tasks. On the basis of holistic scores, length, and T-unit analyses, Tedick did find the field-specific writing to be superior.

In summary, these studies point out the complex nature of the interaction between aspects of external context and language ability: Background knowledge, an important learner internal factor in invoking discourse domains, is relevant to second language performance only when the external context is sufficiently rich and when the learner's level of acquisition is sufficiently high so as to be able to respond to the context. It would appear that there is some "threshold" of contextual specificity (Bachman 1991 has suggested the term *situational authenticity*) required to trigger engagement of a relevant discourse domain in an interlanguage learner, and that there is a similar threshold of interlanguage development necessary before the learner can effectively respond to differences in context. It is clear that much more research is necessary to determine with any kind of precision what the nature of the relationship is and how it affects our interpretation of test and research results. Clapham's (1996) study is particularly provocative. In her investigation of the relationship between background knowledge and reading proficiency level, she found no significant relationship among students at a low reading proficiency level and a greater subject effect as students became more proficient at reading. In an earlier paper on the same study, Clapham speculates,

It might be that low level students are so desperately trying to make sense of the grammar and vocabulary in a text that they are not able to bring background knowledge to bear, or perhaps their English is so poor that they do not yet distinguish between specialist and non-specialist expressions. On the other hand, further up the proficiency scale, where students have good enough English to be competent at reading passages in their own subject area, they may not yet be able to cope so well with texts in other areas. (Clapham 1991: 8)

Clapham worries that such a finding as hers is "contrary to received wisdom," apparently alluding to a compensatory model of reading comprehension (e.g., Stanovich 1980), but, as she rightly goes on to say, much more research is needed on the interaction between background knowledge and language proficiency. We simply do not know enough about the component abilities and how they interact. For example, in a study of field-specific reading tests for chemical engineering students, Hudson (1993) found little evidence for sharply defined, separable reading skills, except at the lowest ability levels, and suggests that a compensatory model of reading, based on a notion of hierarchical levels, may need modification.

To make further progress in understanding the nature of second language acquisition, then, language test developers need to operationalize the notion of context in their tests. As a way of doing so in LT and SLA research, we can follow Bachman's (1990) conclusions on the method effect in testing theory: "While it is generally recognized that [specification of the task or test domain] involves the specification of the ability domain, what is often ignored is that examining content relevance also requires the specification of the test method facets" (p. 244). I would argue (see Douglas & Selinker 1991) that any factor one changes in the test environment – personnel, physical conditions, time, organization, instructions, level of precision, propositional content, and so on – can lead to changes in learner perceptions and assessment of a communicative situation, and thus to changes in interlanguage performance on a test. Douglas and Selinker (1991) have related the concept of discourse domains in SLA to that of contextualization cues in ethnomethodology (Gumperz 1976) and hence to the concept of test method facets in language testing (Bachman 1990). Thus, seen from this perspective, test method facets in language tests are the functional equivalent to contextualization cues in natural language use.

As a way of summarizing, I offer the following suggestions concerning testing methods as guidelines for context-based LT and SLA research:

1. Any factor researchers change in the test domain can lead to changes in an interlanguage user's perceptions and assessment of the communicative situation, and thus to changes in interlanguage performance on the test.
2. Rather than attempting to minimize the effects of test method facets on the interpretation of results, LT and SLA researchers should make use of them to design tests for particular populations.
3. Context-based language tests (i.e., those designed with the express intent of engaging specific discourse domains) can be constructed by manipulating a number of test method facets, such as test environment (administration, personnel, and location), instructions (domain-specific reasons for carrying out the test tasks), and language (subtechnical as well as technical language, context-embedded discourse, level of precision, field-specific topic, authentic genre, and pragmatic and sociolinguistic domain-related features).
4. There is likely to be a threshold level of context-based method facets, or situational authenticity, necessary for domain engagement, and a corresponding threshold level of communicative competence necessary to respond to the context.
5. Subjects taking context-based tests will be more likely, as a result of domain engagement, to focus on content than on form.
6. Context-based test tasks may be inherently more complex than those on general purpose tests.
7. The interlanguage produced by subjects taking context-based tests will not necessarily be more complex or even more targetlike, compared with that produced in general tests, but performance on context-based tests will allow for interpretation of language ability for specific purposes.
8. Raters or judges of context-based tests may need to have some sense of the content accuracy of responses, and may rate context-based test

responses more conservatively as a function of not knowing how accurate the responses are.

9. Rhetorical/grammatical interlanguage analysis may be necessary to disambiguate gross subjective ratings on context-based tests.

10. Context-based tests may provide more useful information than general purpose tests when the goal is to make field-specific judgments about subjects' interlanguage communicative competence.

To conclude, with regard to the focus on test method as a distinguishing factor in performance, we should consider a notion discussed by Bachman (1990) as "the dilemma of language testing" – that language is both the object and the instrument of measurement. For Bachman, a way out of the dilemma is to understand more explicitly both the nature of language ability and the nature of test methods, so that we can "minimize the effect of test method" in the interpretation of results as indicators of language abilities. The perspective in this paper is focused differently: Rather than attempting to *minimize* the method effects, I have argued that we need to *capitalize* on them by designing tests for specific populations – tests that contain instructions, content, genre, and language directed toward that population. The goal is to produce tests, useful to both LT and SLA professionals, that would provide information interpretable as evidence of communicative competence in context.

References

Alderson, J. C., & A. H. Urquhart. 1985. The effect of students' academic discipline on their performance on ESP reading tests. *Language Testing, 2,* 192–204.

Bachman, L. F. 1989. Language testing–SLA research interfaces. *Annual Review of Applied Linguistics, 9,* 193–209.

Bachman, L. F. 1990. *Fundamental considerations in language testing.* Oxford: Oxford University Press.

Bachman, L. F. 1991. What does language testing have to offer? *TESOL Quarterly, 25*(4), 671–704.

Bialystok, E. 1990. *Communication strategies: A psychological analysis of second-language use.* Oxford: Blackwell.

Bialystok, E., & M. Sharwood Smith. 1985. Interlanguage is not a state of mind: An evaluation of the construct for second language acquisition. *Applied Linguistics, 6,* 101–117.

Brown, P., & C. Fraser. 1979. Speech as a marker of situation. In K. Scherer & H. Giles (eds.), *Social markers in speech* (pp. 33–62). Cambridge: Cambridge University Press.

Bruner, J. S. 1978. The role of dialogue in language acquisition. In R. J. Jarvella, W. J. M. Levelt, & A. Sinclair (eds.), *The child's conception of language* (pp. 241–256). Berlin: Springer Verlag.

Canale, M. 1983. From communicative competence to communicative language pedagogy. In J. C. Richards & R. W. Schmidt (eds.), *Language and communication* (pp. 2–25). London: Longman.

Canale, M., & M. Swain. 1980. Theoretical bases of communicative approaches to second language teaching and testing. *Applied Linguistics, 8,* 67–84.

Carroll, J. B. 1968. The psychology of language testing. In A. Davies (ed.), *Language testing symposium: A psycholinguistic perspective* (pp. 46–69). London: Oxford University Press.

Chapelle, C., & D. Douglas. 1993. Interpreting L2 performance data. Paper presented at the Second Language Research Colloquium, Pittsburgh, PA, March.

Chomsky, N. 1965. *Aspects of the theory of syntax.* Cambridge, MA: MIT Press.

Clapham, C. 1991. The effect of academic discipline on reading test performance. Paper presented at the Language Testing Research Colloquium, Princeton, NJ, March.

Clapham, C. 1996. *The development of IELTS: A study of the effect of background knowledge on reading comprehension.* Cambridge: Cambridge University Press.

Dorr-Bremme, D. W. 1990. Contextualization cues in the classroom: Discourse regulation and social control functions. *Language in Society, 19,* 379–402.

Douglas, D., and C. Pettinari, 1983. Psychiatric interview training modules: A grounded ethnography approach to needs analysis in ESP. Paper presented at the annual TESOL Convention, Toronto, March.

Douglas, D., & L. Selinker. 1985. Principles for language tests within the "discourse domains" theory of interlanguage: Research, test construction and interpretation. *Language Testing, 2,* 205–226.

Douglas, D., & L. Selinker. 1989. Markedness in discourse domains: Native and non-native teaching assistants. *Papers in Applied Linguistics, 1,* 69–82.

Douglas, D., & L. Selinker. 1991. SPEAK and CHEMSPEAK: Measuring the English speaking ability of international teaching assistants in chemistry. Paper presented at the Language Testing Research Colloquium, Princeton, NJ, March.

Douglas, D., & L. Selinker. 1993. Performance on a general versus a field-specific test of speaking proficiency by international teaching assistants. In D. Douglas & C. Chapelle (eds.), *A new decade of language testing research* (pp. 235–254). Alexandria, VA: TESOL.

Douglas, D., & L. Selinker. 1994. Research methodology in context-based second language research. In E. E. Tarone, S. M. Gass, & A. D. Cohen (eds.), *Research methodology in second-langauge acquisition* (pp. 119–131). Hillsdale, NJ: Lawrence Erlbaum.

Educational Testing Service. 1983. *Test of spoken English.* Princeton, NJ: ETS.

Ellis, R., & C. Roberts. 1987. Two approaches for investigating second language acquisition. In R. Ellis (ed.), *Second language acquisition in context* (pp. 3–30). London: Prentice-Hall.

Erickson, F., & J. Shultz. 1981. When is a context? Some issues in the analysis of social competence. In J. Green & C. Wallat (eds.), *Advances in Discourse Processes. Ethnography and language in educational settings* (Vol. 5, pp. 147–160). Norwood, NJ: Ablex.

Faerch, C., & G. Kasper. 1983. Plans and strategies in foreign language communication. In C. Faerch & G. Kasper (eds.), *Strategies in interlanguage communication* (pp. 20–60). London: Longman.

Fagundes, R. 1989. Strategies used in the SPEAK test: A discourse analysis. Master's thesis, Iowa State University, Ames.

Gumperz, J. J. 1976. Language, communication and public negotiation. In P. R. Sanday (ed.), *Anthropology and the public interest* (pp. 273–292). New York: Academic Press.

Hale, G. A. 1988. Student major field and text content: Interactive effects on reading comprehension in the Test of English as a Foreign Language. *Language Testing, 5*, 49–61.

Hornberger, N. H. 1989. *Tramites* and *transportes:* The acquisition of second language communicative competence for one speech event in Puno, Peru. *Applied Linguistics, 10*, 214–230.

Hudson, T. 1993. Testing the specificity of ESP reading skills. In D. Douglas & C. Chapelle (eds.), *A new decade of language testing research* (pp. 58–82). Alexandria, VA: TESOL.

Hymes, D. 1972. On communicative competence. In J. B. Pride & J. Holmes (eds.), *Sociolinguistics* (pp. 269–293). Harmondsworth: Penguin.

Hymes, D. 1974. *Foundations in sociolinguistics: An ethnographic approach.* Philadelphia: University of Pennsylvania Press.

Hymes, D. 1985. Toward linguistic competence. *AILA Review, 2*, 9–23.

Larsen-Freeman, D., & M. H. Long, 1991. *An introduction to second language acquisition research.* London: Longman.

Oller, J. 1979. *Language tests at school.* London: Longman.

Perdue, C. (ed.). 1984. *Second language acquisition by adult immigrants: A field manual.* Rowley, MA.: Newbury House.

Read, J. 1990. Providing relevant content in an EAP writing test. *English for Specific Purposes, 9*, 109–122.

Rounds, P. 1987. Characterizing successful classroom discourse for NNS teaching assistant training. *TESOL Quarterly, 21*, 643–671.

Sang, F., B. Schmitz, H. J. Vollmer, J. Baumert, & P. M. Roeder. 1986. Models of second language competence: A structural approach. *Language Testing, 3*, 54–79.

Selinker, L.,. & D. Douglas. 1985. Wrestling with "context" in interlanguage theory. *Applied Linguistics, 6*, 190–204.

Selinker, L., & D. Douglas. 1989. Research methodology in contextually-based second language research. *Second Language Research, 5*, 93–126.

Smith, J. A. 1992. Topic and variation in the oral proficiency of international teaching assistants. Doctoral dissertation, Department of Linguistics, University of Minnesota.

Stanovich, K. E. 1980. Toward an interactive-compensatory model of individual differences in the development of reading fluency. *Reading Research Quarterly, 17*, 157–159.

Tedick, D. J. 1990. ESL writing assessment: Subject-matter knowledge and its impact on performance. *English for Specific Purposes, 9*, 123–144.

Widdowson, H. G. 1989. Knowledge of language and ability for use. *Applied Linguistics, 10*, 128–137.

Widdowson, H. G. 1990. *Aspects of language teaching.* London: Oxford University Press.

Zuengler, J., & B. Bent. 1991. Relative knowledge of content domain: An influence on native–non-native conversations. *Applied Linguistics, 12*, 397–415.

7 How can language testing and SLA benefit from each other? The case of discourse

Elana Shohamy

Second language acquisition (SLA) and second language testing (LT) both focus on "what" and "how" issues of language: SLA is concerned with what the learner's language is at a given point and how further language can best be acquired, and LT is concerned with what language ability (knowledge) is and how it can best be measured. This chapter examines the extent to which each discipline can benefit from advances made in the other, using the example of discourse. It begins by focusing on the contribution of LT to SLA, with emphasis on the following areas: (a) defining the construct of language ability, (b) applying findings from LT to confirm and/or test SLA hypotheses, and (c) providing SLA researchers with quality criteria for tests and tasks. We then turn to the contribution of SLA to LT, focusing on: (a) identifying the language components that need to be elicited, (b) proposing innovative tasks that can be used for language assessment, and (c) informing language testers about language variations so tests can be constructed accordingly. Each of these contributions is discussed using the case of discourse.

Contributions of LT to SLA

Defining the construct of language ability

While SLA researchers have focused on the description of the learner's language, language testers have concentrated on the definitions and theory of language ability. Valid theories of language ability can be useful for SLA researchers in examining the validity of the findings about second language acquisition, that is, the extent to which the second language has actually been acquired.

Since the 1980s language testers have made theories and definitions of language ability the most important focus of discussion, the rationale being that a clear identification of the construct and structure of language

Some sections of this chapter relating to discourse analysis are based on Shohamy (1990); sections on the connection between SLA and LT appeared in Shohamy (1994a).

ability will make it possible to design tests to match such descriptions. Work in this area has been conducted by a number of LT researchers. Oller (1979, 1983), for example, defined language ability as a unitary factor underlying language behavior competence, based on the learner's expectancy grammar and operationalized through integrative tests such as cloze and dictation. Canale and Swain (1980) hypothesized that language competence comprised linguistic, sociolinguistic, discourse, and strategic competencies, implying that a valid measure of language needed to include these components. They were the first to give special attention to discourse competence as a separate component within communicative competence, and defined it as the ability to process language at a level beyond that of a single sentence, enabling participation in conversations and processing of written texts of some size. The main question concerning the construct of language ability was whether discourse could be considered an independent component along with the other proposed components.

Since the relationship between discourse and other components of language competence was not entirely clear, a number of studies were carried out to examine this question. One such validation study failed to confirm the hypothesized four-trait structure of language proficiency (Harley et al. 1990). Other studies also failed to find support for the separate existence of a discourse component (Swain 1985; Milanovic 1988; Harley et al. 1990). In response to the negative findings of the Harley et al. (1990) study, it was pointed out that the discourse trait was not well defined and that discourse knowledge of text seems to be closer to microsociolinguistic knowledge (Schachter 1990). Since, according to Schachter, discourse knowledge involves both cultural conventions and appropriate grammatical choices, this component of knowledge has been referred to as textual knowledge and, to some extent, as pragmatic knowledge as well. Schachter found a number of items used to test discourse in the Harley et al. study problematic because it was not clear which trait the items actually represented. In fact, she contended that the status of the discourse component would become clear, not from tests attempting to validate it, but rather from more clearly delineated theoretical models. In another reaction to Harley et al.'s study, Bachman (1990a) claimed that the discourse instruments in the study were questionable because the definition of discourse conflated formal and functional aspects of discourse. Final conclusions about the independence of discourse in this framework of language ability could not be made.

Building on the seminal work of Canale and Swain (1980), Bachman (1990b) described a framework of language ability that consisted of a number of components, concentrating on organizational and pragmatic competencies. In this model, there was a component similar to discourse competence that he termed *textual competence*. He hypothesized that textual competence was separate from grammatical competence and included "knowledge of the conventions for joining utterances together to form a text, which is essentially a unit of language – spoken or written – consisting of two or more utterances or sentences that are structured according to rules of cohesion and rhetorical organization" (p. 88). Although Bachman's model has not yet been fully validated (i.e., empirical data indicating the independence of textual competence are not available and there is no definite answer as to the question of the relationship between discourse and the other components that make up the structure of language ability), it is widely accepted nowadays among both language testers and a large number of SLA researchers as a framework for guiding research. It can therefore be considered a working model in the construction of valid language tests and in conducting SLA research.

These models and frameworks have expanded the scope of language testing theory by offering a broader view of language competence, and thus can provide a significant contribution to SLA theory that can be used by SLA researchers to examine the validity of their findings. Yet there may be a problem with the potential contribution of LT to SLA in defining the construct of language ability, as testers have relied almost exclusively on tests for validating their theories, whereas language competence – a broader and more complex construct – needs to be examined through a variety of procedures. For example, it is likely that language learners behave differently in test and nontest situations. One study claims that writing an essay for a test requires a different set of strategies and skills (e.g., decisions about audience, purpose, style, tone, length) than writing for nontest situations (Connor & Carrell 1991). Consequently, there is a need for language testers to validate theories of language ability via procedures that are less "testlike" (e.g., observations of natural behaviors, documents, interviews).

Moreover, recently a major change has been taking place in the language testing field, as language testers employ not only tests but a variety of different types of assessment procedures. Thus, it is not uncommon to see language samples that are obtained via procedures such as observations, portfolios, self-assessment, and a variety of performance tasks. In fact, the use of such alternative procedures increases the potential for language testing to contribute further to SLA. Hence, while in the past testers attempted to identify what knowing a language meant only in testing situations and viewed performance on tests as a subset of general language ability or in the context of discourse only in testing situations, current practices of alternative assessment make it more likely that these models can be used effectively in SLA research.

The recent trend toward performance testing, as a means of alternative assessment, may eventually provide better and more expanded definitions of language ability. McNamara (1996), for example, claims that there is a need for a broader concept of communicative competence, consisting of variables that relate language to other cognitive and affective areas. These areas would include subject matter knowledge, integration of language knowledge with other performances, communication skills, personalities, gender of the communicators, and attitudes and beliefs, as well as other variables that affect the communication process. It is likely that such expanded models and theories can be useful to SLA researchers in defining language constructs.

Applying LT findings to test SLA hypotheses

Despite continuing controversy over the construct of language ability in language testing, LT researchers do have findings about language behavior from tests that can be useful to SLA researchers for generating, testing, or confirming SLA hypotheses. For example, through the analysis of phenomena such as differential item functioning (DIF), it is possible to identify groups of language learners for whom specific test items function differently (Pollitt 1991; Ryan & Bachman 1992). This procedure is especially powerful with tests such as the TOEFL (Test of English as a Foreign Language), where it is possible to observe such differences in performance across groups. For example, one study showed that differences in the performance of native speakers of several Asian languages on individual items were related to differences in their respective first languages (Ryan & Bachman 1992). Pollitt (1991) reports on a study in which a group with a certain first language (L1) performed differently on a language test than did groups of test takers using other languages. This study also identified biases in specific test items based on L1 differences. These kinds of data can be instrumental in confirming and testing hypotheses, such as the differential success in test taking of respondents from different language and SLA backgrounds (i.e., formal vs. informal, processes of language development, different teaching methods).

There are numerous LT studies that examine how specific discourse features manifest themselves in testing situations. Findings on discourse by type, domain, style, and processing can provide useful information about the role of discourse in testing situations. In a representative study on discourse types, for example, Douglas and Selinker (1985, 1990) investigated the effect of subject matter scores on reading comprehension test scores. Their research demonstrates how performance can vary according to choice of topic (e.g., professional specialization vs. everyday subjects). They found that familiarity with the content domain affected performance and, as a result, the nature and fluency of communication. They concluded that generalizations from one discourse domain to another on language tests may not be justified. Another study tested comprehension difficulties in reading scientific discourse that contained implicit and explicit definitions and found differences in scores depending on the type of definition (Flick 1980). Although both types of information were difficult to comprehend, the difference in scores remained the same even when proficiency increased.

On oral tests that represented different discourse styles and genres, studies have found significant differences in the scores according to whether the respondent was engaged in an interview or a reporting task, for example (Shohamy 1983). In another study on discourse styles, it was found that the interview, which represented a specific discourse style, did not provide a valid assessment of other discourse styles, such as discussion and report, or of a variety of speech acts, as exemplified in role-play situations (Shohamy, Reves, & Bejarano 1986). Only moderate correlations were obtained between scores of test takers who took tests representing these discourse genres. Yet another study (Shohamy & Inbar 1991) investigated the effect of different genres along the oral-written continuum on test takers' listening comprehension scores, controlling for the topic across the genres (Ong 1982). Three types of discourse styles were selected for the research – an interview (characterized by a large number of "oral features"), a short lecture (characterized by a mixture of oral and written features), and a news broadcast (characterized by mostly written features). The results revealed significant differences among test takers' scores on each of the discourse types, despite identical content. The interview resulted in the highest scores, followed by the lecture; the news broadcast resulted in the lowest scores, thus coinciding with the oral-written continuum. Yet Clapham (1994) examined the effect of background knowledge on English for academic purposes reading test performance on the IELTS (International English Language Testing Service) test and found no such effect.

Some discourse processing studies have examined the transfer of discourse competence and features from L1 to L2 tests. One study looked at the transfer of organizational features in writing from L1 to L2 and found that organizational structure did transfer (Vignola & Wesche 1991). A similar finding was obtained by Cumming (1990). In their validation study of discourse tasks, Harley et al. (1990) found that the discourse coherence scores of immersion students were close or equivalent to those of the native speakers (unlike the other aspects of competence that they investigated), and that there were relatively few significant between-group differences. The nativelike performance of second language learners in coherence can be explained by their ability to transfer discourse competence already gained via their first language.

Research on discourse processing is also reported by Jonz (1987, 1989, 1991), who experimented with a discourse-type cloze test. He found that nonnative speakers' scores on a cohesion-based test showed that they were far less able to cope with the loss of redundant cohesive information than were native speakers. However, when such information was available, nonnatives employed it comparatively more than did native speakers. On cloze tests, nonnative speakers appeared to rely far more on text in comprehension than did natives. Discourse adaptation to the audience has also been examined among L1 respondents (Rubin 1982). The research demonstrated the effect of audience adaptation and social cognitive abilities on the syntactic strategies employed by different age groups in tasks requiring persuasive discourse. Findings showed that older writers adapted their discourse to the audience more than younger ones. Discourse adaption has been examined by Spolsky (1994), who claimed that different discourse interpretations of tests may come from the miscomprehension of different sources.

In discourse processing on L1 reading comprehension tests, one study showed that the customary discourse genres on tests represented a genre that was used only on standardized tests (Fillmore 1981). Further, the procedures for processing such discourse types differed from those that learners normally used in nontest reading situations. For example, readers referred to the test questions as guides to information in the text.

Other studies have examined textual processing on L2 reading comprehension tests via different question types – multiple choice and open ended – presented in both L1 and L2 (Shohamy 1984; Gordon 1987). Each study found significant differences in the test takers' scores. It was shown that the strategies test takers utilized in processing discourse were heavily dependent on the type of discourse of the question. Specifically, the multiple choice form, consisting of a statement plus a number of additional statements (the alternatives), represented a special text type that readers processed differently.

A number of studies have examined the type of discourse features produced on oral tests. Van Lier (1989) called for examination of the oral interview test with respect to the extent to which the interview resembles conversation – in degree of planning, predictability of sequence of outcomes, equal distribution of rights and duties to talk, and other conversational principles. He provided examples of various degrees of planning that enter certain discourse styles and that may be responsible for pragmatic failure in oral proficiency testing interactions. Qualitative studies have examined discourse features and rhetorical styles exemplified on oral interview tests (Lazaraton 1992; Young & Milanovic 1992). Lazaraton (1994) conducted qualitative studies on various aspects of the Cambridge Assessment of Spoken English (CASE). In analyzing the test she described the language used by native speakers in communicative situations, the ways that native speakers accommodated themselves to situations, and the ways that they accommodated themselves to their less-than-proficient interlocutors. She focused on the interactional and pragmatic roles that questions play in native speakers' accommodation process.

Course placement interviews have also been analyzed for their discourse features. Lazaraton (1991, 1992) showed that interviewers routinely modify their question prompts in response to perceived trouble on the part of the nonnative interlocutors. She suggested that the systematic and recurrent patterns of question design that emerge are best accounted for by the interactional perspective that conversation analysis employs. Ross (1992) identified a set of factors that contributed to the occurrence of accommodation and found that the extent of accommodation can be a powerful factor in determining oral proficiency. Ross (1992) showed that formulaic speech plays a crucial role in helping the interviewer frame new topics in major portions of an interview.

Shohamy (1994a) compared the discourse features of the Oral Proficiency Interview (OPI), developed by the American Council on the Teaching of Foreign Languages (ACTFL), with those on the Semi-Direct Oral Proficiency Interview (SOPI), the test developed by the Center for Applied Linguistics (CAL) (Stansfield & Kenyon 1988; Shohamy & Stansfield 1990). The different analyses revealed that different speech genres emerged on the two tests, and test takers used different discourse strategies and features, despite the high correlations that were obtained between scores on the two tests. For example, there were more paraphrasing and more error correction on the SOPI, and more switches to L1 on the OPI. The discourse obtained from the two tests differed in rhetorical functions and structure, genre, communicative properties, discourse strategies, prosodic paralinguistic features, speech functions, and discourse markers.

Building on the previous research, Shohamy, Donitze-Schmidt, and Waizer (1993) examined the types of discourse obtained from five different elicitation procedures, using identical tasks. Some procedures required interacting with humans, and others with different types of machines (telephone, video recorder, and audio recorder). Results showed that the discourse obtained with the different procedures differed in a number of features. The language obtained in interactions with machines was more direct and did not involve pragmatic devices, while the language elicited from face-to-face interactions was more elaborated and indirect, and involved a large number of pragmatic and social devices. Differences were also found between the types of machines, with telephone elicitations being the most elaborated and including the highest number of pragmatic devices.

Interestingly, the work of Tarone (1983) on elicited versus spontaneous tasks, which indicates that task and context have an effect on the language samples obtained, was a method effect study. Yet one wonders if Tarone's conclusions can be interpreted as an indication of variation or of testing method effect. Here again, LT research can be instrumental in interpreting findings. In the testing literature, there are procedures for finding out whether differences are a result of the method of eliciting the data regarding the trait (that is, method) or the language (that is, the trait). This is a very important area in which language testers can contribute to SLA research by virtue of their own research and experience in applying different validation methods, such as multitrait multimethod, in a number of major studies.

Differences in conversational styles according to proficiency level have also received attention. Young (1995), for example, compared the conversational styles of intermediate and advanced learners of ESL in language proficiency interviews and found differences in the amount of talk and rate of speaking (advanced learners talked more and faster than intermediate learners), in the extent of context dependence (advanced learners elaborated more in answers to questions), and in the ability to construct and sustain narrative (advanced learners did so, intermediate learners did not). There was no difference between the two groups in the frequency of initiation of new topics, or in the reactivity to topics introduced by the interviewers. Interviewers did not vary in their interviewing styles with the two groups.

Another area of research that has direct relevance to SLA is the choice of criteria for judging the quality of the language obtained on performance tests. The question of whether to use native speaker performance on rating scales has been the subject of long debate. While traditionally the native speaker was acceptable as the "correct" or most appropriate criterion for appropriacy, currently there are debates as to whether the so-called native speaker should be used as the criterion for appropriate language. It has been pointed out that there are variations in discourse among native speakers in the same region and across regions. For example, in a series of studies of native speaker performance using the IELTS assessment battery, a study found that the great variability in the performance of the native speakers was related to educational level and work experience, and it was concluded that native speakers should not be considered the criterion (Hamilton, Lopes, McNamara, & Sheridan 1993). Likewise, in another study done on French Canadian speakers, it was revealed that the Oral Interview Proficiency test was not sensitive to the issue of regional variants, and hence the question was raised as to how to define nativeness. Thus, means for determining the quality and level of appropriate discourse for rating scales and other assessments should be considered seriously.

In summary, with the increased interest and focus on conversational and discourse analysis in language testing, there is a growing body of findings that can be very useful to SLA and discourse researchers. Findings obtained by LT researchers who utilize procedures of discourse and conversational analysis can provide SLA researchers with ample hypotheses for testing and confirmation. Also of interest is the question of the extent to which these findings from testing research can be extended to nontesting situations.

Providing SLA researchers with quality criteria for tests and tasks

One of the most important contributions of LT to SLA research is in the area of validity of the methods that are used for collecting SLA data. Language testers have expertise and experience in the development and validation of language tests and are in a position to provide both guidance and actual tests for obtaining reliable and valid SLA data. SLA elicitation tasks can be distinguished from LT tests on the basis of their purpose. SLA tasks are used to elicit language for answering research questions, while LT tests are used for making decisions about individuals (see Douglas, Chapter 6, this volume, for an alternate view). Since the external and internal validity of SLA studies depends on the reliability and validity of the data obtained through these tasks, research involving elicitation tasks that did not undergo reliability and validity checks may yield unreliable results.

Yet another issue concerns the use of appropriate research methods. Most studies in discourse analysis utilize descriptive research methods. While descriptive methods are powerful for some research questions, they are not appropriate for others because descriptive research does not lend itself to making predictions and inferences about specific hypotheses and theories. After discourse patterns are obtained through descriptive studies, there is a need to make predictions about the emergence of different features in certain texts.

The following are examples of different types of tests that have been developed for assessing various aspects of discourse. A discourse-type cloze test from which discourse chunks were deleted was used to collect data on discourse processing (Jonz 1987). This type of test supports the use of cloze for assessing text processing. Another approach involved the deletion, based on discourse rules, of discourse elements in a cloze test (Deyes 1984). Harley et al. (1990), applying the Canale and Swain framework, constructed tests based on the definition of discourse competence that centers on the ability to produce and understand coherent and cohesive texts. One of these tests required test takers to retell the story of a silent movie to others in a way that would convince them not to carry out some harmful action. A second discourse test was a multiple choice test consisting of short written passages, each of which omitted one sentence. The student was required to select from three alternatives the sentence that best fit the context of the passage. Written discourse production tests consisted of a narrative and a request letter. All four written production tasks were rated for discourse coherence and cohesion.

With regard to different discourse types, Pollitt and Hutchinson (1987) developed a test battery that assessed writing skills and included a variety of different tasks such as letter writing, report writing, and storytelling.

These tasks provided a wider sample of discourse performances. Similarly, Shohamy, Reves, and Bejarano (1986) developed an oral proficiency test battery that consisted of different spoken discourse tasks, such as interviews, reports, discussions, and different types of role plays. A variety of contextual variables were applied to these tasks, such as status, formality level, audience, topic, and setting, so that the speaker produced a variety of oral discourse types (Shohamy 1988).

Lazaraton and Riggenbach (1990) reported on a semidirect oral test that they developed for measuring the functional ability to accomplish a variety of rhetorical tasks. Similarly, Stansfield and Kenyon (1988) and Shohamy and Stansfield (1990) developed semidirect oral proficiency interviews in a large number of languages that tap different discourse functions and rhetorical styles. These tests have been piloted on large samples in many languages and are reported to have very high interrater reliability and concurrent validity.

In addressing different discourse domains, Sarig (1989) reported on a testing procedure that considered differences in domains. This procedure was based on a meaning-consensus criterion that was derived from analyses of model answers by a sample of readers with diverse professional backgrounds. The work of Douglas and Selinker (1985, 1990) has also resulted in a number of tests that are matched to specific discourse domains.

Thus, various assessment procedures developed by language testers may be useful for researchers in the field of SLA if they access them. In the next section, the focus shifts to the contribution of SLA to LT within the context of discourse analysis.

Contributions of SLA to LT

SLA contributions to LT can be made by (1) identifying language components for elicitation and criteria for their assessment, (2) proposing tasks that can be used for assessing language, and (3) informing language testers where differences may occur and accommodating these differences. Each of these areas is discussed using the example of discourse analysis.

Identifying language components for elicitation and criteria for their assessment

An important contribution of SLA to LT is in identifying the constructs necessary for language testers to develop second language tests – specifically, in defining components for testing. For example, research into task variability may provide valuable insights into the roles that such variables as interlocutor, topic, social status, and discourse domain play in proficiency tests. Similarly, L1 research indicates that writing is a process that requires revision, implying that testers must design tests that allow test takers the opportunity to review their writing samples prior to assessment. Brindley (1991) has claimed that SLA research can make a contribution to the development of empirically derived criteria for language assessment. This contribution is relevant to the assessment of discourse because until recently research findings on discourse features have not been applied to the construction of language testing. For example, cloze tests that utilize a rational deletion system may well focus on discourse features or apply discourse rules for deleting words (Olshtain & Feuerstein 1989).

However, only limited attention is being given to the discourse criteria used for assessing the quality of the language samples collected from oral proficiency measures. For instance, the ACTFL OPI, now one of the major instruments for assessing oral language in the United States, overlooks numerous aspects of discourse. ACTFL guidelines (American Council on the Teaching of Foreign Languages 1986) are based on a view of language as unitary, hierarchical, and homogeneous – a view that is detached from our understanding of language consisting of discourse features. Thus, while the OPI elicits language in discourse through an interview and a role play, it focuses not on specific discourse features either in the elicitation tasks or in the assessment of the speech samples, but rather on holistic and general ones. Even in the SOPI test developed by the Center for Applied Linguistics, which does attempt to elicit different discourse styles and genres, the rating is based on a holistic criterion that overlooks a variety of discourse features.

Raffaldini (1988) noticed this deficiency and claimed that even when the tests include elicitation tasks that could tap different types of discourse, there is no guarantee that they are really doing so. In fact, such tests provide very limited information about the discourse competence of language learners because the types of communicative functions and discourse domains that are included are limited. Therefore, these tests fail to give an account of the ability of the learner to influence and be influenced by the discourse of an interlocutor, and they reflect only in part the purposefulness and unpredictability that characterize authentic communicative exchanges.

As an alternative, Raffaldini proposed two situational tests to assess discourse skills: one written and one oral. Both tests use prompts in the form of situations written in English, and both center on sociocultural and discourse contexts in which the learners are expected to be able to perform. Each situation parallels a variety of discourse contexts found in real-life language use tasks, and each reflects different moments in a communicative exchange. The speech samples are assessed with specific rating scales for discourse, sociolinguistic, and linguistic categories. The discourse scale consists of *function* (a measure of expressive effectiveness), *message* (a measure of how well the response conveyed factual information), *cohesion* (a count of each structural and lexical form that violated the cohesion of the response), and *coherence* (a count of each utterance that violated the coherence of the response).

Researchers on SLA discourse are providing insights concerning other discourse features as well. For example, Chun (1988) contends that intonation, a discourse feature, has received little attention in communicative competence or proficiency testing, despite the fact that it is a powerful tool for negotiating meaning, managing interaction, and achieving discourse coherence. In the assessment of discourse there is a need to measure other discourse features, such as turn-taking, sharing information, expanding ideas, and elaborations.

Similarly, Fulcher (1988) claims that in assessing the rating scales used by the Interagency Language Roundtable (ILR) Oral Interview, the concept of vocabulary is too vague. This claim is based on a study that examined the differences in strategies used by fluent native speakers and nonfluent, nonnative speakers to avoid disruption of communication in real conversation when lexical items were not available to them. Fulcher further states that a data-based discourse analysis technique needs to be used in order to construct scales that would lead to the development of new communicative discourse tests.

It has been argued that features of connected discourse identified through discourse analysis need to be recognized in the evaluation of oral proficiency in a second language (Litteral 1980). For example, in the area of semantics, a speaker's control of cause-effect relationships involves, among other things, the ability to produce the different grammatical and lexical manifestations of such relationships. Other testable discourse features may be the ability to make inferences from texts and the ability to place stress on the proper element according to the preceding context. Examples of cohesion that can be evaluated in the discourse context are pronominalization and classification of lexical items within a hierarchy. Such competencies should be evaluated using a variety of procedures, such as comprehension questions and paraphrasing in context. The work of Biber (1988) is relevant as it demonstrates the usefulness of multidimensional analysis of register variation as a language test validation tool (Connor-Linton & Shohamy 1996).

The focus on different elements of discourse as provided by SLA research may well be essential for providing meaningful information about the quality of the discourse of oral and written language used in tests. Language testers may want to apply features from discourse analysis to the development, and especially to the assessment, of language tests.

Proposing tasks for assessing language

SLA researchers have used varied and creative tasks beyond traditional tests for collecting language data. One beneficial contribution that SLA research and experience can make to LT is to broaden the kinds of measurement instruments that are used. Tasks such as judgment tests, observation, documentation, narration, elicited imitations, modified interactions, and small group interactions are only a few of the varied and creative elicitation tasks used by SLA researchers that might be applied to LT (see Seliger & Shohamy 1989 and Larsen-Freeman & Long 1991 for examples of a variety of data collection tools used in SLA research). The following are examples of such data collection tasks used by researchers in discourse analysis.

A study of the accommodation process in interlanguage discourse in a foreign language focused on the effect of various accommodation and negotiation strategies (Ross 1986). The study found that EFL students paired at different proficiency levels accommodated each other in ways similar to interactions between native and nonnative speakers.

Narrative procedures have been widely recommended for assessing discourse. Jax (1986) discusses several procedures for assessing the nature of discourse in children's school language and suggests that language assessment should use tasks that elicit different story structures. She describes seven types of narrative story structures for use in schools in determining the relationship between language proficiency and academic performance. The use of narrative abilities with learning-disabled students is reported by Ripich and Griffith (1988). One ability was the reconstruction of stories, a skill that requires narrative analysis of both original and retold stories and that can provide useful information on language skills beyond the sentence level. Connelly and Clandinin (1990) have also advocated the use of stories and narrative inquiries as effective procedures for assessment.

Likewise, Ross (1986) reports on the use of narrative tasks to test the oral English proficiency of first-year Japanese university students who were nonnative speakers of English. The subjects were shown an animated cartoon of a Japanese folk tale, with narration in Japanese, and later asked to narrate the story in English. The recorded speech samples were rated for pronunciation, accuracy, and fluency. T-unit analyses, common in SLA research, were performed on portions of the recording. Ross recommends this process for obtaining written data as well. Aside from elicited narratives, it is also possible to collect natural data. Berdan and Garcia (1982), for example, discuss the use of observations of natural language interaction as a measure of language proficiency. The study also examines the impact of discourse characteristics on children's use of Spanish and English as measured by length of utterances.

In addition, different types of qualitative tools are used. For example, van Lier (1989) calls for an in-depth examination of the type of discourse that takes place in oral testing situations. He recommends an examination of: (1) the features used in the oral interview, (2) their similarity to or difference from the features of actual conversations, and (3) those features that prevent a successful oral test. He contends that conversation analysis and microethnography must be used to identify and describe performance features that determine the quality of conversational interactions on tests.

In addition, the case has been made for finding out which speech acts are being tapped by the different oral tests and by other elicitation procedures. Olshtain and Blum-Kulka (1985) describe the development of several different types of elicitation techniques for collecting speech act data on a learner's acquisition of the rules of language use. The procedures varied in degree of structuring. They first discuss ethnographic procedures that elicited natural data based on observations. These procedures led to role-play activities, which in turn could produce even more structured testing techniques, such as situations in which the learner was expected to produce in writing the appropriate speech act. Thus, data obtained from a less structured procedure, for example, could be useful in constructing other tasks. The use of multiple procedures for collecting language samples, widespread in SLA research, is also supported by the current move in educational measurement toward the use of alternative assessment procedures that are authentic and performance based.

Informing language testers about differences and accommodating these differences

SLA researchers can at times alert language testers to potentially problematic areas in test construction. For example, if SLA research has concluded that the L1 makes a difference in SLA, then language testers should not treat test takers from different L1 backgrounds in the same way. There may be a need to make accommodation for these differences by devising different versions of a test for different test takers. The evidence that the type of elicitation task significantly affects the type of language that is elicited should be of special interest to language testers.

In the assessment of discourse, the findings of Tarone (1982, 1983) and Ellis (1985) can provide the language tester with important information regarding the kind of instruments that should be developed for measuring language. Their research indicates that the language sample obtained in natural discourse more closely reflects the vernacular (i.e., everyday informal language) and therefore may be a more authentic representation of language as it is actually used, as opposed to language in samples obtained via structured elicitation tasks. Thus testers may want to choose testing instruments with this in mind. Similarly, the use of the article system may be more accurate when applied to chunks of text discourse than when it is elicited in isolated sentences (Tarone 1988), suggesting that language tests should elicit language in a narrative task, since the language sample obtained in this way seems to be more stable. Further, the work of Berdan and Garcia (1982) shows that discourse contexts have an effect on the length of utterances. All of these findings provide useful information from SLA research that can inform the type of elicitation tasks that language testers should use.

Conclusion

This chapter examines interfaces between LT and SLA by identifying ways in which each field can contribute to the other in the area of discourse analysis. For example, LT can contribute to SLA by providing models of language ability that can inform models of second language acquisition. The move of language testing toward the use of assessment procedures other than tests implies another potential area of contribution to SLA.

Findings obtained by researchers in LT can also be useful for generating, testing, and confirming SLA hypotheses. One of the important areas of study in LT has been the effect of testing method on test takers' scores. Results of such studies show that the procedure used for collecting the data, the type of instrument, and even the type of question (multiple choice vs. open ended) affect language test scores. Other studies show that familiarity with the topic, background knowledge, genre, and a variety of other contextual variables affect test takers' scores.

LT can provide SLA researchers with quality tests to be used in discourse research. In addition, language testers can inform SLA researchers about psychometric criteria for evaluating tasks and instruments to ensure that the information obtained from these tasks is reliable and valid.

Many findings obtained in SLA have been overlooked by language testers, and many testing instruments do not take discourse analysis into consideration. Thus, tests that are used for decisions about individuals may not be assessing language within the framework of discourse analysis. While many of the communicative tests elicit discursive language, discourse features are not considered in many of the test tasks and rarely figure in the rating scales that are used to judge the quality of the language. Therefore, there is a need to develop tasks and rating scales that will focus on a variety of aspects of discourse.

Assessing the variety of discourse aspects is probably more costly than ignoring them, because it may mean that the tester will need to provide multiple scores for a language sample, rather than giving a single general score that overlooks such information. If discourse competence is an accepted feature in the definition of language ability, then information about it needs to be delivered to the consumer. Consequently, testers need to incorporate this feature in both the elicitation devices and the criteria for assessing the quality of the language sample.

The recent trend by language testers to expand their repertoire of assessment procedures by experimenting with the various elicitation tasks is due, in part, to the influence of SLA. Most language tests have followed traditional patterns of data collection and are suited to large-scale application. However, SLA researchers use a larger assortment of assessment procedures. Testers often view the elicitation tasks of researchers as devices that do not pass the measurement criteria of reliability and validity and therefore cannot qualify as tests for decision making. Yet the current trend in language testing to use various types of assessment procedures and performance tasks shows that these procedures can be used confidently for eliciting language data with high levels of reliability and validity and could conceivably be adopted for use in language testing as well. The procedures suggested by Olshtain and Blum-Kulka (1985) for using ethnographic data to construct more structured tasks, for example, may be appropriate for language testers.

SLA researchers can also advise language testers of the effects on testing of differences in L1s, a variety of instrument types, and informing testers about differences. Language testers then can adjust their tests according to these findings, especially as they relate to differences among groups and individuals.

In summary, discourse analysis would benefit from closer cooperation between SLA researchers and language testers. The construction of quality language tests necessitates the integration of knowledge from the domains of language learning and measurement theory. Olshtain and Blum-Kulka (1985) argue that the development of testing instruments for discourse analysis and pragmatics cannot be divorced from the field of cross-cultural pragmatics. Cooperation between the two groups means that SLA researchers can devise hypotheses and questions that will then be addressed by LT; these results should lead to new or revised hypotheses and continuation of the process.

There are many unresolved questions that can best be answered through this type of cooperation. For example, to what extent can discourse competence be viewed as a separate competence? How is it related to other competencies of language proficiency in testing and nontesting situations? If discourse can be viewed as an independent competence, how is it related to discourse performance? How can discourse processing be assessed? What is the relationship between discourse competence and performance in test situations? What are the best ways of eliciting language in discourse? Which discourse features are most important to assess, and what is their relevant importance in comparison to other features?

A team approach to many of the issues raised here will make it possible to develop tests and other assessment procedures that can provide a broader picture of the language of the learner and that will match current views of language. In return, researchers in discourse analysis and other areas of SLA will be able to obtain from language testers empirical evidence that can confirm the reliability and validity of instruments and theories used in discourse analysis research. SLA researchers could turn to language testers to evaluate the quality of their instruments, tests, or other elicitation tasks. At the same time, SLA researchers could use their findings to help interpret language test results and advise testers of potential problems. It is clear that researchers who collect language acquisition data and testers who measure language for making decisions must begin to pay attention to one another's work. In this way, it will be possible both to derive more valid theories from research and to make more sound decisions about individual learners. This chapter has highlighted the example of discourse; it remains to be seen whether similar claims can be made for other areas of language use and language acquisition.

References

American Council on the Teaching of Foreign Languages. 1986. *ACTFL proficiency guidelines*. Hastings-on-Hudson, NY: ACTFL.

Anderson, P. 1980. Cohesion as an index for written and oral composition of ESL learners. Paper presented at the annual meeting of the Midwest Modern Language Association, Minneapolis, MN, November. ERIC Document ED 198529.

Bachman, L. 1990a. Constructing measures and measuring constructs. In B. Harley, P. Allen, J. Cummins, & M. Swain (eds.), *The development of second language proficiency* (pp. 26–38). Cambridge: Cambridge University Press.

Bachman, L. 1990b. *Fundamental considerations in language testing*. Oxford: Oxford University Press.

Berdan, R., & M. Garcia. 1982. *Discourse-sensitive measurement of language development in bilingual children*. Los Alamitos, CA: National Center for Bilingual Research.

Biber, D. 1988. *Variation across speech and writing*. Cambridge: Cambridge University Press.

Brindley, G. 1991. Defining language ability: The criteria for criteria. In S. Avivan (ed.), *Current developments in language testing* (pp. 139–164). Singapore: Regional Language Center.

Canale, M., & M. Swain. 1980. Theoretical bases for communicative approaches to second language teaching and testing. *Applied Linguistics, 1*, 1–47.

Chun, D. 1988. The neglected role of intonation in communicative competence and proficiency. *Modern Language Journal, 72*(3), 295–303.

Clapham, C. M. 1994. The effect of background knowledge on EAP reading test performance. Doctoral dissertation, Lancaster University, Lancaster, England.

Connelly, F., & D. Clandinin. 1990. Stories of experience and narrative inquiry. *Educational Researcher,* 19(4), 2–14.

Connor, U. M., & P. Carrell. 1991. The interpretation of tasks by writers and readers in holistically rated direct assessment of writing. Paper presented at the annual TESOL Conference, New York, March.

Connor-Linton, J., & E. Shohamy. 1996. Discourse variation and oral proficiency interview sampling. Paper presented at the annual American Association of Applied Linguistics Conference, Chicago, IL, March.

Cumming, A. 1990. Expertise in evaluating second language compositions. *Language Testing,* 7(1), 21–29.

Deyes, R. 1984. Towards an authentic "discourse" cloze. *Applied Linguistics,* 5(2), 128–137.

Douglas, D., & L. Selinker. 1985. Principles for language tests within the "discourse domains" theory of interlanguage: Research, test construction and interpretation. *Language Testing,* 2, 205–226.

Douglas, D., & L. Selinker. 1990. Performance on a general vs. a field specific test of speaking proficiency by international teaching assistants. Paper presented at the 12th Language Testing Research Colloquium, San Francisco, CA, March.

Ellis, R. 1985. *Understanding second language acquisition.* Oxford: Oxford University Press.

Fillmore, C. 1981. Ideal reader and real reader. In D. Tannen (ed.), *Analyzing discourse: Text and talk* (pp. 248–270). Washington, DC: Georgetown University Press.

Flick, W. 1980. Rhetorical difficulty in scientific English: A study in reading comprehension. *TESOL Quarterly,* 14, 345–351.

Fulcher, G. 1988. Lexis and reality in oral evaluation. Paper presented at the annual meeting of the International Association of Teachers of English as a Foreign Language, Edinburgh, Scotland, April.

Gordon, C. 1987. The effects of testing method on achievement in reading comprehension tests in English as a foreign language. Master's thesis, School of Education, Tel Aviv University, Tel Aviv, Israel.

Hamilton, J., M. Lopes, T. McNamara, & E. Sheridan. 1993. Rating scales and native speaker performance on a communicatively oriented EAP Test. *Melbourne Papers in Language Testing,* 2(1), 1–25.

Harley, B., P. Allen, J. Cummins, & M. Swain. 1990. The nature of language proficiency. In B. Harley, P. Allen, J. Cummins, & M. Swain (eds.), *The development of second language proficiency* (pp. 7–25). Cambridge: Cambridge University Press.

Jax, C. 1986. Understanding school language proficiency through the assessment of story construction. Paper presented at the Ethnic and Multicultural Symposia, Dallas, TX.

Jonz, J. 1987. Textual cohesion and second language comprehension. *Language Learning,* 37(3), 409–438.

Jonz, J. 1989. Textual sequence and second language comprehension. *Language Learning,* 39(2), 207–249.

Jonz, J. 1991. Cloze item types and second language comprehension. *Language Testing,* 8(1), 1–22.

Larsen-Freeman, D., & M. Long. 1991. *An introduction to second language acquisition research.* New York: Longman.

Lazaraton, A. 1991. A conversation analytic perspective on interaction in the language interview. Paper presented at the 13th annual Language Teaching Research Colloquium, Princeton, NJ, March.

Lazaraton, A. 1992. The structural organization of a language interview: A conversation analytic perspective. *System, 20*(3), 373–386.

Lazaraton, A. 1994. Questions turn modification in language proficiency interviews. Paper presented at the annual conference of the American Association of Applied Linguistics, Baltimore, MD, March.

Lazaraton, A., & H. Riggenbach. 1990. Oral skills testing: A rhetorical task approach. *Issues in Applied Linguistics, 1,* 196–217.

Litteral, R. 1980. Discourse factors in the evaluation of language ability. Paper presented at the Regional Seminar of the Southeast Asia Ministers of Education Organizational Regional Language Center, Singapore, April.

McNamara, T. 1996. Second language performance assessment. London: Longman.

Milanovic, M. 1988. The construction and validation of a performance-based battery of English language tests. Doctoral dissertation, University of London.

Oller, J. 1979. *Language tests in schools: A pragmatic approach.* London: Longman.

Oller, J. 1983. *Issues in language testing research.* Rowley, MA: Newbury House.

Olshtain, E., & S. Blum-Kulka. 1985. Crosscultural pragmatics and the testing of communicative competence. *Language Testing, 2*(2), 16–30.

Olshtain, E., & T. Feuerstein. 1989. Using a computerized cloze for teaching and assessing reading comprehension. Paper presented at the 8th ACROLT Colloquium, Kiryat Anavim, Israel, May.

Ong, W. 1982. *Orality and literacy.* London: Methuen.

Pollitt, A. 1991. Construct validation of some cloze tests. Paper presented at the East/West Symposium, Jyväskylä, Finland, August 27–29.

Pollitt, A., & C. Hutchinson. 1987. Calibrating graded assessments: Rasch partial credit analysis of performance in writing. *Language Testing, 4*(1), 72–92.

Raffaldini, T. 1988. The use of situation tests as measures of communicative ability. *Studies in Second Language Acquisition, 10,* 197–216.

Ripich, D., & P. Griffith. 1988. Narrative abilities of children with learning disabilities and nondisabled children: Story structure, cohesion, and propositions. *Journal of Learning Disabilities, 21*(3), 165–173.

Ross, S. 1986. An experiment with a narrative discourse test. Paper presented at the Language Testing Research Colloquium, Monterey, CA, March.

Ross, S. 1992. Accommodative questions in oral proficiency interviews. *Language Testing, 9,* 173–286.

Rubin, D. 1982. Adapting syntax in writing to varying audiences as a function of age and social cognitive ability. *Journal of Child Language, 9,* 497–510.

Ryan, K., & L. Bachman. 1992. Differential item functioning on two tests of EFL proficiency. *Language Testing, 9*(1), 12–29.

Sarig, G. 1989. Testing meaning construction: Can we do it fairly? *Language Testing, 6*(1), 77–94.

Schachter, J. 1990. Communicative competence revisited. In B. Harley, P. Allen,

J. Cummins, & M. Swain (eds.), *The development of second language proficiency* (pp. 39–49). Cambridge: Cambridge University Press.

Seliger, H., & E. Shohamy. 1989. *Second language research methods*. Oxford: Oxford University Press.

Shohamy, E. 1983. The stability of the oral proficiency trait on the Oral Interview Speaking Test. *Language Learning, 33,* 527–540.

Shohamy, E. 1984. Does the testing method make a difference? The case of reading comprehension. *Language Testing, 1*(2), 147–180.

Shohamy, E. 1988. A proposed framework for testing the oral language of second/foreign language learners. *Studies in Second Language Acquisition, 10*(2), 165–180.

Shohamy, E. 1990. Discourse analysis and language testing. *Annual Review of Applied Linguistics, 11,* 115–131.

Shohamy, E. 1994a. The role of language tests in the construction and validation of second-language acquisition theories. In E. E. Tarone, S. M. Gass, & A. D. Cohen (eds.), *Research methodology in second-language acquisition* (pp. 133–144). Hillsdale, NJ:: Lawrence Erlbaum.

Shohamy, E. 1994b. The validity of direct versus semi-direct oral tests. *Language Testing, 11,* 99–124.

Shohamy, E., S. Donitze-Schmidt, & R. Waizer. 1993. The effect of the elicitation method on the language samples obtained on oral tests. Paper presented at the Language Testing Research Colloquium, Cambridge, England.

Shohamy, E., & O. Inbar. 1991. Construct validation of listening comprehension tests: The effect of text and question type. *Language Testing, 8*(1), 23–40.

Shohamy, E., T. Reves, & Y. Bejarano. 1986. Introducing a new comprehensive test of oral proficiency. *English Language Teaching Journal, 40*(3), 212–220.

Shohamy, E., & C. Stansfield. 1990. The Hebrew Oral Test: An example of international cooperation. *AILA Bulletin, 7,* 83–95.

Spolsky, B. 1994. Comprehension testing, or can understanding be measured? In G. Brown, K. Malmkjaer, A. Pollitt, & J. Williams (eds.), *Language and understanding*. Oxford: Oxford University Press.

Stansfield, C., & D. Kenyon. 1988. Development of the Portuguese Speaking Test. Final Report to the U.S. Department of Education. Washington, DC: Center for Applied Linguistics. ERIC Document ED 296586.

Swain, M. 1985. Communicative competence: Some roles of comprehensible input and output in its development. In S. Gass and C. Madden (eds.), *Input and second language acquisition* (pp. 235–253). Rowley, MA: Newbury House.

Tarone, E. 1982. Systematicity and attention in interlanguage. *Language Learning, 32*(1), 69–82.

Tarone, E. 1983. On the variability of interlanguage systems. *Applied Linguistics, 4*(2), 143–163.

Tarone, E. 1988. *Variation in interlanguage*. London: Edward Arnold.

van Lier, L. 1989. Reeling, writhing, drawling, stretching and fainting in coils: Oral proficiency interviews as conversations. *TESOL Quarterly, 23*(3), 480–508.

Vignola, M., & M. Wesche. 1991. L'écriture en langue maternelle et en langue seconde chez les diplomes d'immersion française. *Études de Linguistique Appliquée,* April-June, 94–115.

Young, R. 1995. Conversational styles in language proficiency interviews. *Language Learning, 45*(1), 3–42.

Young, R., & M. Milanovic. 1992. Discourse variation in oral proficiency interviews. *Studies in Second Language Acquisition, 14*(4), 403–424.

Appendix: Language testing – SLA research interfaces

Lyle F. Bachman

Introduction

Language testing [LT] research and second language acquisition [SLA] research are often seen as distinct areas of inquiry in applied linguistics. To oversimplify slightly, SLA research takes a longitudinal view, concerning itself primarily with the description and explanation of how second language proficiency develops, while LT research typically observes a "slice of life," and attempts to arrive at a more or less static description of language proficiency at a given stage of development. While LT research has tended to focus on the complexities of the language proficiency that are the result of acquisition, SLA research has concerned itself more with the factors and processes that affect or are part of acquisition. That is, SLA research has tended to focus on the *antecedents* of proficiency, without concerning itself unduly with the complexity of that construct, while LT research has investigated the *results* of acquisition, largely ignoring questions of how proficiency develops. Finally, LT and SLA research have lent themselves to different research methodologies: SLA research has historically utilized the linguistic analysis of learners' interlanguage utterances, descriptive case studies, experimental and quasi-experimental designs, and ethnographic research, while LT research has more typically employed *ex post facto,* correlational methods.

In recent years LT researchers have probed the nature of language proficiency, not only to develop more useful measures of it, but also to better understand its complexity. One result of this research has been the emergence of a general consensus that language proficiency consists of a number of distinct but related component abilities. Concomitant with this theoretical research has been the development of "communicative" language tests – tests that include a range of abilities and types of tasks that are consistent with current views about communicative competence and communicative language use. This multicomponential view of language

Journal Review of Applied Linguistics (1988) 9, 193–209. Printed in the USA. Copyright

177

proficiency presents a set of complex questions for SLA research. First, it raises questions about the relative effects of different factors, such as context of language use, learning purpose, motivation, and attitude, on the development of different components of language proficiency. Do these factors exert equal or differential influences on the development of different components of proficiency? And if differential, which factors have the strongest effects on which components? A second set of questions has to do with the development of the different components. Specifically, do these develop more or less autonomously, each following its own predetermined sequence, or are they interrelated in various and complex ways? Finally, there are questions about whether the same cognitive processes are involved in the acquisition of the different components of language proficiency. One implication of these questions is that SLA research needs to investigate not only multiple predictors, or independent variables, but also multiple criteria, or dependent variables.

Recently, both LT and SLA researchers have become increasingly aware of the limitations of attempting to assess language proficiency as a more or less static construct. Recognizing that taking a language test involves a complex set of interactions between the facets of the testing environment, the test input, the response expected of the test taker, and the test taker's own language abilities, personal characteristics, and cognitive processes, LT researchers have begun to examine more closely the processes involved in taking language tests. At the same time, SLA researchers have been exploring alternative approaches to assessing language abilities that are based on SLA developmental considerations.

In this section I will first review recent LT research into the nature of language proficiency, along with some recent innovations in the development of tests of communicative competence. I will then discuss the rationale and need for continued multivariate correlational studies in both LT and SLA research, arguing that this research approach provides a powerful means for simultaneously addressing questions both about the nature of language proficiency and about its acquisition, and hence constitutes an interface between LT and SLA research. Finally, I will give an overview of recent qualitative research into the processes involved in taking language tests and into developmental approaches to assessing language proficiency.

Language proficiency as multicomponential

In the early 1980s, informed largely by emerging discussions of communicative competence (e.g., Hymes 1972, Savignon 1972, Widdowson 1978, Canale and Swain 1980a), a number of language testing researchers re-opened an investigation of the hypothesis that language proficiency consists of several distinct abilities. Studies by Bachman and Palmer (1981a; 1982a), Upshur and Homburg (1983), and Carroll (1983) all found support for a multicomponential view of language ability. More recently, Sang, *et al.* (1986) have found empirical support for a multi-componential view of language proficiency that varies along three dimensions. While this research clearly supports a multicomponential view of language proficiency, several questions are yet to be answered. One question, obviously, is "how many component abilities are there, and what are they?" A second set of questions has to do with how the various component abilities are related to each other; that is, are they simply correlated to each other in varying degrees, or are there higher order abilities that affect the primary language abilities? While the research to date seems to support the latter interpretation, there is still no consensus as to what the primary abilities of language proficiency are, what the higher order ability or abilities might be, and how these are related to each other. Finally, there is a more complex question as to whether there is a common or "universal" set of language abilities that may be tapped to differing degrees in different language use contexts, or whether there are actually different sets of abilities for different contexts.

Recent developments in testing communicative language abilities

While LT research has yet to provide clear answers about the nature of language proficiency, a number of language testers have begun developing tests of language proficiency based on notions of communicative competence and communicative language use. Canale (1988a) and in his contribution to the *Annual Review of Applied Linguistics VIII,* provided an excellent review of the major issues and considerations, as well as recent achievements, problems and challenges in assessing communicative competence, and I would refer interested readers to that work for a full discussion of assessing communicative competence.

Early efforts to develop tests of communicative competence included those of Morrow (1977), Canale and Swain (1980b), and Bachman and Palmer (1981b; 1982b; 1982c; 1983). The past two years have witnessed a rapid expansion in the development of language tests based on current views of communicative competence and communicative language use. These include the English Language Testing Service [ELTS] (British Council and University of Cambridge Local Examinations Syndicate 1987; n.d., Criper and Davies 1988), the examinations in the Communicative Use of English as a Foreign Language (Royal Society of Arts Examination Board 1985), and the Institute of Linguists syllabus development project (Institute of Linguists 1987) in England; the Development of Bilingual

Proficiency Project at the Ontario Institute for Studies in Education (Swain 1985, Harley, *et al.* 1987) and the Ontario Ministry of Colleges and Universities (Wesche, *et al.* 1986, Wesche 1987) in Canada.

Two characteristics are shared by the tests developed by these programs. First, all attempt to measure a wide range of language abilities including, but not limited to, those associated with the formal characteristics of language. Second, these tests all attempt to capture the essence of communicative language use in the methods that are used for testing. This characteristic is referred to as *authenticity* and, although there is considerable debate among language testers as to exactly what this is and how best to achieve it, authenticity generally refers to the extent to which the tasks required by the test involve the test taker in communicative language use, or the negotiation of meaning (see Bachman [1990] for an extensive discussion of this issue).

The concern for authenticity has resulted in the use of test tasks that are quite different from those encountered in most currently available language proficiency tests. First, these tasks present the test taker with a relatively greater variety of types of stimuli or input and require a greater variety of tasks in processing this input. A second difference is that, in many of these tests, tasks are linked together sequentially, so that the entire test, or individual sections of it, constitutes a single piece of discourse. This theme-oriented approach is an important design characteristic of the subject-matter specific test modules in the *Ontario Test of English as a Second Language* (Wesche 1987) and the ELTS.

Current LT research into the nature of language proficiency and practical language test development efforts are informed by theories of communicative competence and communicative language use. Progress in the empirical investigation of language proficiency has often been painstakingly slow, while innovations in language test development have been numerous in the past half dozen years. And, while one must certainly pay heed to Alderson's (1986) cautions about the need for accountability in innovation, it is difficult not to feel encouraged by the amount and variety of current research and development in language testing. It is this feeling of encouragement that has led to the proposal of a plan for future language testing research and development.

An agenda for language testing research and development

The problems related to our inadequate understanding of the nature of language deficiency and the resulting inadequacy of many current language tests on the one hand, and the relative success of several recent innovative approaches to language proficiency testing on the other, are the major motivations for a program of language testing research and development proposed by Bachman and Clark (1987). Pointing to the lack of a sound theoretical basis for measures of language proficiency, along with an increasing practical need for "measures of language proficiency for use in language acquisition and attrition research, [and] in program evaluation" (1987:21), Bachman and Clark have proposed a coordinated program of research and development that would investigate the nature of language proficiency and at the same time develop a wider range of practical measures of its various components. This program would proceed in four interrelated areas; it would:

continue to refine the theoretical model of communicative language proficiency . . . with particular attention to defining the specific ability domains in operational terms;

develop . . . highly authentic measures of performance within these domains . . . ;

survey currently available proficiency testing instruments with respect to their degree of congruence with the requirements of a more fully elaborated model . . . ; and

develop and validate, through a joint effort of language testing practitioners, applied linguists, evaluators and psychometricians, batteries of new instruments of optimum reliability, validity and practicality for use in a variety of real-world testing contexts (Bachman and Clark 1987:30).

The proposed program would include a wide range of research approaches and analytic procedures, ranging from the discourse analysis of test content and answer protocols, to introspective recall of test-taking processes, to multivariate statistical analyses. Bachman and Clark argue that such a program would not only expand and solidify our understanding of language proficiency, but would also result in a large battery of practical tests of different abilities for use in applied linguistics research. Many of the studies that would be part of this research agenda constitute interfaces, or areas of mutual interest and common research methodology, between LT and SLA research.

Ex post facto correlational designs

Within the quantitative approach to empirical SLA research, one can identify a wide range of specific designs and analytic techniques. One of the most common of these has been the use of experimental and quasi-experimental designs to investigate relationships between one or more antecedents and the degree or level of acquisition, often as measured by a language test. One problem with experimental or quasi-experimental designs is that, as the number of variables to be investigated increases, so does the complexity of the design and the number of separate groups of subjects that are required, thereby decreasing the feasibility of effectively implementing such designs. Thus, as SLA research has found evidence for an increasing number of different factors and processes that affect SLA, and as LT research has provided support for a number of distinct component language abilities, there has been a need for quantitative research designs and analytic procedures that are more effective for investigating multiple relationships among multiple variables.[1] This is not to say that well-designed and rigorously implemented experimental studies are not useful, but simply that their feasibility is generally limited to the study of a relatively small number of variables.

An alternative to the experimental design is the *ex post facto* correlational design, which differs from the experimental design in that it is not necessary for subjects to be assigned to separate comparison groups and that there is no experimental treatment. The advantage of this approach is that it permits the researcher to investigate a relatively large number of variables in a single study. In order to make use of this advantage, however, the researcher must carefully control the sampling design and obtain a large enough sample to assure that it is representative of the population to which he or she wants to generalize.

Multivariate statistical analyses

Correlational designs are most appropriately used when the researcher wishes to examine relationships among a large number of independent variables, or predictors, and one or more dependent variables, or criteria. A number of "multivariate" statistical procedures for analyzing the results of correlational studies have been devised, of which exploratory factor analysis, multiple linear regression analysis and, more recently, covariance structure analysis, are the most commonly used in LT and SLA research.

Within the past two years several articles utilizing multiple linear regression analysis have appeared. In a series of studies, Chapelle, Jamieson, and Roberts (Chapelle and Jamieson 1986, Chapelle and Roberts 1986, Jamieson and Chapelle 1987) investigated the effects of such variables as time spent using, and attitude toward, computer-assisted language learning; working styles on computers; field independence; ambiguity tolerance; motivational intensity; and English-class anxiety on ESL proficiency. Their results generally support the hypothesis that field independence and, to a lesser degree, ambiguity tolerance are positively related to performance

---

1 Sage Publications' series, *Quantitative Applications in the Social Sciences,* is an excellent reference library for empirical research methodology. The papers are written by practicing social scientists, and emphasize applications and interpretations of procedures, rather than mathematical proofs. The series includes several particularly good papers in the area of causal modeling, or covariance structure analysis. Several titles are cited in the bibliography.

on different measures of ESL proficiency. Clément (1986) used both exploratory factor analysis and multiple regression analysis to investigate differences between majority and minority Francophones in the effects of a wide range of learner affective characteristics on oral production in English and on degree of acculturation. His results suggest that self-confidence is the best single predictor of oral production in English for the majority Francophones, while self-confidence and affectivity were both significant predictors for the minority Francophones. There was less of a difference between the two groups in the predictors of acculturation, with self-confidence and affectivity both being significant. In a study directed toward LT research, Perkins and Linnville (1987) investigated relationships among characteristics of stimulus words and keyed responses in an ESL vocabulary test and test takers' responses to items. Their results indicate that for their sample the best predictors of item responses were the frequency, abstractness, distribution, number of letters, number of response synonyms, and number of syllables.

Causal modeling

Causal modeling refers to the logic and family of statistical procedures "designed to evaluate the utility of causal hypotheses and to support inferences regarding causality among naturally occurring events" (James, Mulaik, and Brett 1982:11). It grew out of "the need to pursue questions of causality and causal inference with non-experimental data" (1982:11). Causal modeling, in other words, has evolved specifically to test hypotheses about causal relations among variables collected in *ex post facto* correlational designs of the type discussed above (although its use is not limited to such designs). Of the many statistical procedures that have been developed to perform causal modeling, two – path analysis and covariance structure analysis – have been applied in the recent LT and SLA research literature.

Path analysis is an extension of multiple linear regression that provides a means for simultaneously investigating multiple relationships among several predictors and more than one criterion. A recent study that illustrates the usefulness of path analysis in SLA research is that of Ely (1986), who tested hypotheses about relationships among various attitudinal variables, classroom participation, and language proficiency. Using an *ex post facto* design, Ely collected measures of his theoretical variables from a group of 75 first-year American college students in Spanish courses. On the basis of these data, he was able to test the specific hypotheses represented in the model. While Ely points out that his results are limited by the small sample size, his inability to cross-validate the results with another sample and possible concerns with some of his measures, particularly the self-reports of affective states, his study is nevertheless an exemplary application of path analysis to an SLA research question.

Covariance structure analysis is an analytic procedure that enables the researcher to investigate relationships among both observed variables and unobserved, or latent, variables, thus combining the advantages of factor analysis and path analysis. Covariance structure analysis is generally performed with a computer package called "LISREL" (Jöeskog and Sörbom 1984), an acronym for the analysis of *linear structural relationship.*" In applying covariance structure analysis, the researcher begins by specifying, on the basis of substantive theory, a model in which hypothesized relationships among observed variables (measures) and latent variables (constructs) are explicitly stated in terms of a set of mathematical formulae. Appropriate measures of the variables in this "LISREL model" are then collected and the interrelationships among them (correlations or covariances) computed. The LISREL model is then tested statistically to determine how well it explains or "fits" the inter-relationships observed among the measures in the study.

Covariance structure analysis with LISREL was introduced to the field of applied linguistics in the early 1980s by LT researchers (Bachman and Palmer 1981a; 1982a) and SLA researchers (Purcell 1983, Gardner 1983, Gardner, Lalonde, and Pierson 1983, Clément and Kruidenier 1985). While the studies of Bachman and Palmer provided empirical support for the multicomponential view of language proficiency, the studies of Gardner and his colleagues were important in that they empirically tested, for the first time, the relationships among integrativeness, attitudes, aptitude, motivation, and second language proficiency that Lambert (1963; 1967) and Gardner (1979) hypothesized in their models of SLA – models which have had considerable influence on both SLA theory and L2 teaching since their formulation.

An illustrative LISREL study

The potential for LT and SLA research of *ex post facto* correlational design combined with LISREL modeling can perhaps best be illustrated by the discussion of a recent article by Gardner, *et al.* (1987), who investigated the effects of motivation and use on language attrition, or loss. This study is of importance to SLA research for two reasons. First, as Gardner, *et al.* (1987) point out, there is a growing body of research on language attrition indicating that many of the same factors that are at play in SLA also influence language loss. According to the model of language loss proposed by Gardner (1982), there is an "incubation" period following learning or acquisition during which language proficiency is either retained, improved, or lost, depending upon the extent to which opportunities to use the L2 are sought, as well as upon motivational factors. Gardner argues that this characterization of attrition as taking place in an incubation period provides a basis for linking L2 attrition to L2 acquisition. This suggests that something may be learned about language acquisition by investigating the factors and processes involved in its loss.

This study is also important methodologically in that it deals with many of the same problems SLA researchers face in attempting to trace SLA longitudinally. These include the practical problem of finding subjects who have had either relatively uniform exposure to language, longitudinally, or for whom the type of exposure has differed in specific ways, and the statistical problem of relating measures of change to other variables. This application of the method also illustrates how relationships among multiple predictors and multiple criteria can be investigated *over time.*

Gardner, *et al.* (1987) began with a model of attrition that consists of two time periods: an *acquisition phase,* during which some type of language training or exposure occurs, and an *incubation period,* marked by the cessation of training or opportunities to use the language. The model further hypothesized that language attitudes and motivation would affect L2 proficiency during the acquisition phase, and that these, along with use, would influence L2 proficiency during the incubation phase. The subjects for the study were 98 English-speaking students in Grade 12 French classes in schools in London, Ontario. At the end of the school year, in June, these subjects were given measures of French achievement, attitudes, and motivation, and a self-rating questionnaire of their proficiency in French. At the beginning of the next school year, in September, they were given the same measures of French achievement, the same self-rating questionnaire, and a questionnaire on how much they used French during the summer.

The LISREL model that Gardner, *et al.* (1987) investigated is represented in the figure on the next page.[2] In this model the observed variables ("AFC," "INT," . . . "LC") are represented by rectangular boxes. Associated with each observed variable is a "unique" component, or factor, represented by the Greek letters *delta* and *epsilon.* The unobserved variables ("LANGUAGE ATTITUDES," "MOTIVATION," and "ACHIEV. 2") are represented by circles. Straight, single-headed lines indicate paths of directional causal relationships, while double-headed lines represent paths of correlations, with no causation implied. The numbers associated with the paths are estimates of parameters, or "path coefficients," which indicate the relative strength of the relationships with values theoretically ranging from +1.00 to –1.00.

---

2 The figure is taken from Gardner, *et al.* 1987:43 and is reprinted with the permission of Robert C. Gardner, Howard Giles, and Multilingual Matters Ltd.

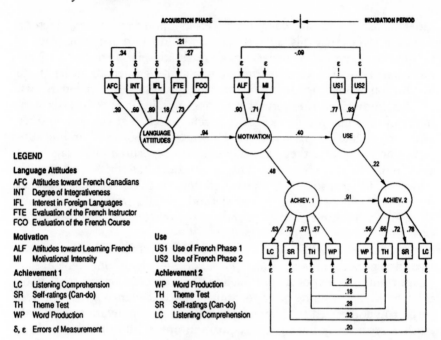

Causal model linking attitudes and motivation to language achievement, use and retention (Gardner, et al. 1987: 43)

The LISREL model (Gardner, *et al.* 1987) includes one predictor ("exogenous variable") – LANGUAGE ATTITUDES – and four criteria ("endogenous variables") – MOTIVATION, USE, achievement in French at the end of the acquisition phase (ACHIEV. 1), and achievement in French at the end of the incubation period (ACHIEV. 2), which are related to each other as specified by the directional paths. One of the strengths of this particular study, it should be noted, is that every latent variable has at least two observed variables as indicators.

One result that can be seen in the LISREL model (Gardner, *et al.* 1987) pertains to the measurement characteristics of the observed variables in the study. An inspection of the factor loadings of the observed variables reveals that virtually all of these load quite heavily on the latent constructs they represent, the single exception being "FTE," which has a loading of only .18. Unfortunately, Gardner, *et al.* (1987) do not provide the coefficients for the paths between the error terms and their respective observed variables, so that it is not possible to assess the relative influence of these errors on the measures.

The primary focus of this study, however, is on the hypothesized relationships among language attitudes, motivation, use, and language retention or attrition. For the subjects in this study, language attitudes show a strong positive influence on motivation (.94), which in turn exerts about equal effects on achievement at the end of the acquisition phase (.48) and on the extent to which individuals continue to use the L2 during the incubation period (.40). L2 achievement at the end of the incubation period can be seen to be a function primarily of the level of achievement attained at the beginning of the incubation period (.91), and to a much lesser degree (.20) of the amount of L2 use during it.

This study provides an excellent example of the usefulness of the causal modeling of data obtained from *ex post facto* designs, as do the others that Gardner and his colleagues have conducted. At the same time, however, all these studies suffer, in my opinion, from two weaknesses with respect to the language abilities they have used as criteria. First, although all of these studies include measures of different aspects of language ability, in every case these measures are treated as if they measure a single ability. In the study just discussed, for example, Gardner, *et al.* (1987) used ten different indicators of language proficiency, but grouped these together more or less according to the test method used, rather than by the language abilities measured. The self-ratings, for example, included indicators of speaking, understanding, reading, and writing, but these were aggregated into a single indicator, "SR." And although the factor loadings indicate that the measures included in the model are all reasonably good indicators of some "general" L2 achievement, treating indicators of different abilities as if they were all measuring the same ability ignores, it seems to me, recent LT research.

Rather than specifying a general L2 achievement construct, Gardner, *et al.* (1987) might have specified three latent achievement constructs – vocabulary, writing/grammar, and listening comprehension – which would have permitted the researchers to investigate hypotheses about the different effects of motivation and use on different language abilities.

A second weakness, in my opinion, is in the measures of language achievement that were used as criteria for the study. As indicated above, much current thinking in applied linguistics views language proficiency as consisting of competencies in both the formal – syntactic, lexical, and morphological – and the functional or pragmatic aspects of language, a view that is also generally supported by recent research in language testing. Furthermore, as indicated above, there is a growing corpus of language tests that attempt to operationalize this broadened view of language ability. One would, therefore, reasonably expect SLA researchers to begin utilizing as criteria for their studies language tests that are based on more current views of language proficiency and more in keeping with current practice in the measurement of communicative competence.

An example of an SLA study that examined different components of language proficiency as part of its LISREL model is provided by Sang, *et al.* (1986), who hypothesized that different types of L2 instruction would differentially affect three dimensions of language proficiency. They examined a LISREL model that included two different language teaching methods ("modern" and "traditional") and three hypothesized dimensions of language proficiency ("elementary," "complex," and "communicative"). Their results suggest that for their sample of subjects, the "modern" teaching method had a stronger effect on all three dimensions of proficiency than did the "traditional" method. Furthermore, the "modern" method appeared to have the strongest influence on the "communicative" dimension of language proficiency.

In summary, covariance structure analysis appears to provide an ideal tool for simultaneously investigating questions about the nature of language proficiency and about its acquisition. This is so because it enables the researcher to bring together, in a single empirically verifiable model, hypotheses about the abilities that language tests measure and about the relationships among these abilities and the antecedents of their acquisition. However, it should be emphasized that covariance structure analysis may not be applicable to any set of *ex post facto* data the researcher happens to have at hand. Because of the logic of causality that must go into the design of the LISREL model, and because of the requirements of the statistical procedures for estimating the path coefficients, both in terms of model specification and assumptions about the nature of the data, covariance structure analysis is an extremely demanding procedure and can be applied most successfully to data that have been collected with a specific model or set of models and specific hypotheses in mind. Nevertheless, the usefulness of this approach for both LT and SLA research has already been amply demonstrated, I believe, by the studies mentioned above. Its potential for truly advancing these fields lies in the utilization of language tests that tap the wider range of language abilities hypothesized to be part of communicative language use.

Qualitative analyses of language tests and test-taking

A second empirical approach to the complexity of SLA research is the careful observation and detailed *qualitative* analysis of events and processes related to the language acquisition of a single individual or group of individuals, combined with the linguistic analysis of the language use of these individuals. Recently, LT researchers have begun to utilize certain qualitative empirical research procedures to understand the processes involved in taking language tests better. Cohen (1984), for example, reported on several studies that were based on verbal self-report data which identified a variety of strategies followed in completing cloze and multiple-choice reading tests. More recently, Cohen has utilized verbal report data to investigate test-taking strategies in composition tests (Cohen 1987) and summarization tasks in a foreign language reading comprehension test (Cohen forthcoming).

In a recent paper, Grotjahn (1986) outlined an integrated program of research that combines quantitative psychometric analyses of test data with qualitative analytic methods. He argues convincingly that the validation of language tests may include, in addition to the quantitative analysis of test-takers' responses, the qualitative analysis of test-taking processes and the test tasks themselves. He describes a strategy of "logical task analysis" that "can suggest what kinds of cognitive processes may be involved when the subject is confronted with the task or that a specific solution may be generated by several alternative processing strategies" (1986:165–166). For the investigation of test-taking processes, he recommends the types of self-report data (thinking-aloud and retrospective interview) utilized by Cohen.

While the utilization of self-report data has produced impressive results in SLA research and is now considered a "standard" research method, it has begun to be applied to LT research only relatively recently. The few studies in which it has been used, however, clearly demonstrate its usefulness, not only in understanding what test takers actually do when they take tests, but more importantly, what it is that language tests actually measure.

A developmental approach to L2 assessment

A third area of interface between LT and SLA research is that of the incorporation of SLA developmental considerations into the design and interpretation of language assessment instruments. The primary work in this area derives from the research of Clahsen and his colleagues with L2 speakers of German, and from Johnston and Pienemann with L2 speakers of English. Building upon research into the sequential regularity of morphological and syntactic development in L2 speakers of German, Clahsen has described a procedure for providing "detailed information as to the learners' level of linguistic development," for purposes of language instruction (1985:283). The procedure incorporates an approach to deriving profiles of language disorders that was developed by Chrystal and his colleagues (e.g., Chrystal and Fletcher 1979). Although Clahsen's work with this profile analysis has so far been limited to the acquisition of morphological and syntactic features of German by nonnative speakers, he claims that the approach is generalizable to other languages, other groups of L2 learners, and other linguistic skills (1985: 283).

Clahsen proposes five criteria that L2 assessment tests should satisfy:

1) they should be based on oral L2 speech production;
2) they should be based on samples of spontaneous speech;
3) the procedure should provide a description of the learners' interlanguage;
4) the procedure should focus on syntax and morphology, and
5) the linguistic structures used by learners should be graded in terms of order of acquisition in natural L2 development (1985:286–288).

He further argues that most currently available L2 proficiency tests fail to meet these criteria, whereas the profile analysis he advocates does.

In an article that is both provocative and challenging, Pienemann and Johnston (1987) begin with the proposition that proficiency needs to be distinguished from development. Based on their work in the L2 acquisition of English, they develop a "multidimensional model" of SLA acquisition that includes two dimensions: 1) development, which they posit as being regular and predictable, and 2) variation, which is largely the result of individual differences. They then argue that differences in accuracy, as often measured by standard language proficiency tests, cannot be regarded as reasonable indicators of development, since accuracy will vary as a function of both the regular developmental sequence and individual variations across that sequence.

Pienemann, Johnston, and Brindley have applied profile analysis to the assessment of the acquisition of L2 English morphological and syntactic features, emphasizing that "the assessment procedure proposed . . . is *not a proficiency test*. It is an initial attempt to devise a practical method of obtaining information about a learner's stage of grammatical development in the second language" (1988:22). In this study, a group of assessors listened to recorded oral interviews that had been collected as part of a prior research study. Using a checklist of the morphological and syntactic features that were of interest, the assessors checked those items which occurred and, for obligatory contexts, those which did not occur. On the basis of these observation protocols, the assessors were asked to indicate the highest stage of acquisition, based on a description of six stages, for which there was evidence. Pienemann, Johnston, and Brindley (1988) are careful to point out that this study is a preliminary investigation but, as the procedure is reasonably practical and consistent across assessors, continued research and development of the procedure are thus warranted. They also wisely caution against possible misuses of the instrument by educational administrators or funding authorities.

This approach to the assessment of L2 acquisition is, I believe, promising, since it addresses the need to consider acquisition history in the assessment of L2 proficiency. It is also encouraging from a methodological perspective in that it involves the application of an empirical method, developed for SLA research, to LT research questions. At the same time, there are some serious questions that must be addressed before this approach can be considered a viable approach to L2 proficiency assessment. Although there may be evidence for the regularity of morphological and syntactic development in the L2 acquisition of German and English, whether Clahsen's claims for generality will hold across other languages and other groups of L2 acquirers is, it seems, an empirical question for further research. A greater problem, I believe, is the application of the procedure to other aspects of communicative competence, such as socio-linguistic appropriateness and pragmatic functions, which have not been investigated as extensively in the SLA research as have formal linguistic features such as morphology, syntax, and lexicon. Another question pertains to the relative effect of regular developmental sequence versus that of individual variation, across different contexts, on the types of accuracy data collected by the profiling procedure; that is, to what extent is the procedure sensitive to individual variations that may result from different elicitation contexts, and to what extent will this affect the determination of the developmental stage? Finally, there is the whole question of the authenticity of the methods utilized in obtaining the sample of language use, which is endemic to all language tests, and from which profile analysis is not exempt, despite its claim to be based on naturally occurring language use in "real-life" situations. The problem of eliciting "authentic" language use is one that language testers have grappled with for years and, from their collective experience, it would seem impractical, to say the least, to attempt to impose authenticity as an absolute requirement for an L2 assessment procedure.

Summary

Researchers in language testing and SLA are finding an expanding area of common ground in terms of both the research questions they address and empirical approaches to those questions. Three such interfaces have been discussed in this review: the covariance structure analysis of *ex post facto* correlational data, the qualitative investigation of test-taking processes, and the development of L2 assessment instruments based on developmental sequences in L2 acquisition. It would appear that LT and SLA research have much to gain from each other and can be viewed more productively as complementary approaches to inquiry into the nature of language proficiency and its acquisition. To this area of mutual inquiry LT research brings a multicomponential view of language proficiency that is consistent with current thinking in the field, a wide range of instruments for measuring these different components, and a multivariate approach to empirical research. SLA research, on the other hand, contributes a rich body of information about the factors that affect SLA, the processes that are part of it, and the developmental sequence it follows, along with a well-developed set of qualitative approaches to empirical research.

In the conclusion of their report on the five-year longitudinal "Development of Bilingual Proficiency" [DBP] project, Harley, *et al.* (1987) distinguish three stages of development in the history of empirical research into the nature of language proficiency. The first stage was characterized by the use of exploratory factor analysis as the primary statistical tool for investigating both the formal and functional, or pragmatic, dimensions of language proficiency. The second stage has been characterized by increasingly complex and comprehensive frameworks of language proficiency and sophisticated research designs. The third stage, which has been stimulated in no small degree by the DBP study itself, will be marked, according to Harley, *et al.*, by the interpretation of language performance "explicitly in terms of how different aspects of communicative competence have developed as a function of specific language acquisition/learning experiences" (1987:58). Research during this stage will also incorporate a much wider range of research approaches and analytic procedures. I would take their analysis one step further, asserting that the third stage is upon us, and is bringing together LT and SLA research in designs that permit the application of the full range of multivariate quantitative and qualitative analytic methods that have been discussed above.

Unannotated bibliography

Alderson, J. C. 1986. Innovations in language testing? In M. Portal (ed.) *Innovations in language testing.* Windson: NFER-Nelson. 93–105.
Asher, H. B. 1983. *Causal modeling.* 2nd ed. Newbury Park, CA: Sage Publications.
Bachman, L. F. 1990. *Fundamental considerations in language testing.* Oxford: Oxford University Press.
———— and J. L. D. Clark. 1987. The measurement of foreign/second language proficiency. *Annals of the American academy of political and social science.* 490.20–33.
———— and A. S. Palmer. 1981a. The construct validation of the FSI oral interview. *Language learning.* 31.1.67–86.
————. 1981b. Self-assessment of communicative competence in English. Salt Lake City, UT: University of Utah. Mimeo.
————. 1982a. The construct validation of some components of communicative proficiency. *TESOL quarterly.* 16.4.449–465.
————. 1982b. Test of communicative competence in English: Multiple-choice method. Salt Lake City, UT: University of Utah. Mimeo.
————. 1982c. Test of communicative competence in English: Writing sample method. Salt Lake City, UT: University of Utah. Mimeo.
————. 1983. Oral interview test of communicative proficiency in English. Urbana, IL: University of Illinois. Photo-offset.
Berry, W. D. 1984. Nonrecursive causal models. Newbury Park, CA: Sage Publications.
British Council and the University of Cambridge Local Examinations Syndicate.

1987. *An introduction to English Language Testing Service.* London: The British Council.

———. n.d. *English Language Testing Service: Specimen materials booklet.* London: The British Council.

Canale, M. 1988a. The content validity of some oral interview procedures: An analysis of communication problems and strategies. Paper presented at the 10th Annual Language Testing Research Colloquium. Urbana, IL. March.

———. 1988b. The measurement of communicative competence. In R. B. Kaplan, et al. (eds.) *Annual review of applied linguistics, VIII.* New York: Cambridge University Press. 67–84.

——— and M. Swain. 1980a. Theoretical bases of communicative approaches to second language teaching and testing. *Applied linguistics.* 1.1.1–47.

———. 1980b. A domain description for core FSL: Communication skills. In *The Ontario assessment instrument pool: French as a second language, junior and intermediate divisions.* Toronto: Ontario Ministry of Education. 27–39.

Carroll, J. B. 1983. Psychometric theory and language testing. In J. W. Oller, Jr. (ed.) *Issues in language testing research.* Rowley, MA: Newbury House. 80–107.

Chapelle, C. and J. Jamieson. 1986. Computer-assisted language learning as a predictor of success in acquiring English as a second language. *TESOL quarterly.* 20.1.27–46.

——— and C. Roberts. 1986. Ambiguity tolerance and field dependence as predictors of proficiency in English as a second language. *Language learning.* 36.1.27–45.

Chrystal, D. and P. Fletcher. 1979. Profile analysis of language disability. In C. Filmore, J. Kempler, and W. Wang (eds.) *Individual differences in language ability and language behavior.* New York: Academic Press. 167–188.

Clahsen, H. 1985. Profiling second language development: A procedure for assessing L2 proficiency. In K. Hyltenstam and M. Pienemann (eds.) *Modelling and assessing second language acquisition.* Clevedon, Avon: Multilingual Matters. 283–331.

Clément, R. 1986. Second language proficiency and acculturation: An investigation of the effects of language status and individual characteristics. *Journal of language and social psychology.* 5.4.271–290.

——— and B. G. Kruidenier. 1985. Aptitude, attitude and motivation in second language proficiency: A test of Clément's model. *Journal of language and social psychology.* 4.1.21–37.

Cohen, A. D. 1984. On taking tests: What the students report. *Language testing.* 1.1.70–81.

———. 1987. Studying learner strategies: Feedback on compositions. *PASAA* 17.2.29–38.

———. 1994. English for academic purposes in Brazil: The use of summary tasks. In C. Hill and K. Parry (eds.) *From testing to assessment: English as an international language* (pp. 174–204). London: Longman.

Criper, C. and A. Davies. 1988. *Edinburgh ELTS Validation Project: Project report.* London: The British Council.

Davis, J. A. 1985. *The logic of causal order.* Newbury Park, CA: Sage Publications.

Dillon, W. R. and M. Goldstein. 1984. *Multivariate analysis: Methods and applications.* New York: John Wiley and Sons.

Ely, C. M. 1986. An analysis of discomfort, risktaking, sociability, and motivation in the L2 classroom. *Language learning.* 36.1.1–25.

Gardner, R. C. 1979. Social psychological aspects of second language acquisition. In H. Giles and R. St. Clair (eds.) *Language and social psychology.* Baltimore, MD: University Park Press. 193–220.

———. 1982. Social factors in language retention. In R. D. Lambert and B. F. Freed (eds.) *The loss of language skills.* Rowley, MA: Newbury House. 24–43.

———. 1983. Learning another language: A true social psychological experiment. *Journal of language and social psychology.* 2.2.3&4.219–239.

———, R. N. Lalonde, and R. Pierson. 1983. The socio-educational model of second language acquisition: An investigation using LISREL causal modeling. *Journal of language and social psychology.* 2.1.1–15.

———, *et al.* 1987. Second language attrition: The role of motivation and use. *Journal of language and social psychology.* 6.1–47.

Grotjahn, R. 1986. Test validation and cognitive psychology: Some methodological considerations. *Language testing.* 3.2.159–185.

Harley, B., *et al.* 1987. *The development of bilingual proficiency: Final report.* Toronto: Modern Language Centre, Ontario Institute for Studies in Education.

Hymes, D. 1972. On communicative competence. In J. B. Pride and J. Holmes (eds.) *Sociolinguistics.* Harmondsworth: Penguin. 269–293.

Institute of Linguists. 1987. *Institute of Linguists syllabus development project.* London: Institute of Linguists.

James, L. R., S. A. Mulaik, and J. M. Brett. 1982. *Causal analysis: Assumptions, models and data.* Newbury Park, CA: Sage Publications.

Jamieson, J. and C. Chapelle. 1987. Working styles on computers as evidence of second language learning strategies. *Language learning.* 37.1.109–122.

Jöreskog, K. G. and D. Sörbom. 1984. *LISREL VI. User's guide.* Chicago: National Educational Resources.

Lambert, W. E. 1963. Psychological approaches to the study of language. 2 parts. *Modern language journal.* part II.14.114–121.

———. 1967. A social psychology of bilingualism. *Journal of social issues.* 23.1–109.

Long, J. S. 1983a. *Confirmatory factor analysis.* Newbury Park, CA: Sage Publications.

———. 1983b. *Covariance structure models: An introduction to LISREL.* Beverly Hills, CA: Sage Publications.

Morrow, K. 1977. *Techniques of evaluation for a notional syllabus.* London: Royal Society of Arts.

Pedhazur, E. J. 1982. *Multiple regression in behavioral research.* 2nd ed. New York: Holt, Rinehart and Winston.

Perkins, K. and S. E. Linnville. 1987. A construct definition study of a standardized ESL vocabulary test. *Language testing.* 4.2.125–141.

Pienemann, M. and M. Johnston. 1987. Factors influencing the development of language proficiency. In D. Nunan (ed.) *Applying second language acquisition research.* Adelaide: National Curriculum Resource Centre. 45–141.

——— and G. Brindley. 1988. Constructing an acquisition-based procedure for second language assessment. *Studies in second language acquisition.* 10.121–143.

Purcell, E. T. 1983. Models of pronunciation accuracy. In J. W. Oller, Jr. (ed.) *Issues in language testing research.* Rowley, MA: Newbury House. 133–151.

Royal Society of Arts Examination Board. 1985. *The communicative use of English as a foreign language.* Orpington, Kent: Royal Society of Arts Examination Board.

Sang, F., et al. 1986. Models of second language competence: A structural equation approach. *Language testing.* 3.1.54–79.

Savignon, S. J. 1972. *Communicative competence: An experiment in foreign language teaching.* Philadelphia: Center for Curriculum Development.

Sullivan, J. L. and S. Feldman. 1979. *Multiple indicators: An introduction.* Newbury Park, CA: Sage Publications.

Swain, M. 1985. Large-scale communicative language testing: A case study. In Y. P. Lee, et al. (eds.) *New directions for language testing.* Oxford: Pergamon. 35–46.

Upshur, J. A. and T. J. Homburg. 1983. Some relations among language tests at successive ability levels. In J. W. Oller, Jr. (ed.) *Issues in language testing research.* Rowley, MA: Newbury House. 188–201.

Wesche, M. 1987. Second language performance testing: The Ontario Test of ESL as an example. *Language testing.* 4.1.28–47.

————, et al. 1987. *Ontario Test of English as a second language (OTESL): A report on the research.* Ottawa: Ontario Ministry of Colleges and Universities.

Widdowson, H. G. 1978. *Teaching language as communication.* Oxford: Oxford University Press.

Index

Note: Page numbers followed by n indicate footnotes.